The New Lafayette Theatre Presents

ED BULLINS is a producer, editor, teacher and filmmaker. He is the author of *The Duplex, Five Plays, The Hungered One, Four Dynamite Plays*, and *The Theme Is Blackness*. His play *The Fabulous Miss Marie* won the Obie Award. Mr. Bullins is former playwright-in-residence at The New Lafayette Theatre in Harlem. And he is currently working on *The Twentieth-Century Cycle*, which is a series of plays.

The New Lafayette Theatre Presents

PLAYS WITH AESTHETIC COMMENTS BY 6 BLACK PLAYWRIGHTS

ED BULLINS

J. E. GAINES

CLAY GOSS

OYAMO

SONIA SANCHEZ

RICHARD WESLEY

Edited by Ed Bullins

ANCHOR BOOKS

ANCHOR PRESS/DOUBLEDAY
GARDEN CITY, NEW YORK
1974

ACKNOWLEDGMENTS

Grateful acknowledgment is made to the following for permission to reprint the plays contained in this anthology:
Ed Bullins for *The Fabulous Miss Marie,* reprinted by permission of Ed Bullins. Copyright © 1971 by Ed Bullins.
J. E. Gaines for *What If It Had Turned Up Heads,* reprinted by permission of J. E. Gaines.
Clay Goss for *On Being Hit,* reprinted by permission of Clay Goss.
Oyamo for *His First Step.* Copyright © 1970 by Charles F. Gordon. Reprinted by permission of Charles "Oyamo" Gordon.
Sonia Sanchez for *Uh, Uh; But How Do It Free Us?* Copyright © 1971 by Sonia Sanchez. Reprinted by permission of Sonia Sanchez.
Richard Welsey for *Black Terror.* Copyright © 1970 by Richard Wesley. Reprinted by permission of Richard Wesley.

The Anchor Press edition is the first publication of THE NEW LAFAYETTE THEATRE PRESENTS.

Anchor Books edition: 1974

ISBN: 0-385-04126-8
Library of Congress Catalog Card Number 73–83586
Copyright © 1974 by Ed Bullins
All Rights Reserved
Printed in the United States of America
First Edition

Dedicated to The New Lafayette Theatre

Contents

The Black Drama of Now

Two of the positive characteristics of contemporary Black writing have been the attempt at honesty by the newer writers and the turning away from addressing Black writing to white audiences and readership.

In the past decade the Black writer/artist/intellectual has been able to acquire an urban Black audience in the Black theatre, for the independent and Hollywood-type Black film, and a wider range of Black readership for Black poetry, fiction and drama.

In the early 1960s, with the advent of the new Black nationalism as espoused by Malcolm X and the Nation of Islam, the contemporary Black writer was influenced to migrate psychically away from strictly European values in his art and aesthetics. The Black people, in their struggle to survive in hostile white America, through revolutionary or reactionary means, again became worthy subject matter for the artists, especially when the examples of the Cuban Revolution, the African Liberation movement, the Civil Rights movement, the Black militant/revolutionary/student movement were spread by the media and influenced, perhaps even created, the Black arts movement of today.

Introduction

The Black masses were sought out in their ghettos and enthusiastically set upon by the new Black revolutionary artists through almost seemingly spontaneous eruptions of Black street plays. An inevitable round of benefits appeared with revolutionary rhetoric and rap interlinked by Black revolutionary theatre, film, music, dance and art, to aid Black political prisoners that the social and political climate of the times generated. Black arts festivals proliferated, with numerous conferences and symposiums created to discuss the criteria for evaluating Black arts, the role of the artists in the movement and the creation of an alternate Black communications and media system throughout the Black communities of America. New Black magazines specialized in Black poetry, Black theatre, Black scholarship and Black community and Pan-African issues. The Black revolutionary theatre did its thing upon the at first makeshift stages of Harlem, San Francisco, Detroit and New Orleans, while the new Black poets institutionalized the street rhetoric of the day as Black arts centers and groups grew from Baltimore to Santa Barbara, having in common activities and arts efforts that incorporated an African motif and Afro-American soul ethos, a commonality of words couched in Black ideological expression and using a Third World iconology.

The present phase of Black writing is in the dialectic period of evolution. Black artists are discussing ideas, discoursing about the problems and concerns of their Black audience, readers and peers, among a body of evolved Black consciousness; hence, it is a dialectic of Black contemporary literature/art/theatre in which this generation's artists are engaged.

In the recent past, preoccupation in addressing mainly social and political issues may have been Black literature's major flaw. Richard Wright, James Baldwin and LeRoi Jones (now Imamu Baraka) have each in turn called for a Black literature that plumbed the human spirit for Black beings, but each has been mainly concerned by the social and political aspects of Black existence in America.

With the present Black writers turned away from addressing an anticipated white readership and appealing the plight of Blackness in America to their masochistic delight, the literature has changed from a social-protest oriented form to one of a dialectical nature among Black people—*Black dialectics*—and this new thrust has two main branches—the *dialectic of change* and the *dialectic of experience*. The writers are attempting to answer questions concerning Black survival and future, one group through confronting the Black/white reality of America, the other, by heightening the dreadful white reality of being a modern Black captive and victim.

These two major branches in the mainstream of the new Black creativity, the dialectic of change (once called protest writing, surely, when confronting whites directly and angrily, then altered to what was called Black revolutionary writing when it shifted a decade ago through the pioneering work of Baraka away from a white audience to a Black), and the dialectic of experience (or being), sometimes merge, but *variety* and *power* in the over-all work are the general rule. And there is little conflict among the artists working within the forms.

The dialectic of change has a distinguished history founded in the slave narrative/abolitionist/protest phases of Black literature. The dialectic of experience has roots that antecede the arrival of Black slaves on this continent and is traceable to oral literatures of Africa and cultures of temperate zone non-European peoples. Both are strong strains in Black art and play vital functions in the Black ethos of Black American writing.

The six plays in this collection demonstrate the best dramatic writing of today coming out of the contemporary Black dialectic movement.

Richard Wesley's *Black Terror* is a play discussing the revolutionary ideas and situations of evolutionary change in the Black community among a cadre of revolutionaries. And *What If It Turned Up Heads*, by J. E. Gaines, perfectly represents the other side of this creative coin of Black dramatic writing. His character J.J. could almost be Richard Wright's symbolic "man who lived underground," but Jacob Jones is somehow more horribly real and grass-roots original.

The works of Goss, Oyamo, Sanchez and Bullins are fully realized works of the modern Black theatre writers and are the best of the plays that are being done in the rising number of Black theatres throughout America, and sometimes Off Broadway.

ED BULLINS
Harlem

The Fabulous Miss Marie

(No. 4 of the Twentieth-Century Cycle)

BY ED BULLINS

THE PEOPLE:*

MARIE HORTON: *mid-forties*
BILL HORTON: *Marie's husband*
ART GARRISON: *early twenties*
WANDA: *Marie's niece, early twenties*
MARCO POLO HENDERSON: *late twenties*
STEVE BENSON: *mid-twenties*
RUTH: *Marie's cut-buddy, thirty-five*
TONI: *Marie's home girl, thirty*
BUD: *Toni's husband, thirty-three*
GAFNEY: *Marco's friend, early twenties*
WHITIE: *Marie's lap dog, invisible*

* Some of the ACTORS *can be doubled over to play the stag movie figures, the TV announcer, the news victims, etc.*

NOTE: *This work should be played in ensemble style—as fluid and free form as possible, short of being pretentious. It should be scored to music, live if possible, and not have a fixed, heavy set—in fact, if the company can pull it off, their bodies and persons could be the scenery.*

The Fabulous Miss Marie opened at The New Lafayette Theatre of Harlem on March 5, 1971. The production was directed by Robert Macbeth. Settings and lights were designed by Ademola, James Macbeth, Toby Macbeth, Morgan Morris and Alfred Smith.

THE CAST:

MARIE HORTON	Rosanna Carter
BILL HORTON	Sonny Jim
ART GARRISON	Roscoe Orman
WANDA	Yvette Hawkins
MARCO POLO HENDERSON	Bill Lathan
STEVE BENSON	Gary Bolling
RUTH	Vaughn Reddie
TONI	Martha Charles
BUD	Whitman Mayo
GAFNEY	George Miles

MUSIC BY:

Chief Bey	Sonny Morgan
Naji Ibrahim	Nadi Qamar
Kahlil	Louis Williams
Pat Patrick	

The people in this play are Black.

Time: early 1960s; the past, etc. Place: MARIE HORTON's *house—a single-story, two-bedroom bungalow in Los Angeles, near Pico and Western.*

Stage black. Slowly, a bizarre Christmas tree lights up. Its bulbs wink and glare colorfully in contrast to the shadows and blackness of the rest of the stage.

A small dog yaps abruptly, offstage, then quiets.

The tree commands the area for some moments, then a Rhythm 'N Blues number of the period rises from a cheap, portable, imitation-alligator-covered phonograph.

A television set lights up without sound, its picture out of focus at first, then clearing to show a white face smiling and speaking wordlessly.

Giggles in the dark. The dog sounds offstage. A VOICE: *"Damn!" Silence except for the music.*
Lights of the tree and television show figures on stage.

MARIE'S VOICE
(*Impatient*) C'mon, Bud!
(*More giggles. And the whirring sound of a film projector*)

TONI'S VOICE
Damn, Bud . . . Little-ass Whitie could have done better than you. (*Dog yaps*)

RUTH'S VOICE
You hear her tellin' you to let her in so she can take care of business, can't ya?
A screen lights up feebly, at first, then the film begins. It is apparent from the start that it is a pornographic film.
There is a sound track of heavy lovemaking pervading the space, mixed with the other mechanical and human sounds.
If the technology of the cinema proves too difficult to nego- tiate for the Black Theatre *group that does the play, then a framed scrim, lighted from behind, can serve as the movie screen, with actors playing there, their silhouettes simulating the lewd and obscene performances.*
Female laughter and giggles of delight.

MARIE HORTON
(*Giggles*) Ohhh . . . gawd, Horton! . . . Ohhh . . . this is awful, Bill. Heee heeee . . . ha ha ha . . . Hey, Mr. Hor- ton! . . . this the best you can find, huh? . . . This old sad things is as about as sexy as my grandmammy's drawers.

RUTH
Shhh . . . quiet, Marie . . . I can't hear the slurpin' . . .
(MARIE HORTON *goes into a fit of giggling*)

BILL
(*Drunk, stretched out upon the floor*) Hey, Marie . . . Hey, stuff . . . I brought you back a dirty movie . . . didn't I? . . . Heeyyyy . . . that's a dirty movie, ain't it?

MARIE

(*Giggles*) Oh, stop it . . . Bill. Ha ha . . . you're killing me.

RUTH

Slurp . . . slurp . . . slurp . . .

MARIE

(*Screams and laughs*) Oh . . . Ruthie . . . Ha ha ha . . . hee
hee . . .
   (*As the television glare lowers to blackness and the music
from the phonograph drifts away to silence, the lights rise
to show* MARIE HORTON's *Christmas party*)

TONI

I don't know what you're laughin' at, Marie. That's the vul-
garest thing that I've ever seen.

BUD

You're just sayin' that, baby . . .
   (*Winks*)
Wait till I get you home tonight and try out some of that
French kissin' stuff on ya.

TONI

Bud! . . . Have you lost your mind? . . . Man . . . you better kiss me like you civilized or don't even get to the first
pucker.
   (MARIE HORTON *is sprawled upon a couch.* BILL HORTON *lies
drunkenly upon the floor,* ART GARRISON *is in an alcoholic stupor
upon the floor, his back propped up by the couch,* RUTH *and*
TONI *stand, peering at the movie screen, and* BUD *operates
the projector*)

MARIE

Awww . . . Toni, girl . . . You so crazy.

RUTH

Sho is.

TONI

Why, Ruth . . . I would never say anything like that to you.

RUTH

Well, you know I was kiddin', Toni.

TONI

But you said it anyway.

RUTH

Well it wasn't nothin' . . . Marie says far worse things to you than . . .

TONI

(*Cuts*) Now I wasn't talkin' about . . .

MARIE

(*Cuts*) Hey . . . you two ole hens! . . . Stop all that cacklin'.

BILL

(*Slurs*) Damn . . . Marie . . . nobody can say anything . . .

MARIE

(*Jovial*) Shut up, Horton . . . man . . . you so drunk. Get up from there and fix me a drink.

BILL

(*Groggy*) When I fix you a drink I'll be fixin' us a drink.

TONI

You gonna let him talk to you like that, Marie?

RUTH

Sho she is.

BUD

I thought you folks were gonna look at this movie?

MARIE

(*Shrugs*) Well . . . Mr. Horton pays the bills . . . and if he don't want to get me a drink . . . well . . . the ole red nigger don't have to do nothin' for yours truly . . . Nawh . . .

nobody don't have to do nary a thing for Miss Marie . . .
Miss Marie is quite independent . . . Hummp!

BILL

(*Groans*) Ohhhh . . . Marie . . .

MARIE

Shit! . . . I still want me a Scotch on the rocks, man.

TONI

Turn that filthy thing off, Bud! Nobody wants to look at that.
(*Dog yaps*)

MARIE

Awww . . . c'mon, Toni . . . Let's look at the old dull thing.

TONI

You should turn that filthy shit off, Marie. Look at it.

RUTH

You lookin' at it so hard yourself, Toni . . . Why you want it
off?

TONI

Now, Ruthie . . . you can't say that I'm lookin' at that junk
seriously . . . can you?

BUD

Yeah.

TONI

Oh, keep quiet, Bud!

    (TONI *pulls out the power cord to the movie projector. It
grinds to a stop with a mechanical groan. If* ACTORS *are used
behind a scrim,* THEY *make the noise of their being unplugged.
    Lights change; the dog yaps*)

(*Ladylike*) Marie, honey . . . why don't you let that goddamn
dog in?

RUTH

She can't . . .

BUD

Can't?

TONI

Bud!

MARIE

Nawh . . . she's in heat. She's gotta keep her little white ass out in the back yard.

BILL

Ha ha ha . . . and she pees on Marie's new rugs.

TONI

Gawd . . . leave the little bitch out then. I wouldn't have her wetting on my new nylon carpets.

(*Lights change. Sprawled upon the couch,* MARIE HORTON *slips her slipper from her foot, lets it drop to the carpet, and with her stockinged toe nudges* ART GARRISON's *head, leaning beside the end of the couch*)

MARIE

(*Teases* ART) Hey, you . . .

RUTH

Hey, Marie . . . let him sleep.

BUD

Ha ha . . . don't woke him . . . let him slept . . . ha ha . . .

TONI

Damn . . . I forgot that guy was still here.

MARIE

(*Pulls her leg back*) Hey . . . don't you hear what I'm sayin' to you? . . . I want you to get me a drink . . . Scotch on the rocks, baby. Ambassador Scotch . . . my brand . . . you know where it is, don't you? . . . And take out your coffee cup on your way out.

BUD

He knows the Scotch's out in the kitchen . . . Ha ha . . . out in the kitchen . . . to your right . . . beside the 'frigerator.

. . . Hey . . . remember when everybody thought that Frigidaire meant all 'frigerators?

MARIE

(*Rises*) Hey . . . Art . . . hey! You gonna get me my drink, huh?

BILL

(*Groggy, half conscious*) I'll take a V.O. and water . . . champ.

(ART GARRISON *stirs. Bleary-eyed* HE *looks up at* MARIE *standing over him, and he smiles drunkenly*)

MARIE

Oh, now you're awake . . . 'bout time. Man . . . you were snoring to beat the band.

(BILL *falls asleep and begins snoring.* TONI *giggles as* BUD *whispers into her ear and tries to feel her butt. The lights change and sensual melody comes from the phonograph and the TV comes dimly on, as the lights change color. The dog yaps outside.* ALL FIGURES *drift into the shadows except for* ART *and* MARIE, *and* BILL, *who snores upon the floor, just beyond the spill of the confined light*)

MARIE

You've slept so long . . . baby. And you've missed the movie and my guests have gone an' everything. Look at ole Bill over there . . . drunk to the world . . . and it's so quiet except for our breathing . . . I want me a Scotch on the rocks, baby. Ambassador . . . Scotch . . . my brand . . . And while you're up, honey . . . ha ha ha . . . see how the V.O. and the ale is holdin' out. Bill will be thirsty when he wakes up . . . and Ruth'll be wantin' her ale when she comes over.

ART

(*Drowsy*) Huh?

MARIE

Now . . . Art . . .

(SHE *stands, moves around in front of him, reaches down*

and pulls her fingers through his shaggy head of hair. HE
takes her hand, climbs to his feet and kisses MARIE HORTON
passionately for a long moment
  Catches breath)
Oh . . . Art . . . not here, baby.
  (HE *kisses her again*)
Let's go into the bedroom, Art . . . Yes, I know that Bill is
stone cold drunk and it's impossible to wake him . . . but let's
go in the bedroom anyway . . . Doin' it in front of him makes
me feel creepy . . . Uhhggg . . . Oh . . . don't kiss me so
hard, baby . . . Remember . . . I'm a soft, tender woman
. . . ha ha . . . well taken care of . . . not plump, ya understand . . . ha ha . . . not even pleasingly . . . but first you
have to get me a drink, Art. My motor won't turn over too
tough with a dry battery, honey . . . you know what I drink,
don't you? . . . Ambassador . . . Ambassador Scotch . . . top
shelf . . . imported . . . yeah, that's what I drink . . . yeah
. . . that's what you have to bring Marie Horton to clean her
pipes . . . umhmmmm . . . *Miss Marie* . . . takes it on the
rocks, honey . . . that's right . . . you better believe it!
  (ART GARRISON *withdraws into the shadows. The music plays
and the lights and TV's glare throw strange patterns across
the stage*)
What chou say? . . . I been drinkin' Scotch for quite some
time now . . . ever since I got accustomed to tryin' to
live like I would like to become accustomed to . . . ha
ha . . . damn right I do. I used to live in Buffalo, ya know
. . . I'm really from Pittsburgh, you understand . . . but I
used to live in Buffalo with my granny . . . just like Wanda
lives here with me . . . but god knows I wasn't stupid like
Wandie . . . god knows I wasn't. Damn . . . I was a slick
little chick. That's when I started bein' called Miss Marie . . .
It used to snow real deep up in Buffalo and I had my little
red boots that I used to tip 'round in . . . and everybody
used to say: "There goes little cute Miss Marie . . . down to
get a bucket of beer for her Granny." And that's where I'd be
on my way to . . . and I'd get there and get inside where it

was warm by the coal stove and blow my breath into my hands
and take my bucket around to the back end of the bar . . .
that's where they filled your bucket . . . back 'round the side
there . . . back in those days. And it ain't had nothin' to do
with discrimination . . . I'm from the North . . . and I ain't
never known anything 'bout no discrimination. . . . I always
did have my freedom . . . Yes sir . . . Miss Marie will tell you
. . . I want to thank you.

(*During the remainder of* MISS MARIE's *speech,* BILL *rises
from the shadows and enters a lighted area, opposite* MARIE,
and begins a shuffling dance. BILL *does the dance of a 1930s
negro showman, the Black Bottom, the Soft-shoe, the Buck 'n
Wing;* HE *appears a young man at the start of his dance but
toward the end of* MARIE's *monologue* HE *becomes the man* HE
is on Christmas day, 1961.

*Meanwhile, the Christmas tree glows and pulsates dimly
to the rhythm of the scene, as the television casts its mute
image outward, and the phonograph plays softly*)

MARIE

If I couldn't have my Scotch every day, honey . . . I'd quit!
I'd just give it up, baby. Nawh . . . I ain't kiddin' . . . Hummp.
And it better be Ambassador too. Those old cows in my clubs
would swear that I was slippin' if they saw me sippin' a Miller's
High Life . . . Wouldn't they? . . . Yeah . . . sure would.
Bad as me havin' no fur coat. Marie Horton . . . without even
a stole. Ohhh . . . that Bill . . . he says I don't need a fur in
Los Angeles. Sheet . . . I've had a fur ever since my granny
gave me my first one when I was nine . . . 'cept now that we
out here.

You know I'm president of three negro women's clubs . . .
really the founder as well as president. And I have to keep
myself together . . . or what would the girls say? Hell, I
know what they'd say . . . They'd say: "Who does Miss
Marie" . . . that's what they call me. "Miss Marie" . . . "Who
does Miss Marie think she is?" they'd say . . . "she hasn't even
got a fur coat." they'd say . . . "Everytime you see her she's

in that old red print dress . . . with her fat gut stickin' out so far it looks like the middle button's gonna pop off" they would say. "Probably needs to wear her house dress, poor dear, with that little bit of money Bill brings in" they would say . . . If I stood for them 'n let them . . . Shoot . . . I ain't never gonna let them say nothin' about Marie Horton. Nawh suh! That's for somebody else to tolerate . . . not Miss Marie.

We been out here in L.A. for twelve years now . . . Bill and me. Came out a couple years after the war. And it's groovey, baby . . . nothin' but high life. Bill makes three times as much . . . maybe four . . . as he made back East. He used to dance . . . before he went out and had to get a job. Yeah. I don't know how anybody can stay back there in the cold. Give me L.A. any day, baby. It's got everything . . . And the men . . . the men . . . makes a girl like me drool all over her cocktail frock . . . 'cause this is the place to keep an old hen scratchin' like a spring bird. Ooooo . . . yeah. In the warm California sun.

(SHE *does a large bump and grind, snaps her fingers and humps the audience as* WANDA *enters* BILL's *area of light and is snatched by the hand and is made to reluctantly dance with the now drunk man*)

MARIE

(*Grinds, grimacing as if during orgasm*) You can take it if you can make it . . . 'cause you ain't gonna break it . . . yeah. Miss Marie wants to thank you.

(BILL *and* MARIE *stop still in their pools of light and speak. Together*) Bill brings home two hundred stone cold dollars a week . . . to me, Miss Marie . . . and puts it in my hand. And the tips he makes parkin' cars out to the studio in Beverly Hills is more than that. We make almost as much as some colored doctors make . . . 'n we spend it too. 'Cause it's party time every day at Miss Marie's house.

(WANDA *tries to pull away from* BILL; HE *pulls her back*)

WANDA
Ahhh . . . Uncle Bill . . . I'm tired.

(*Lights come up. Christmas tree lights dim and dissolve into the background with the TV. The dog yaps outside*)

BILL

(*Dances*) Heeyy . . . Wandie . . . you ain't gonna let your ole uncle out-dance you . . . are ya?
(*Does high kick and step*)
Whheee . . . swing it, girl . . . Oeeeee . . . yeah . . .
(*Lights up on* RUTH, TONI *and* BUD)

WANDA

(*Dancing*) Ahhh . . . Uncle Bill . . .

MARIE

Bill! . . . hey, Bill . . . leave that broken-down little broad alone. She ain't nothin' but a young girl . . . hummmp . . . but she acts like she's got an iceberg up her twat . . .
(WANDA *holds down her skirt as* SHE *is flung about by* BILL)

WANDA

Ohh . . . Aunt Marie . . .

TONI

Bill . . . why don't you leave that child alone . . . you can see that she don't want to dance with you.

BUD

Well I don't care if she don't want to dance with ole Bill . . . as long as I got nex' dance.
(BUD *begins to do the Twist and moves into* BILL *and* WANDA's *area and dances with* WANDA)

MARIE

Do it, Bud. . . . What's that new dance that you and Wandie does so good?

RUTH

It's called the Twist . . . Marie.

MARIE

Ohh . . . well . . . Bud sho can do it . . .

TONI

Sho can . . . chile . . .

(*The telephone begins to ring.* MARIE *dances a fast rumble to the phone, while* BUD *and* WANDA *do the Twist and* BILL *Soft-shoes, Buck 'n Wings almost in the shadows.* TONI *watches, tapping her foot. The dog yaps.* ART *enters, carrying a tray of drinks*)

Well . . . here's our boy . . . Art.

(*On her way to the telephone* MARIE *sweeps a drink from the tray, almost upsetting the mess in* ART's *hands*)

ART

(*Catching balance*) Hey! . . .

MARIE

(*Answers phone, a high, false young voice*) Hey . . . what's happenin'?

TONI

(*To* ART) Did you bring my Southern Comfort?

MARIE

Oh, Bea . . . how ya doin', girl?

ART

(*To* TONI) Ahuh . . .

(HE *hands her a drink*)

BILL

Mine's V.O. and water, Art. That's Canadian . . . ya know . . .

(*The television lights up.* ART *serves* BILL *and* BUD *and is politely refused by* WANDA. *The dog yaps outside. In a lighted area at back, an* ACTOR *pantomimes what is supposed to be happening on the television screen. There is the negro evening news announcer, in bow tie and serious face, wordlessly mouthing about the dreary events of the day*)

MARIE

(*On phone*) Yeah, girl . . . we still partyin' . . . yeah, this is some Christmas. Yeah . . . really, Bea. We started at

Shadow's place two days ago, girl. I really wanted to wait to
at least Christmas Eve, honey . . . but those niggers couldn't
wait to swill some liquor and call themselves having a good
time . . . Sure she's with him! . . . yeah! . . . Ruth's still with
that nigger, child . . . Ahuhnnn . . . it should have been somethin' . . . Ahuhnnn . . . would be still over to Shadow's but
you know how he is . . . wouldn't give Ruth a moment, girl
. . . Ha ha . . . that man is the biggest cockhound in town
. . . Gawd! . . . Didn't give anybody a chance . . . ha ha . . .
bad enough for Ruthie it was her old man who forever had
a sweaty . . . and I mean *sweaty!* . . . wet palm on her booty
. . . but we other girls had to suffer the consequences . . .
NO! . . . Nawh, whore . . . don't put that off on me . . . he
ain't my type . . . none of ours . . . ha ha . . . not even Ruth's
. . . Heee ha ha ha . . . I want to thank you, chick . . . him
and Bill . . . ha ha ha . . . Toni calls them the Gold Dust
Twins, honey . . . Yeah! . . . Bill's still fucken that funky ole
white bitch, girl. Yeah . . . sho is corny . . . He swears to me
that it's all a product of my imagination . . . yes, he does . . .
but he don't know I know he's got that little old red baby by
her . . . I hear tell it looks like a wrinkled-up pink baboon . . .
yeah . . . Ha! . . . Iris tell me that
    (*Whiny voice*)
"Maybe you should have a baby for Bill." . . . WHOOP! . . .
hee ha ha ha . . . ain't that the limit, Bea? . . . The only thing
Bill Horton's gettin' from me is a hard time if he don't bring
some money in here, and I mean some money . . . Ha! . . .
The Gold Dust Twins . . . but Bill's the drunky half, girl.
Shadow's dizzy . . . an' Bill's drunky, honey . . . I want to
thank ya.
    (SHE *snaps her fingers and wiggles to the music and the
rhythm of her voice*)
. . . Yeah, preach, baby. Tell it like it is . . . ha ha ha . . .
ooooeee . . . you a wicked heifer, woman . . . Geezus! . . .
what Ruth and I got to go through, girl . . .

WANDA

But you should do somethin' . . . somethin' . . . anything not
fall into a grave of middle-age remorse . . .

BILL

What you say, Wandie?

MARIE

(*To* WANDA) Get out of that spotlight, broad . . . this is my
story, understand?

WANDA

Oh, nothin' . . . Uncle Bill . . . nothin' . . . and I'm sorry,
Aunt Marie.

BILL

(*Cutting a fancy step*) Wheee! . . . See that, Marie! . . . See
that!

MARIE

Child . . . Bill's here really cuttin' the fool now . . . ha ha . . .
you should just see him with his ole timey self.

(*The TV news announcer has disappeared and has been
replaced by* FIGURES *simulating a non-violent civil rights dem-
onstration of the early sixties' vintage.* THEY *pray,* THEY *kneel,*
THEY *appeal,* THEY *sing "We Shall Overcome" respectfully,
then* THEY *are beaten mercilessly*)

WANDA

Oh . . . look . . . look y'all . . . the civil righters.

TONI

The civil who? . . .

BUD

Rights, sweet cake . . . rights.

RUTH

(*In her cups*) What they rightin' about?

BILL

(*Dancing*) Hey, Marie . . . looka here, stuff . . . watch this one . . . wheee . . . C'mon, Wandie . . .

WANDA

Nawh, Uncle Bill . . . Nawh, . . . I want to watch the Freedom Marchers.

MARIE

Bea, . . . they got some fools on this television that ain't got no sense, girl . . . They gettin' their natural ass kicked by some crackers, chile . . . big ugly-lookin' red-necks.

(ART *returns with more drinks, sets them down and takes one.* HE *stands apart from the group watching.* GAFNEY *enters*)

ART

Niggers always look so cool because they don't want anybody to know how bad things are.

GAFNEY

Just as I thought. These people are drinking and carouseling.

WANDA

He's in my class, Art . . . I know you and Aunt Marie and Uncle Bill don't like Gafney, but try and be nice to him, huh?

MARIE

(*Still on telephone*) Shucks, child . . . Freedom Marchers . . . huhnnn . . . I already got my freedom . . . have always had it. I don't need no raggedy-ass niggers beggin' and moanin' and gettin' their behinds whipped for my freedom, honey . . . Nawh, sir, Miss Marie got what she's got . . . and that spells freedom, baby.

WANDA

But you don't understand . . . Aunt Marie, you don't understand. It's not about what you have or what I have but what we all have, need and want as Black people.

GAFNEY

Teach, sister! . . . Tell 'em where it's at!

(*The dog yaps. Lights change. The TV images fade, and* ALL *on stage disappear into shadows except* BILL)

BILL

It ain't been a bad life. Hell no, not a bad one. It could have been worse, ya know . . . Yeah, chief . . . it could have been a buster . . . wow . . . But I met Marie, see . . . and . . .

(*In dim, tinted light,* MARIE *appears, swaying and humming to soft music, cradling an imaginary bundle in her arms, as if it were a baby*)

it started straightenin' out for me from then on. Until now. Which ain't so bad, actually . . . Me and Marie been makin' it close to sixteen years. We make it pretty well together. Yeah that's my ole lady, Marie. . . . Hardly ever get hassled by the world. She keeps the kinda house I like to live in . . . and we drink and party together and like some of the same people . . . it could have been worse. . . . I coulda stayed in Pittsburgh and kept on pluggin' away at nuttin' . . . but me and Marie came out here. Out here where the sun almost never stops shining, where palms wag above the dog-days Boulevards . . . yeah . . . it coulda been worse. . . . We coulda broken up . . . yeah . . . we coulda but we stuck it out. I guess our most serious hassle was when we was three—four years into our thing.

(*The lights dim on* MARIE)

I usta run numbers some back in Pittsburgh . . . and I got busted. Yeah, I got busted. Got sixty days . . . which wasn't so bad, ya understand . . . but bad enough. And I got out in thirty-three. Don't know how. Wasn't good time or nothin' like that. I forget now. Probably my boss, Big Time, gave somebody some juice downtown.

(MARIE'S *face is seen—startled, apprehensive*)

I was one of his best boys. And I come home to where Marie and I were stayin'.

MARIE

(*Nervous, angry*) Big Time! . . . nigger, why didn't you tell me that you put in a fix for Bill? He's home and here we are —caught! Damn! I don't care if you thought he wasn't gettin' out until after the weekend. Gon' man, you got a second to get out the back door before he sees you. I can handle him. . . . Don't worry . . . I can take care of Bill Horton. . . . Just get your ass out of here, ya hear?

BILL

. . . and I was so happy I hollared out: "HEY, STUFF . . . HEY, MARIE!"

MARIE

(*Aside*) Which saved my dark behind. . .

BILL

. . . and I came through my front door. . . . A dim light was on in the back . . .

(*A black* FIGURE *is portrayed upon the movie screen: it is seen tipping with clothes and shoes in hand, then sneaking with exaggerated movements, then disappears from the screen*)

BILL

I saw a shadow. "Marie?" I called. Then there was some movement and noise. The bathroom door opening and closing. Footsteps in the kitchen and then the soft slam of the back door. . . . After Marie came out of the bathroom we had our worse argument. . . . We nearly busted up right then and there. . . . The bitterness lasted in our lives for over a year. . . . She never did tell me who it was. Said it was my dirty mind, my nasty, jailbird imagination and the drinks I had had before I got home. . . . But I know my woman . . . and now I don't blame her too much. There are just some things about a woman that you understand if you've been together long enough and are tryin' to make it. But that was an argument we had . . . whew . . . I almost hit her. . . . Yeah, I almost tore her head off. . . . But I didn't. There's something about hitting a woman that means the end. When you raise your hand to a woman that you love and hurt her that way . . . well somethin' just goes out of the relationship. . . . Do you understand what I mean?

MARIE

Yeah . . . you mean that you better not think of crackin' your
knuckles too close to Miss Marie . . . if you know what's good
for your weather-beaten buns.

BILL

Now if I were to strike Marie . . . well there'd be an awful
row . . . she's spoiled, you know. But it would blow over . . .
on the surface . . . after a while. But something would be
gone . . . it would be long gone . . . and perhaps that's the
thing that has made this thing between us work, ya know. And
I don't want to lose that. . . . Nawh . . . it ain't been a bad
life . . . and I ain't about to mess it up, if I can help it. Not
for love or hate or a white woman . . . or nuthin'. HEY,
MARIE! . . . HEY, STUFF! . . . FILL UP MY GLASS
AGAIN. YOU KNOW MY DRINK, BABY. YOU KNOW IT!

(BILL *and* MARIE *fade away; lights alter.* ART *steps forward
as the dog yaps, then quiets*)

ART

I can dig where you comin' from, chief, but you're wastin'
your breath.

GAFNEY

You would think so, wouldn't you? For you this is the best
environment that you could have?

WANDA

(*From the shadows*) Can't you two try and understand one
another?

ART

Hey . . . Gafney . . . if you gonna be talkin' to me, friend,
you gonna have to start talkin' like the rest of us. Some of those
words you use are too much, man.

GAFNEY

Yes . . . that's what you say but you can't fool me none, Art
Garrison. You make out like you don't know nothin', that you're

just a nigger off the streets like everybody else . . . or like lots of people would like to be like . . .

ART
No kiddin'. . . . tell me more.

GAFNEY
But I got you down pat, you . . . you . . .

WANDA
(*From the shadows*) Please don't say it . . .

GAFNEY
. . . YOU CON MAN! You just do that dumb act to fool people. You just around here waitin' to take advantage of these poor Black people. . . . Why . . . why I've even seen you taking night courses at City College!

ART
You know it all don't you, Gafney?

GAFNEY
Yes, I know all about you . . . and you know what?
(*Pause*)
You know what?
(*Pause*)
You know . . . I could tell you something?

ART
You could, huh?

GAFNEY
Yes, I could.
(*Pause*)
I could tell you something that you wouldn't even believe. That hardly no person . . . Black or white . . . would believe.

ART
You can, huh?

GAFNEY

Yes, I can tell you something about me, Art Garrison. . . .
If I really thought for a moment that you could understand.

ART

I might.

WANDA

(*From the shadows*) So would I. Gafney . . . try me.

GAFNEY

Now nobody knows this . . . that means nobody . . . except
people who don't matter to me anymore.

ART

Ummhmmmm . . .

GAFNEY

Now anybody know this, Art.

WANDA

(*From the shadows*) Nobody knows . . .

ART

Yeah, man . . . nobody knows it.

GAFNEY

(*Proudly; after deep breath*) I come from the streets too. . . .
I wasn't born in a well-to-do colored neighborhood in Atlanta,
Georgia . . . and was brought to L.A. when I was a baby . . .
No, brother . . . I come from East Saint Louis.

ART

No kiddin'.

GAFNEY

Yes, brother Art. . . . I am a Soul Brother, too.

ART

Well . . . this is really news. . . . HEY, WANDIE! . . . HEY!
GAFNEY SAYS THAT HE'S A STREET NIGGER! . . . HEY
WANDA DID YOU HEAR THAT? . . . GAFNEY SAYS
THAT HE'S A STREET NIGGER!

GAFNEY

(*Venomous*) Art Garrison . . . you're nothing! You're nothing, Art Garrison. Nothing!

MARIE

(*Off*) Art . . . don't just leave your empty coffee cup around my house, nigger . . . pick it up . . . try and help me keep my place nice.

(*Lights and shadow and music alter;* ART, *alone, speaks*)

ART

I'm on my ass, man. Down, down down . . . I mean down, brother. And my spirit is down. Way down. Down so low I can't fly . . . not right now. So I'm layin' . . . yeah . . . with this bitch and her ole man. It sure is somethin' else. Wouldn't have believed it if I hadn't seen it. . . . Whew . . . but I'm takin' care of business ah little taste. Got this ole sister, Marie, jacked up. And she's keepin' her ole man cool. She tells him that I'm suffering from a bad situation. And I am. Just got out of the slam. Just gettin' myself together. I stay here and eat and sleep and do whatever they want me to do, which is mainly gettin' drinks for them and drivin' them around in their car. Just light work . . . except for the action I give the ole girl when her daddy Bill is out of sight or out like a light . . .

(MARIE *appears*)

Oh oh . . . here she comes again.

(*To music, the* COUPLE *kiss, embrace and dance intimately, then break.* SHE *leaves*)

See what I mean? She's got heavy and hot hot pants for me . . . if she wore them. Nawh . . . she doesn't . . . nawh nawh . . . I'm not kiddin'. Swear I'm not. Marie Horton don't wear no drawers. Not one stitch. . . . Says they slow her down, yeah. She's a pistol, man. But it was lucky I hooked up with her and her ole man, Bill. 'Specially now that I can't do nothin' for me. Wow . . . a broad can really get you down. I'm comin' off one of those bad broad trips myself . . . but that's another play, right, sport? But I got to get my ass up off the ground. Yeah, I got to make it. I got places to go, things to do, people to see and myself to be, yeah. Gotta clear my head. Get this pain in my brain in gear. Gotta get Garrison in gear. And this is the place to make it for the moment. Good grease, man. More drinks than I can stand to drink. And then there's Miss Marie . . . and maybe there's her little niece . . . Wanda.

(*Lights alter. Dog yaps off.* MARIE *and* BILL *are seen*)

MARIE

Did you have to take her around our friends, Bill? Did you have to take that white woman where we go?

BILL

I was drunk, Marie. . . . High as a kite. . . . It shouldn't have happened, I know, but I just couldn't help it.

MARIE

(*Resigned*) No . . . I guess you couldn't. . . . You done so much to me over the years . . . I guess doin' just one more thing like this don't really matter.

BILL

But, baby, if we could . . ; if we could . . .

MARIE

Well I can't . . . you saw to that, didn't you?

BILL

. . . If we could have only had kids, Marie.

MARIE

It was the abortion that did it. It was that . . . that damn quack that you got me that messed me up for life.

BILL

I never wanted you to do it, Marie.

MARIE

It was your fault, Bill Horton! It was your fault! You got me pregnant!

BILL

But I never wanted you to get that operation. I never wanted you to get rid of the baby.

MARIE

But the other one went okay. . . . Nothing happened to the first one.

BILL

Your grandmother saw to that.

MARIE

Granny had her place in the community. . . . Granny couldn't have me do something terrible like that and ruin our good family name.

BILL

But you should have never gotten rid of our baby, Marie.

MARIE

But I could have never had a baby by that ole nigger from The Hill. . . . I couldn't do that to Granny, Bill . . .

BILL

It would have been so nice if . . .

MARIE

If you just hadn't told our friends . . . I would have let you keep her quietly . . . as long as you kept up my house.

BILL

I was drunk . . . drunk as a skunk . . . and I wanted the world to know that I could have kids . . . even if she was white.

MARIE

You shouldn't have gotten me pregnant. . . . You shouldn't have been younger than me and got me pregnant . . . and give in to me and gotten the operation for me like Granny had . . . and married me 'cause you ruined me. . . . That's right, Bill, we wouldn't have been married now . . . and out of love.

BILL

Sometimes when I get drunk I'm sorry afterwards . . . sometimes . . .

(*Lights and shapes alter; the Christmas tree glows from the darkness. The dog yaps outside*)

TONI

(*Off*) Why don't that damn mutt keep quiet?

RUTH

(*Off*) Whitie just wants something to eat. . . . Marie'll feed her soon.

TONI

(*Off*) I sure as hell hope so, honey . . . that's a noisy little bitch.

RUTH

(*Off*) Marie's gotta wait until Bill gives her some shoppin' money . . . she only feeds her dog steak.

TONI

(*Off*) Sheet . . .

MARCO

You don't know me. I just got here. . . . My name's Marco . . . Marco Polo Henderson . . . now ain't that a handle? My folks really hung one on me. . . . I sure won't get confused with a lot of other niggers. 'Cause my name is strange. And I'm a pretty yellow nigger anyway with curly curly hair that all the little Black mamas like to run their hands over. And the white bitches speak to me in my tongue too, baby . . . and it ain't forked, dig? Nor is it cold, hmmm . . . ha ha ha . . . Yeah, man, if I only had that piece of paper. If I only had that degree . . .

(*During* MARCO's *speech*, BILL, ART, STEVE BENSON *and* BUD *swing and sway together, harmonizing Christmas carols.* GAFNEY *stands to one side with folded arms and impatiently taps his foot until* WANDA *comes near enough for him to corner and wordlessly exhort to her his truths.* SHE *patiently hangs on his every word while attempting to listen to* MARCO)

. . . Damn . . . I could get out of this chickenshit level of existence. . . . Man, my ass is on the ground. . . . Wow, my ass eats grass if this ain't a bad scene for me, Jim. All I got to show for nothin' is a little ass chickenshit government check to go to school on. . . . If it wasn't for my gettin' disability from the VA for my asthma I would really be up shit creek without proper means of locomotion. . . . Wow, my dick would be in the sand, man. I'd just be humping along, my balls draggin' . . . if I wasn't a fuckin' invalid. Yeah! That's right, boss. Couldn't do nothin'. Now they expect me to finish this last year on my degree with no dough. The court's after me. My ole lady's screamin' for support. . . . Support, shit! . . . She knows I can't pay no support for Adrienne and Keith. I gotta finish school. Why did she wait till now to start this shit. Been outta the service for almost three years. No word from her. She was doin' alright . . . and the kids were so much hers that I couldn't even see them if I wanted to. Didn't even know where she was for a while. Then bam . . . before I knew it I was in court. She wants all kinds of money, even back money for the times she didn't get no money when I didn't have no money after my service checks stopped. Sheet . . . she's at the other end of the state and got me sneakin' around like Robert F. Williams . . . yeah, there might be a nab behind every bush, man. What if they bust me at school? And this dizzy-ass bitch I'm messin' with, Wanda, ain't nothin' but a drag. . . . Damn . . . how chickenshit . . . what kinda goddamn luck do I have anyway? If I only had that piece of paper, man. I could split and get me a job somewhere . . . but, man, I dig California . . . I really dig it . . . yeah yeah yeah . . . in the warm California sun.

(*As the* CAROLERS *disintegrate into shadowy figures,* ART *steps away from the forms and joins* WANDA *and* GAFNEY)

ART

What cha doin' these days, Wandie?

WANDA

Nothin' . . . I was goin' to school . . . but I'm not even doin' that now. Aunt Marie's on me to get a job.

MARIE

(*Momentarily appears*) You better believe it! She's gonna get a job or my name ain't what yawhl know it to be. Wandie! . . . you gonna stop your funky ass from comin' in here with a wet twat after stayin' out all night . . . layin' up with Marco!

WANDA

Ohhh . . . Aunt Marie.
   (MARIE *disappears*)

GAFNEY

(*To* ART) Yes . . . I was just informing the sister here that there was many positive things she could be doing with herself . . .

ART

(*Ignores* GAFNEY) I know of a little job that you can have, Wandie.

GAFNEY

Day care centers are always in need of young, energetic and sensitive people to work with the children.

ART

You could bring home maybe two . . . three hundred bucks a week, Wandie.

WANDA

I could?

GAFNEY

And there are tutorial programs . . . in the ghetto . . . mainly voluntary, of course . . .

ART

I got a buddy who's got this masseur parlor over on Crenshaw.

WANDA

But, Art . . . I don't know.

GAFNEY

Wanda! I believe that would be completely wrong for you.

ART

Easy man . . . I'm talkin' to the girl, okay. . . . Listen, Wanda, you don't know how to massage nobody . . . and you don't need to know. My friend needs somebody straight-lookin' to front for his business in the back. All you'd have to do is welcome the chumps, check them out and refer them to the people in the back. . . . Oh, yeah . . . and answer the phone.

WANDA

Art, you couldn't think . . .

ART

But he'd dig your nicey style, baby. . . . You could get almost anything you'd ask for.

WANDA

Ohhh . . . Art.
  (MARIE *laughs in the background*)

GAFNEY

(*Stutters*) Mmmmmmmmaaannn . . . tttthhh . . . ttthhhhhis this is terrible! . . . Ttthhiisss this is the mmmo oooss stt disgusting, fff fffoouuulll act that Iiiii ttthhhaattt Iiiii've evvvver seen!

WANDA

(*Hurt*) Art . . . how could you?

ART

Take it easy . . . think it over . . . two, three hundred bucks a week could mean a lot to you right now. . . . Why don't you think about it, Wanda.
  (*In tears* WANDA *exits.* MARIE *and* MARCO *appear.* MARIE *still laughs*)

MARIE

Ha ha ha . . . ha hee hee . . . Art . . . ha . . . Art, you're too much. Ha ha . . . tryin' to put Wandie's stiff ole corny butt on the block.

GAFNEY

It's disgusting.

MARCO

Look . . . Marie . . . she's your niece, not mine. I got my own problems. You take care of her. She ain't movin' in with me . . . umm umm . . . if she ain't got no place to stay that's her problem.

ART

Maybe I can find somethin' else for her to do.

MARIE

Well, she's gonna have to do somethin'. Draggin' herself in here every night like some ole mangy dawg. Thinks because she hardly eats here and sneaks herself into my bathroom to wash her ole funky drawers that she's not takin' up space. Well, soap costs, you know. And every towel in this house is my towel . . . I've got them counted. And two women in one house is two women too many.

GAFNEY

This is just too awful . . . I have to get out!
(HE *exits. The lights grow dim on the figures. The dog yaps*)

MARCO

I don't care if the broad stays with me now and then. . . . Sure she wants to move in with me . . . and she's got a pretty nice little box . . . but man I'm tryin' to make it . . . and she ain't in my program at the moment.

ART

I was just trying to be helpful . . . people.
(MARIE *whoops with laughter and clutches* ART. THEY *kiss hard and go off together. Black. Lights up on* STEVE BENSON)

STEVE

Well, I'm really not in this one. I just eased through the door.

Came in behind Marc. Kinda by accident. And Art's my cousin
. . . and I know some of the rest of these people. So I guess I
just get pulled into the middle of this. Things haven't been
going too well with me. I've had some bad problems lately
. . . yeah . . . women. Yeah. You can bet on it. Was goin' with
this married broad. Yeah. She has a husband . . . and a lot of
problems. And somehow I got myself into the middle of it.
Sure was scary for a minute . . . but it's over now. We had
several hassles, then she took a shot at him and he realized
that she was in love with him . . . and the memory of me hanging around them screwin' up their new-found love affair was
too much for them. They up and moved back to the sticks
where they came from. And what made it so cold was that
they were my landlords . . . and I had to find a new place to
stay . . . and the whole thing's messed with me, ya understand.
I started hittin' the jug again. Quit my job, dropped out of
school . . . and started staying by myself again . . . sittin' in
the library, browsing in bookstores, driving around with no
place to go . . . yeah, I got a little car now. Sports car. Nawh,
didn't cost me much. I got it with my severance pay from
work. Now all I got to worry about is puttin' gas in it and paying my room rent. But this town is gettin' me down. Time
for gettin' my hat. Maybe I'll head north. Or even get out of
this damn country. Who knows. I'm just makin' it, that's all
and I'm here to see my buddy buddy Marco Polo Henderson
. . . and my cousin . . . Art Garrison . . . and maybe throw a
quick so-long to Miss Marie.

(MARCO *and* ART *enter. Seeing* STEVE, THEY *greet him: slap
hands* ["*Gimme five*"], *eastern embrace* ["*Salaam, brother*"],
and good-natured put-downs ["*Hey, where'd you find this
chump*"]. *Off to one side* MARIE *looks on, smiling, until* BILL
joins her and grabs her thoughts. The dog yaps)

BILL

I don't know how they could do that, Marie . . . I just really
don't know.

MARIE

Did they tell you that they were going to fire you?

BILL

No.

MARIE

You didn't know anything?

BILL

Nawh . . . I don't know how . . .

MARIE

Oh, god! . . . the car payment is already past due . . . the rent has to . . . ohhh, Bill . . . how could this have happened to us?

BILL

I don't know, baby . . . I don't know . . .

MARIE

Well we have to do something. We can't just lay down and die. Have you spoken to your boss again? . . . Have you spoken to Izzy?

BILL

Nawh . . . nawh . . . Izzy sez he don't want to see me no mo'.

MARIE

Not see you! But you built his business. . . . When I got you that job all he had was that little parkin' lot down off the Main Street . . . with his bein' down at the race track more than anything. . . . Now he's in Beverly Hills . . . and Silky Sullivan didn't put him there.

BILL

Marie.

MARIE

(*Angry*) I worked at Izzy's house. I cleaned his house and took care of his brats. And he won't talk to you? I was down too low and have rose up by covering up his shit and patchin'

his ass together . . . 'cause his woman ain't woman enough
to do it . . . and now he won't talk to you? . . . I've come too
long aways to go back to nothin'!

BILL

Marie.

MARIE

Well, if he won't talk to you then he'll talk to me. We've stuck
by that man . . . what's he going to do now that he doin' good
. . . just shove us aside? That's just like a Jew!

BILL

Marie!

MARIE

Yes, Bill . . . what is it? What is it, baby?

BILL

There's been some money missing from the till . . . at least
that's what Izzy said. He said he kept quiet about it and only
hinted around for a while . . . but he said it got out of hand.

MARIE

But you make a good salary, Bill . . . and your tips are more
than your check.

BILL

And Marie . . . Marie, he said he didn't like what I was doin'
with my life.
  (*Pause*)

MARIE

Bill . . . you didn't take her on your job too, did ya?

BILL

I was drunk, Marie. . . . Drunk. I dreamed of how it would
be for me to drive out along Sunset Strip in my convertible
with my top down with a white woman next to me . . . close,
ya know? Right under me . . . baby, I'm sorry. . . . I was
drunk . . . her too . . . and then when we got out to the lot

and she met Izzy she said somethin' to him that I didn't like and I hit her.

MARIE

You did?

BILL

Yes, I did, baby . . . right in front of everybody.
(*Pause*)

MARIE

How much does her apartment cost you, Bill?

BILL

A lot, baby . . . a lot . . . I didn't mean to get into this . . . I really didn't, baby . . . but . . .

MARIE

(*Realistic*) Well, I got to call Izzy's ole lady. . . . I didn't wipe the shit from her little bastards' behinds for nothin'. She owes me what's mine . . . and Izzy does too . . .

BILL

Izzy said that you were a good, hard-workin' woman, baby . . . and that he liked and respect you . . .

MARIE

Bill . . .

BILL

Huh, baby.

MARIE

Fix me a drink will ya?

BILL

Yeah, baby . . . yeah . . . but Izzy wished you all the best.

MARIE

(*Gentle*) Shhss shhhsss . . . Bill . . . I have to get back your job. Fix me a drink, honey.

BILL

You're too good to me, Marie . . . baby, I'm sorry.

MARIE

Shhsss shhssss . . . Bill . . . stop being sorry.
  (*Bright*)
You know there's no despair in Miss Marie's house. Hey, what's
our theme song, lover?
  (THEY *fall into a brief show routine and Buck 'n Wing and
sing*)

BILL and MARIE

(*Together*) Bill brings home two hundred stone cold dollars
a week . . . to me, Miss Marie . . . and puts it in my hand.
And the tips he makes parkin' cars out to the studio in Beverly
Hills is more than that. We make almost as much as some col-
ored doctors make . . . 'n we spend it too. 'Cause it's party
time every day at Miss Marie's house.
  (THEY *dance and sing into the darkness. The dog yaps.
Lights up on* GAFNEY *and* ART)

GAFNEY

Man, you're nothin'.

ART

(*Casual*) I'm not?

GAFNEY

No, you're nothin' . . . just a nothin' nigger . . . you haven't
got any ethics, any values or morals.

ART

Nawh . . . I guess I haven't.

GAFNEY

You'd do anything to get what you want, no matter what.

ART

Well . . . not *anything*.

GAFNEY

What make you be like you are?

ART

Be like I am? . . . I don't know . . . maybe I was just raised properly. Maybe 'cause I was born with a tin spoon in my mouth.

GAFNEY

You can treat it like that, brother, if you want. But lightheartedness concerning your evil nature won't make it.

ART

Tell me more . . . brother.

GAFNEY

(*Preaching*) There are a lot more things . . . yes, a lot more things that you could be doin' . . . doin' in the service of the Black man . . . than draggin' down your brothers and sisters . . . leading them down the crooked path in this vile "wilderness of North America." . . . Yes, there are a lot more things that you could be doin' than draggin' down your brothers and sisters for your own advantage.

ART

Like what?

(*Lights change.* BUD *stands in the movie screen area.* HE *plays out his scene as though* HE *were acting in a documentary film*)

BUD

Sure I'm here . . . And I don't mind it much. Marie and Bill are good sports. We get along good. . . . And they come from my ole home town, though they come from up on "The Hill." . . . Where all the nitty gritty folks are . . . which is okay, ya know. But they're some crazy niggers . . . Marie and Bill . . . sometimes. And they make good buddies. I like them. . . . Yeah, I'm sure of that. And they don't know none of the niggers I work with, which is a treat. I'm a schoolteacher. Math. Junior high school. Nothin' heavy but somethin' nice and steady . . . and the district where I teach is not in the ghetto, if you know what I mean. Where I teach, the kids know how to act. They've had some home guidance.

(*Lights on* BUD *fade; the Christmas tree winks; and* ART *and* MARCO *appear somewhere in the space.* THEY *pass a small brown cigarette between them*)

ART

Hey, man . . . hope you didn't get mad about Wanda.

MARCO

(*Supercool*) Nawh, baby . . . everything's everything. . . . Look, Jim, I want the broad to get out of here and get some coins too, dig? Then she can throw me some change.

(*In the background, off,* WANDA *is heard crying quietly, alone throughout the remainder of this segment*)

ART

I hear ya.

MARCO

If she were makin' enough I might even let her move in with me and take care of things while I finish school, dig?

ART

You got it all figured out. . . . You're pretty hip.

MARCO

(*Sucks deeply*) Well . . . you know . . . I gotta take care of myself.

ART

Yeah . . . I know what you mean, champ. . . . My cousin Steve's pretty quiet . . . and kinda slow, ya know. . . . I didn't think he was associating with real operators like you.

(THEY *pass the cigarette*)

MARIE

(*Off*) DON'T SMOKE MORE THAN A COUPLE OF THEM DOPE THINGS IN HERE . . . STUFF GET IN MY CURTAINS AND MY FRIENDS'LL THINK I'M HAVIN' AN OPIUM DEN IN HERE!

(*The last drags are taken and the cigarette is stamped out*)

BUD

Toni and I don't have any kids. But if we did . . . we would
see that he or she got proper home guidance. . . . And I guess
I'd take a crack at being assistant principal. You know . . . get
up in the world . . . but with Toni working, together, we do
okay, so why work up a sweat, I always say. We have a nice
home, the car's a fairly new "T" bird . . . and I can get in a
couple holes of golf whenever I get the mood. And my ole
lady, Toni . . . she's kinda foxy, huh? Bet you'd like to get a
little taste of that, wouldn't cha? Yeah, I know you would. But
I don't think that's likely.

(*Lights and music change.* ART *and* MARCO *appear again*)

ART

Since we both hustlin' men, Marco . . . I can talk to you, can't
I?

MARCO

(*Suspicious*) Yeah . . . sure . . . you can talk to me.

ART

Well I was thinkin', man . . . since we both playin' this Marie
Horton scene that we shouldn't kill the goose that lays them
good eggs . . . you know what I mean, man?

MARIE

(*Off; young, seductive*) Oh, Art . . .

MARCO

Nawh . . . Now I don't.

ART

Well as I see it, man. There's only so much to be had here, ya
understand? A few chicks at best, some drinks, a little chow
and a warm bed, if things are right . . . see what I'm gettin'
to?

MARCO

Well . . . not exactly.

ART

It's like this, man . . . you take care of your own side of the
street, dig? . . . I'm here already . . . and I don't need that
much company.

MARIE

(*Nearer; soft, sweet*) Oh, Art . . .

MARCO

You tryin' to tell me somethin', man?

ART

Yeah. . . . Like I don't want to see you around here that much
more. All you out here for is to put Wandie through some
changes for your own kicks . . . then screw her a little and
browbeat her a lot. . . . I'm tryin' to get my groceries together,
fellow, and you holdin' up the action. . . . See what I mean?

MARIE

(*Almost on top of them; strange*) I'm here, Art . . .

MARCO

Yeah, man . . . I see what you mean.
  (*Lights change*)

BUD

Don't get me wrong about your not bein' able to hit strong on
chicks. It's just where my ole lady, Toni, is concerned, that's
all. See, I'm not saying that you can't hit harder than me or
anything or that she's got cast-iron drawers, or somethin'. It's
just that Toni don't go for bedwork too strong, if you know
what I mean. Not that she's frigid or anything. She'll get into
it if she's in the mood. But she's always holdin' back, ya know.
Says she don't want any kids, ever. Says that the world is ugly
and she doesn't want to bring her kids into it. I say that the
world is the world; it'll take care of itself like we're takin' care
of ourselves. But she says no. And that's the way it is. So she
takes the pill. And before that it was jelly or grease or somethin'. And when I get affectionate . . . she acts bothered. . . .
I don't mind not havin' kids too much or the pills she takes

. . . but her always pushin' me off . . . damn . . . I can understand why some cats drink, ya know. . . . Hey, Marie . . . how's the booze holdin' out?

(BUD *fades out;* BILL *and* WANDA *appear. The music is low.* BILL *and* WANDA *act as lovers*)

WANDA

But Uncle Bill . . . I told you I couldn't do this.

BILL

Look, Wandie . . . you like me, don't ya? . . . And I like you too.

WANDA

But Uncle Bill . . . I can't . . .

BILL

Just call me Bill, baby. . . . Just call me Bill. You're Marie's niece . . . not mine.

(ART *walks through, observes* BILL *and* WANDA, *and continues out, unseen by them*)

WANDA

But you know this is wrong, Bill.

BILL

(*Takes her in his arms*) I've loved you for so long, Wandie, baby.

WANDA

(*Responding*) You shouldn't do this Uncle . . . I mean, Bill.

BILL

(*Feeling her give in*) Just relax, baby . . . you need some love, don't ya? Just relax and let me love you.

WANDA

Take care of me, please . . . see that no one hurts me any more, Bill.

BILL

You're my little girl, baby . . . my own little girl.

(The Christmas tree lights wink; the COUPLE *fades from sight, and* MARIE *saunters in with a half-filled glass in her hand)*

MARIE

Each glass I raise to my lips, with every drop of Scotch I drain from my mug, the moments pass, my life goes and I am an old woman. No regrets . . . no, no regrets. A few missed parties. Some spent dollar bills. A mistake or two but hell, that's life, ain't it, honey? So no tears here . . . just keep the good times keep on keepin' on. Don't let the music stop. Yeah . . . poppa stoppa . . . go it one again. That's my song . . . yeah . . . play it, yeah . . . go it one again. I'm a good Catholic . . . I go to confession . . . whenever I have to . . . and get up in time. So I ain't studden 'bout a thing. . . . I just tell that cute young priest that Miss Marie's takin' care of business . . . and everybody's cool . . . if the Lawd don't mind you better believe Miss Marie don't give a hummmmp hummmmp hummmmp . . . right, peaches? Say it again, my liddle puttie cat . . . wheeee . . . Miss Marie will tell you . . . ha ha ha . . .

*(*GAFNEY *and* ART *appear)*

GAFNEY

We've come a long way, brother Art . . . and you ain't helpin' us Black people any with your niggerish ways.

ART

Yeah, I know I've come a long ways . . . from all way inside my mama.

GAFNEY

I'm talking about slavery, brother . . . please, don't be *facetious* . . .

ART

Don't be what?

GAFNEY

You know what I'm talking about.

ART

Do I?

GAFNEY

Yes, you do! You know I'm talking about your being a nigger pimp!

ART

Hey . . . watch your foul language, prophet.

GAFNEY

To communicate with you and your kind I find that I must sink to your level.

ART

Level? . . . Then you're on a higher level than me?

GAFNEY

Someone has to lead, my brother.

ART

So niggers like me get out of slavery . . . then they find that niggers like you think they're leading us. Nigger . . . we've been led and misled for four hundred years . . . why don't you leave us alone and let us find our own way for a while?

GAFNEY

I'm not a nigger, Art . . . I'm a Black man!

ART

Yeah . . . I guess we have come a long way.
   (THEY *fade, as* MARIE *winks and blows them kisses*)

MARIE

Why do I like young boys? Didn't think you'd ever ask, sweetie. My my . . . but the things you want to get into . . . ha ha . . . you mean Art, don't you? . . . Yeah? . . . shusssssh . . . ummm mmm . . . yeah, I know what you mean. He's a young boy, or man, if you want to get into that . . . and I like him all right. Oh, I like Art. He makes me feel so good . . . so good . . . you know what I mean, honey? Yeah, I'm sure you do. That's why. 'Cause he makes me feel the way I like to feel. That's all there is to it, baby . . . I'd jump over forty old men's

pooties to get to a young man. You hip to that, honey? Miss
Marie is together . . . but she likes her good times too. . . .

GAFNEY
(*Off*) You're decadent . . . you're indecent . . . you're
counterrevolutionary . . .

MARIE
. . . I wanna thank ya . . .
(SHE *fades out of sight. Lights on* RUTH *and* BUD. RUTH *is
straightening her clothes.* BUD, *his back to the audience, is
fixing himself*)

RUTH
What if Toni finds out?

BUD
Take it easy, baby . . . take it easy.

RUTH
But Toni's one of my best friend-girls.

BUD
(*Turns to her*) There's nothin' to worry about.

RUTH
Ohhh . . . this is all a mistake. I musta drank too much . . .
how could I? . . . Oh, I know what it was now . . . it was that
dirty movie of Marie and Bill's . . .

BUD
(*Chuckles*) Ruth, baby . . . ha ha . . . baby.

RUTH
Get away from me! Don't put your nasty hands on me. What
if Shadow knows?

BUD
(*Incredulous*) The Shadow knows?

RUTH
Shadow! My man . . . Oh, Jesus; how did I get my black ass

into this? . . . Oh, please don't tell Marie . . . *Please* . . .
that damn woman can't keep a thing to herself, 'cept'n her own
business.

BUD

Relax . . . relax . . . everything's gonna . . .

RUTH

Please don't tell Toni . . . *please* . . . Ohh, those dirty movies.

BUD

Well, I wouldn't tell my ole lady, Toni, would I? Not even I'm
that dumb.

RUTH

Oh, god, I need a drink . . . Now Bud, don't you tell anybody
anything, ya hear? . . . If you do, man, you'll be sorry!
(SHE *rushes off. Light fades on* BUD; *then up on* WANDA)

WANDA

Ahhh . . . this is such a miserable, mean existence. Men grabbing at you, grabbing what's yours and what they think is or
should be theirs. Oldness and death around the corners. In
the corners of their aspiring middle-class middle-aged souls.
To drink the drink of youth they think is to buy a fifth of 100-
proof oblivion. Here I am just starting out on this thing called
life and from what I see so far I can't get up enough enthusi-
asm to smile about it any longer. When I came from Pittsburgh I thought I was coming to a better place. Not a better
life, really, but a better place. I could have gone to the university back there but I wanted to get away. I knew I could
stay with my aunt . . . ha ha ha ha . . . Thought I was comin'
to a little ole lady's house who had cats and maybe a budgie,
which is a stinky little bird, and certainly potted plants. No
one's seen Aunt Marie back in Pittsburgh, Buffalo or Brooklyn,
where our family's from, for a long time. She had quite a repu-
tation for being wild. . . . My, my, the stories that they
still tell. They said that her mother died in childbirth, she being

the child and nobody knowing who was the daddy. . . . Aunt
Marie's mother was said to have conceived in college. It was
quite a scandal of the day . . . since not many Black girls
went to college, daughters of undertakers or not. And Aunt
Marie was brought up by her mother's mother . . . who was
one of the first colored teachers in Pottstown, Pa. And they
said that Aunt Marie was very spoiled from receiving almost
anything that she wanted, even when there was a depression
going on in those days . . .

BILL

(*Off*) Wandie . . .

WANDA

They said that Aunt Marie used to drink corn whiskey and
smoke cigarettes in public and cuss and race in cars with their
tops rolled back and she wouldn't go to school . . .

BILL

(*Nearer*) Wandie, baby . . .

WANDA

"Look at what school did for my poor little mamma," she
would say. And she was a showgirl and went to Philly and
New York . . . and somethin' happened that nobody ever talks
about and she ended up out here with Bill.
    (BILL *enters*)

BILL

Wanda . . . there you are. I've been looking all over for you.

WANDA

I've been here, Bill . . . just here.
    (HE *clutches her, holds her close*)

BILL

Baby, you worried me for a while . . . you're not sick, are you?

WANDA

Yes, Bill . . . I'm a little sick.

BILL

You are? . . . Oh. I know a man shouldn't ask about a lady's
illnesses . . . but . . .

WANDA

I'm pregnant, Bill.

BILL

Oh . . .

WANDA

Yes.

BILL

By me?

WANDA

Maybe.

BILL

(*Breathes deeply*) Ahhhhhh . . . I see.

WANDA

I'm leaving soon.

BILL

You are?

WANDA

Yes. I'm going to go stay with Marco.

BILL

You are?

WANDA

Yes. He doesn't want me or love me . . . but he is all I need
and care about.

BILL

Will he let you?

WANDA

I love him . . . and I'm pregnant . . . it doesn't matter now
what he wants.

BILL

I see . . . you know I might be able to help you out some.

WANDA

Thanks.

BILL

You know I love you too, Wandie . . . but I couldn't live
without your Aunt Marie.

WANDA

I know . . . well, I have to go now.

BILL

Yeah . . . I know . . . Wandie?

WANDA

Huh?

BILL

What are you going to name the baby?

(SHE *kisses him;* HE *holds her for a second, then* THEY *part.*
WANDA *exits.* BUD *joins* BILL. THEY *hold drinks in their hands*)

BUD

Hey . . . how's it goin', Capt'n?

BILL

Can't complain, Chief . . . How's it go with you?

BUD

Just another Christmas. . . . A few of the girls are just a bit
younger . . . or seem that way.

BILL

Yeah . . . they're all the same . . . too much food . . . too
much to drink . . . too much heartburn.

BUD

Thanks for havin' us over.

BILL

(*Slightly drunk*) But we always have you and Toni over . . .

BUD

The kids act different.

BILL

Different? . . . Yeah . . . I guess they do. . . . You know . . . these young people are confused . . . they're lost.

BUD

But things were different when we were kids.

BILL

Sure was . . . but I don't want to go back to the good ole days.

BUD

But these kids . . . I dunno . . . maybe it's the revolution.

BILL

What you mean?

BUD

Well, I'm around them all the time, ya understand . . . I know them.

BILL

Yeah.

BUD

And they're just different.

BILL

Oh.

BUD

Hey . . . that's strange.

BILL

What is?

BUD

None of us have kids . . . not me and Toni or you and Marie . . . nor Ruthie . . . or almost anybody that we hang out with.

BILL

(*Chuckles*) Havin' kids must be out of style.

BUD

For some people, at least . . . for us. Hummm . . . maybe we're dying off. Maybe we're a vanishing breed.

BILL

Yeah . . . last of the big-time dodos . . . ha ha . . .

BUD

But we've had some good times.

BILL

Yeah . . . we've had a ball.

BUD

Ha ha . . . but if I can have a choice I'll take a woman any day . . . with no strings attached . . .

BILL

Yeah . . . no strings.

BUD

And no history . . . and no future . . . with me, at least.

BILL

Yeah . . . at least.

BUD

Happy New Year, Bossman! . . . May all your troubles be as fleeting as youth.

BILL

Ha ha . . . well said, Professor. You ready for a fresh one?

BUD

Why not, Maestro.

(THEY *fade away.* RUTH *appears*)

RUTH

Ha ha . . . Marie is crazy. . . . We have a lot of fun. She thinks I'm crazy but she's the one. I'm not like Marie's other friends. I'm a *real* friend. Me and Toni, though Toni's not like me at all. . . . Most of Marie's friends are those ole bags that are in her clubs or are too stuck-up to be in them and have clubs of

their own that Marie would like to be in. . . . I'm from Texas
. . . a high-top-boot-wearin', ten-gallon-hat dusky queen of
the wide open spaces, that's me. Yippeee . . . I run a power
machine over on Sepulveda Boulevard. We make costumes
for TV. That's how I make my money, friend. None of that
waitin' for some man to give me what I deserve stuff. I'm a
gal to get her own. Sure, the guys I go with give me what
they want to give me. But I got better sense than to start de-
pendin' in them, and get let down, ya understand? I'm independent. And I drink beer. And I keep Marie company. 'Cause
Bill is out more than he's in so we two lonesome gals have a
lot to talk about. We talk about Marie's poker parties. And
her pot luck suppers . . . and other socials. And we kid about
my boy friends and about Bill's girl friends and about Wanda
bein' so dumb . . . and lots of things like that. We good
friends, Marie and I. But I don't understand her none. Not
one bit. . . . But we good friends just the same.

(SHE *exits.* ART *and* GAFNEY *appear*)

ART

Well, I don't know, man. . . . All that stuff you tellin' me
sounds okay . . . but I don't see how it's gonna get me any
money . . . and that's my problem right now.

GAFNEY

That is the least of your problems, brother. . . . You're an
African and . . .

ART

I'm a what?

GAFNEY

African, my brother. . . . In these days of the early sixties
with so many newly emerged African states coming to the
fore in world influence . . . the fact of your Black birth, even
in this spiritually desolate place known as North America . . .

ART

Look, man . . . I got a lot of things to do. . . . Why don't
you save that . . .

GAFNEY

You can't continue avoiding the truth, Art.

ART

Well, man . . . my truth right now is that I need some dough. Big dough would be best . . . then I'd feel more like a man, African or not.

GAFNEY

We Black people are in a fight for liberation, brother. That is our manhood! And Africa is at the center of our struggle.

ART

Look, Gafney . . . I say let the Africans struggle for what they want . . . and I'll liberate some green here. . . . My fight is right here . . . and this is where I stand or fall.

GAFNEY

You just don't understand. . . . It's not about the white man's money . . . you just don't understand.

ART

Give me a gun, Freedom Fighter . . . and I'll liberate some dough-ray-mee . . . dig?

GAFNEY

You'd more than likely take it from some helpless Black people.

ART

(Annoyed) Maybe . . . but then I could go to Africa, or jump down to see Brother Castro . . . or smoke some good opium with the master . . . Mao.

GAFNEY

(Indignant) The great Chairman Mao has no use for drugs!

ART

(Angry) CAN'T YOU EVER TAKE A JOKE . . . NIGGER!
    (THEY fade from sight)

TONI

I'm Toni. I'm a social worker . . . not that that matters. But I am that, among other things. I'm kinda fine as well. And I know it. Yes, I know it . . . but I go for it as well. And that's cool. 'Cause Toni's fine . . . you can believe that, baby. I'm Marie's friend. Her home girl, Toni. We grew up together, though I'm at least fifteen years younger than her. We really didn't grow up together, ya know. Came from the same neighborhood. Though my folks had more money than Marie's. This is a true story, ya know. But you can't always believe what you see . . . or hear.

(ART *reappears, a drink in his hand.* HE *stares at* TONI *a long moment.* SHE *tries to ignore him.* HE *hands her the drink;* SHE *nods a nervous "thank you"*

Sips drink, clears throat)

We met out here, Marie and I, and having known some of our same families, mutually, and friends, personally, we have been fast friends ever since, always having someone near and dear close at hand to reminisce over the good ole days. And our relationship has deepened. I know Marie more than I know my ole man, Bud. And she thinks she knows me.

(ART *stands behind her, holding her close about the waist, kissing the back of her neck and whispering in her ear.* SHE *is quite perturbed, but continues to speak and hold onto her self-control*)

We remain dear friends. Even though she has problems. . . . Like Bill . . . now that's a real problem. A grade "A" all-American problem. . . . Whew . . . nigger drink more than the law allow. . . . And his runnin' round with that white bitch. IN FRONT OF HER FRIENDS! L.A.'s a big place . . . stretches moocho miles . . . yeah . . . wide open spaces for days . . . and this *nigger*, when he gets drunk, takes his ole skinny white heifer to his hangouts. Nigger pretends that they ain't Marie's places to play either. . . . Last time the nigger came through with her he was loud . . . yeah, LOUD . . . claimed that she was going to have his baby, bought drinks

for the house . . . isn't that disgusting? . . . this was at the
Sportsman's Inn . . . and then got belligerent with the whore
and ended up slappin' her and takin' her out to the parkin'
lot and beatin' her ass in his car. Niggers are somethin' else,
chile. Let me tell you . . .

(*Though maintaining her discipline,* SHE *begins to respond
visibly to* ART)
I hang out with some of the simplest-behinded Negroes there
is. You can believe that. . . . Toni'll tell ya. Sheet . . . make
me act vulgar sometimes. . . . I wouldn't just let one of these
niggers use me. Come suckin' round me and got a white woman
on the side. I'm takin' care of Toni, that's who . . . and Toni
is precious, special and cold as January in the North Pole.

(SHE *pushes* ART *away.* HE *takes her arm and pulls her. Reluctantly, at first,* SHE *goes with him.* THEY *dissolve into the
shadows.* WANDA *appears and sings*)

WANDA*
It's little enough
to love
and need
It's little enough
to be
for real
It's little enough
to keep
my man
but can
I be myself?

It's more than enough
to have
you near
(the dark

* Copyright, Ed Bullins, lyrics, Pat Patrick, music—"Woman's Song"—
Downpat Music Co. (B.M.I.), 1971.

packed muscle
the desperate
meat)
It's more than enough
to wet
your lips
with the
taste of
me, myself.

It's enough
to have you
It's enough
to be yours
It's enough
to keep you
if you're
really mine.

So here I am
take what's yours
So have me
now
don't pass
the chance
So love me
while
I am hot
and know
my name
was Wanda.

    (*Lights on* MARIE *and* STEVE *standing, drinking and flirting. The dog yaps*)

       RUTH
(*Off*) Shoot the niggers . . . shoot the niggers . . .

MARIE

God . . . what's that?

STEVE

I dunno.

RUTH

(*Off*) We got our right . . . we got 'em . . . shoot the niggers . . .
  (ART *and* TONI *enter*)

MARIE

Damn . . . Toni . . . Art . . . what's happening?
  (SHE *starts toward the noise.* TONI *restrains her*)

TONI

No, sister . . . no . . . don't go back there.

MARIE

What's going on?

RUTH

(*Off; sobs*) Shoot 'em . . . it's not fair . . . I got my rights
. . . I ain't never had no trouble out of white folks . . .

TONI

It's Ruth . . .

MARIE

I know . . . that's Ruth's voice.

STEVE

What's she sayin' that for? Shouldn't somebody . . .

ART

Ruth's cracked up . . . she's havin' a fit back there.

MARIE

(*Struggles*) Oh, my god . . . let me go to her.

TONI

(*Holds her*) Bud's with her . . . he'll do all he can for her.

MARIE

But it should be me . . . or you, Toni. She needs us.

TONI

No . . . she's got who she needs . . . she's with her man.

RUTH

(*Off*) Shoot 'em . . . oh, lawd have mercy . . . I already got my civil rights . . . I'm free as a white lady . . . yes, I am . . .

MARIE

She's with her man? Bud?

ART

Yeah . . . Bud.

   (MARIE *begins laughing slowly, pick up to near hysteria, then weeps.* THEY *stand about her, soothing her, not looking at* EACH OTHER)

MARIE

(*Finally*) Ruth and Bud?

TONI

Yes, they were having a little thing . . . like Art and I . . .

ART

Hey, kid . . . I ain't in it.

TONI

(*Pursues subject*) Like Art and I were having a little thing . . . and somehow we . . .

MARIE

(*Resigned*) You and Art . . .

ART

It wasn't nothin', baby . . . I had a few drinks . . . and I got bored . . .

STEVE

Has this something to do with Wanda's splittin'?

TONI

Wanda's gone?

ART

(*Disgust*) Awww . . . she's gone with that jive-ass nigger of hers . . . Marco.

STEVE

Hey, man . . . that's my friend.

MARIE

(*Tired*) No . . . no . . . I think I know why Wanda left. . . . Art . . .

ART

Huh?

MARIE

You haven't left any dirty coffee cups around, have you?
   (*With great halloing* BILL *enters.* HE *has Christmas-gift-wrapped bottles of liquor and a pink box under his arms*)

BILL

Hey, baby . . . Marie, baby . . . I'm home . . . Dry the tears from your eyes, swweeeet cake. . . . I've kicked the wolf in his tail . . . he won't be sniffin' round our door no mo'. . . . Daddy's done brought home the goose.

TONI

Bill . . . quiet . . .

MARIE

(*Regaining composure*) Take it easy, Toni, dear. . . . HOR-TON, YOU OLE PIRATE . . . WHAT YOU BEEN UP TO, NIGGER?
   (THEY *laugh and clutch one another*)

RUTH

(*Off, lower*) I got all I need, yes, indeed . . . yes, indeed, I got all I need . . .

BILL

You lookin' at a workin' man, mamma . . . not only a workin' man . . . but one with a substantial raise . . . and listen to this . . .

MARIE

Sock it to me, sweetie . . .

BILL

(*Plays it for all it's worth*) AND A MANAGERIAL POSITION! . . .

RUTH

(*Off*) Ohh ohh ohhh . . . ohh oooooohhhhhh . . .

TONI

You . . . you're managing the parking lot now?

BILL

No, my dear . . . I am manager to the entire garage beneath the Beverly Hills Motor Spa . . . and I've already spent my bonus.

MARIE

Leave it to my Bill.

STEVE

Damn.
(*The TV comes on. A Black man is shown exhorting a ghetto crowd. Then flashes of rioting, looting, police, National Guard, etc. The TV personality looks larger*)
Look . . . they've started the revolution . . . Those Civil Rights brothers are really taking care of business.

MARIE

Hummp . . . most of them niggers ain't nothin' but cops . . . tryin' to find out what they can get Black people to do. . . . You should know how sneaky white people is . . . honey. And how they use the Black man against the Black man. . . . Hummp, better than to be that kinda fool.

(ART *has withdrawn to the side;* HE *smokes and looks on as* THEY *unwrap the liquor and* MARIE *tears open her box*)

TONI

(*Squeals of delight*) OH . . . MARIE . . . YOU LUCKY OLE BITCH!

(MARIE *pulls a fur stole from the paper and cardboard*)

BILL

(*Expansive*) Not quite ermine . . . but not dog either. . . .

TONI

(*Envy*) Oh, that's just adorable . . . I'm going to have to push Bud into administration. . . . I see that now . . . there's just no future in being at the bottom.

(MARIE *models the stole, swaggering about the stage*)

BILL

I don't know what you told Izzy, baby . . . or Izzy's ole lady . . . but . . .

MARIE

The past is the past, Bill . . .

BILL

(*Dances*) If you say so, sweetheart. . . . Hey, watch this step . . . got that? Art . . . get old Billy Boy his regular.

MARIE

No, no . . . I'll do it, baby. . . . Art was just leavin' . . . for good.

TONI

He is?

ART

Seems like I've heard this somewhere before.

(GAFNEY *enters*)

GAFNEY

Art, there you are. Have you seen Wandie? Have you, huh?

I see you're still standing around. What are you going to be doing when the revolution comes?

ART

(*Softly*) Gafney . . . without me you won't have a revolution.

GAFNEY

Oh, man . . .
   (GAFNEY *looks at* ART. ART *feints, then jabs him sharply in the nose*)

BILL

Art . . . damn . . . what's going on here?

GAFNEY

Owww . . . you shouldn't have done that. . . . Don't you know I'm non-violent . . . you stupid, ignorant nigger!
   (GAFNEY *rushes off, holding his bleeding nose*)

BILL

Say, Art . . . we can't have any of that in here. This is our home.

MARIE

(*Laughing*) Cool down, poppa Horton. . . . Art's just leaving. . . . He was just giving us his calling card . . . weren't you, lover?

ART

See you folks . . .

TONI

See you, Art . . . call me sometime . . . we're in the book.

STEVE

Guess I'll be leaving with you, man.

MARIE

(*Takes* STEVE's *arm; seductive*) No, you can't go now, Steve . . . my party's just starting . . . besides . . . I want you to do something for me later on.

RUTH

(*Off, low*) I've got everything I need . . . everything, everything, everything.

TONI

(*Nervous*) I'm going back here and talk to Bud about his promotion . . . maybe Ruthie needs me now . . .
  (SHE *exits*)

ART

Why don't you lay . . . cousin Steve . . . I generally travel alone.

STEVE

Okay . . . see you around.

ART

Next time you hear from the folks . . . give 'em my best.

STEVE

I'll do that.

ART

Hey . . . remember how we'd fight all the time when we were kids? Who usta win, huh? . . . I wonder who was the best?

STEVE

We'll never know now . . . will we?
  (ART *exits*)

BILL

(*Dances*) Hey, Marie . . . hey, stuff . . . get me a drink . . . hey, sweet stuff . . . get me a drink, will ya?

MARIE

What you think you got around here, Mr. Horton? . . . brown skin service? . . . Oh, Steve . . . will fix us some drinks, please, honey? . . . the usual.

STEVE

(*Shrugs*) Oh . . . sure . . . why not?
  (HE *goes to get drinks*)

MARIE

Fur or no fur, Bill Horton . . . you got to keep on gettin' out of here and gettin' me some money. . . . Miss Marie is used to havin' what she wants.

BILL

Watch this step, baby . . . remember this one . . . c'mon, let me see if you can still do it.

(THEY *do their brief routine and sing*)

BILL and MARIE

(*Together*) Bill brings home two hundred seventy-five stone cold dollars a week . . . to me, Miss Marie . . . and puts it in my hand. And the tips he makes parkin' cars out to the studio in Beverly Hills is more than that. We make almost as much as some colored doctors make . . . 'n we spend it too. 'Cause it's party time every day at Miss Marie's house.

(THEY *dance off. The stage is left dark with the Christmas tree shining and the TV flickering on. The dog yaps outside. The telephone begins to ring.*

Blackness)

Wisdom Comes to Black People
in Many Disguises

J. E. GAINES

I write to record some of the things that I experience. Certain
ideologies that old people have told me when I was a kid—
things I should look out for, things I shouldn't get involved
with.

Family and other people have told me things. The sayings
of our old people like "Sometimes a hard head makes a soft
behind," etc., are famous with niggers. You know, my whole
feeling about certain things that old folks tell you seems to
have in just a few short words more wisdom than all the uni-
versities, all the conglomeration of . . . well, all the compila-
tion of words that we learn. Our mothers and fathers and
friends and friendly neighbors lay some heavy knowledge on
us. Whites, even in their schools, seldom teach the Black man
what he really needs to know. For instance, you may run up
against a drunk who may not be a drunk, but someone who
drinks wine, and this so-called drunk, after he asks and gets
his fifteen cents or quarter, may listen to you trying to tell
him something, trying to save him from alcohol, and the drunk
may lay something very heavy on you. Something that you'd
never believe that he could come up with, seeing that he was
supposed to be a drunk.

So, I mean, wisdom comes to Black people in many dis-
guises, and I try to write plays according to that wisdom of

the few words, which mean a whole lot. And I experiment with that word "wisdom," and give it my fullest attention.

I would be presumptuous as a Black man to think that I've landed on my feet here in North America, and so when I write a play like *What If It Had Turned Up Heads*, I write for all those Black people hidden away in their private basements when they may have been doctors, lawyers, movie stars or pimps.

Words like "eccentric," "paranoid" might not mean a thing to Black people, because those things, when you see them with the brothers, who seem to have those symptoms—walking around the streets, talking to themselves—are accepted by the people and protested against by the brother who has it. If you were to ask him what's wrong, he would ask you what's wrong with you.

They're special people. I write about some of these special people, whom I love, people who are very important to us, people who are victims of an inhumane environment, people who in spite of their condition struggle to survive. And many of them have a lot of class.

These people are the only ones I really know. I don't know about middle-class niggers. I don't write about white people because I don't know nothing about white people other than the fact that they're white. I mean, if I would write about white people they would say I was a hatemonger or something. That I was prejudiced, and I don't want to use my energy on being prejudiced.

What I write about are my experiences with Black people. The ones found in Harlem bars, pool rooms, theatres and basements. I go into basements that I know. I grew up in a basement. I go where niggers go. Because I don't go nowhere that I ain't wanted.

(*From a conversation with* J. E. GAINES,
a.k.a. SONNY JIM,
Fall '72)

What If It Had Turned Up Heads

BY J. E. GAINES

Thanks Whit, Estelle, Ed, Gary, Scoe

CHARACTERS:

JACOB JONES: *loves his dog*
JENNIE LOUISE HARRIS: *loves music*
MOSE BARTHOLOMEW TUCKER: *loves Mose*
BIMBO: *loves to exaggerate*
DIZZY: *loves to follow*
VOICE: *imitating a dog's voice*

What If It Had Turned Up Heads was first presented as a Studio Production at the American Place Theatre in March 1972. The production was directed by Robert Macbeth. Design and lighting were by Bill Howell and Tobias Macbeth. Stage manager: Alfred Smith.

THE CAST:

J.J.	Whitman Mayo
JENNIE	Betty Howard
MOSE	Sonny Jim
BIMBO	Gary Bolling
DIZZY	George Miles

A later production opened at The New Lafayette Theatre on October 13, 1972, directed by William E. Lathan, featuring Carol Cole in the role of Jennie and Sonny Jim as Mose.

WHAT IF IT HAD TURNED UP HEADS

Lyrics by Sonny Jim Gaines
Music by James Macbeth

There must be more in life for me
Something more than the eyes can see
When you're feeling very low
'Cause there's nowhere to go
Or be.
There must be other things to do
When the world is through with you
And you kinda feel real lost
'Cause you paid the cost
To see.

I try for a while
To give a smile
To a friend or two
But fate took a hand
I lost my man
And my child in her youth
I was abused, and misused
So I'll find love where I can
And give to the bitter end
So lovers don't you wail
'Cause fate has turned up tails

Wwwwwhat iffff itttt haddd turned up heads.

ACT I
Scene I

As the play opens there is a dim light on a tin-covered door, a few garbage cans by the door, empty wine bottles by the cans. The set should have the appearance of a basement flat. An elderly WOMAN *comes through the audience,* SHE *is dressed very plain, but raggedy.* SHE *bangs on the door, making a lot of noise.* SHE *has a shopping bag with a shabby rope tied around it. As the* WOMAN *bangs on the door, you hear a growling dog and a man's voice.*

JACOB JONES
Hush, dog, hush, goddammit, hush!
    (HE *shouldn't be seen at this time; his voice comes from behind the door*)
Who is it?

JENNIE
Jennie.
    (*The dog should be barking very loud now*)

JACOB
Hush, dog, hush. . . . Who?

JENNIE
Jennie.

JACOB
Jennie?

JENNIE
Yeah, Jennie!

JACOB
What you want?

JENNIE
I want to buy a bottle of wine.

JACOB

Sold out! Come back tomorrow.

JENNIE

Mister, I can't wait until tomorrow, I need a drink now.

JACOB

It's all gone, lady, sold out!

JENNIE

Mister, I need a drink bad.
   (*There is a silence*)
Mister? Mister?!
   (SHE *bangs on the door again*)
Mister!!
   (*The dog starts to bark again*)
Mister, please . . .
   (HE *cracks the door. There's a bright light behind him,* HE *peeks through the crack at the* LADY, *looks her up and down*)

JACOB

Wait let me put my dog away.
   (HE *closes the door and in a few seconds returns*)
You by yourself?

JENNIE

Yes.

JACOB

Come in, come in.
   (*Pulling her by the arm. The room is practically empty, a mattress on the floor, a table with two chairs, open newspapers by the mattress with some dog food on it, and a record player*)
Sit.
   (*Offering her a chair*)

JENNIE

Thank you.

JACOB

What do you want, port or sherry?

JENNIE

Sherry.

JACOB

You drink port?

JENNIE

Sometime.

JACOB

Well you'll drink it now, 'cause that's all I got.
(HE *goes over to the mattress, pulls out a bottle and hands it to her*)
This is my private stock.
(SHE *grabs the bottle and takes a large drink*)
That's seventy-five cents!
(*Ignoring him and still drinking*)

JENNIE

Uh huh.
(*Taking another large drink*)

JACOB

That's seventy-five cents, lady!!
(*Ignoring him and still drinking*)

JENNIE

Uh huh.
(HE *snatches the bottle*)

JACOB

I want my seventy-five cents.
(*Very stern*)

JENNIE

Oh?
(SHE *begins to search herself, then* SHE *unties her shopping bag.* SHE *takes out a red satin dress, very wrinkled, some*

*cheap beads, a pair of dirty white shoes, a record album and
a pair of black panties)*
I must've lost my purse.

JACOB

Lady, what do you take me for?

JENNIE

I had it, honestly I had it.
  (HE *smacks her off the chair, the dog barks in the background.* HE *goes to where* HE *has locked up his dog and yells)*

JACOB

Hush, dog!!
  (HE *returns and stands over* JENNIE)
I want my seventy-five cents.
  (HE *leans over and grabs her by the collar and begins slap-
ping her.* JENNIE *is screaming, the dog is barking)*
I want my money.
  (HE *releases his grip and yells at the dog)*
Shut up, dog!
  (JENNIE *still crying,* HE *goes over to the table and gathers
up her stuff off the table and dumps it in her shopping bag
with her other memoirs)*
Here, lady, is your bag. Now leave.

JENNIE

(*Still crying*) But I had it honestly, mister.

JACOB

Yeah, uh-huh, look I got to get up early and mop down the
house.
  (JENNIE *looks at the bottle as* SHE *ties the cord around her
bag)*
Here take it with you.
  (*Giving her the remains of the bottle and escorting her to
the door; it's raining)*
You got a umbrella?

JENNIE

No sir.

JACOB

You live far?

JENNIE

I don't live anywhere.

JACOB

Well, where are you going to stay?

JENNIE

I don't know.

JACOB

You don't know?

JENNIE

No.

JACOB

Arrr . . . come back . . . you can stay the night, seeing that it's raining so.

JENNIE

(SHE *steps inside and hugs him*) You're not so mean after all.

JACOB

(*Pushing her aside*) Stop dat! Stop dat!! Now jest 'cause I'm gonna let you stay, is no reason for all of dat. The way it's raining, it ain't fitting for a dog nor cat, much more a lady.

JENNIE

(SHE *places her shopping bag on the chair and looks around,* SHE *places her coat on the floor and lies down*)
Thanks, mister.

JACOB

(HE *lies on his mattress*) I said it wasn't fitting for dog nor cat, lady.

JENNIE
Jennie.

JACOB
What?

JENNIE
My name is Jennie.

JACOB
Okay, lady, Jennie.
(HE *reaches behind the mattress and opens a fresh bottle of wine.* SHE *looks at him very sadly*)

JENNIE
Private stock?

JACOB
Huh.

JENNIE
I said private stock.

JACOB
Um hum.

JENNIE
That was some good port you gave me. What was the name of that?
(*Looking at her empty bottle*)
Oh, Five Stars.

JACOB
Hum.

JENNIE
Yes sir, Five Stars is sure good, no wonder you call it your private stock.

JACOB
Hum.

JENNIE
From now on that's going to be my drink.

JACOB
Good night.
(HE *turns his back to her, the bottle is lying beside him.*
A few minutes pass)

JENNIE
You sleep, mister? Mister? Mister?
(SHE *begins to crawl over to the mattress and just as* SHE's
about to grab the bottle HE *turns over*)

JACOB
No.

JENNIE
Oh.

JACOB
Look, take the bottle, didn't I tell you dat I got to be up early,
dammit.

JENNIE
Thanks.
(SHE *softly touches his head*)

JACOB
Um.
(JENNIE *returns to the other side of the room with her shop-*
ping bag. SHE *lays her clothes gently on her coat while* SHE
drinks and sings "I Gotta Right to Sing the Blues." SHE *can*
sing as long as the director wishes)

JENNIE
Mister?
(SHE's *good and high now*)
Mister, I'm hungry, mister.
(SHE *notices the paper by the mattress with the dog food*
on it. SHE *stands and stumbles against a chair creating a little*
noise, SHE *makes it to the mattress, sits down by the paper. The*

paper should be at what appears to be the foot of mattress, the paper makes noise as SHE *eats her first mouthful.* JACOB *looks up and smacks her hand*)

JACOB

What in the hell you doin'?

JENNIE

(*Startled by the smack*) What?!

JACOB

That's dog food, gal!

JENNIE

I'm hungry, pal.
  (*It should be delivered with finesse and humor*)

JACOB

So is my dog.
  (*Rising up and gathering his dog's food and folding the paper neatly,* HE *should be in long drawers, preferably dirty white ones*)

JENNIE

You think more of your dog than me.
  (*Easing herself sexy-like to him, and blocking his movements*)
I use to be a star. You don't believe me?

JACOB

(*Getting sexually upset*) Um hum, now let me pass so that I can see what I got to feed you with.
  (*Walking around her. There's a short silence, from in the back*)
You eat sardines?
  (SHE *doesn't answer.* HE *enters carrying a can of sardines and a large bowl, mumbling to the audience*)
You just order 'cause that's all I got.
  (HE *sets the bowl and sardines down*)
I ain't got no bread.

JENNIE

How about crackers?
   (HE *stares at her strangely*)
Thanks, daddy.
   (THEY *should have time to open the can and eat a few be-*
fore SHE *returns to her coat bed and lies down humming her*
song)
Mister, mister.

JACOB

Gawd damn, what is it now?
   (*Very angry and pleased*)

JENNIE

The floor's hard.

JACOB

It's cement.

JENNIE

And cold . . .

JACOB

What do you want me to do?

JENNIE

The gentlemanly thing . . .

JACOB

The which? The what????

JENNIE

The gentlemanly thing . . .

JACOB

What's dat, a Chinese dessert?

JENNIE

No, silly.
   (*Rising and coming over, very very sexy-like to* JACOB)
What I mean is . . .

JACOB

What?

JENNIE

(*Touching his head softly*) You know . . .

JACOB

What? Give you my bed, is you drunk????

JENNIE

No, not that, I mean . . .

JACOB

Let you lay down here beside me.

JENNIE

(*Moving right into the covers*) Thanks, daddy.

JACOB

Don't thank me, just go to sleep.

JENNIE

Okay.
    (*A few minutes should pass*)
Mister.
    (HE's *not as angry as before, it should be his softest moment*)

JACOB

Yes ma'm.

JENNIE

Don't say that. I told you my name is Jennie, Jennie Lou Harris.

JACOB

Jennie Lou.

JENNIE

Yes. What's yours?

JACOB

Mine, oh, Jacob Jones.

JENNIE

Jacob Jones, that's a good Christian name. I suppose the boys call you Jake.

JACOB

No.
   (*Proudly*)
J.J.

JENNIE

J.J. J.J. That's nice.
   (*Some moments pass*)
J.J.? Your body sure is warm . . .

JACOB

You think so?

JENNIE

Yes I do, daddy.

JACOB

J.J.!

JENNIE

Oh, that's right.
   (*A few moments pass*)
J.J., daddy.

JACOB

(*As sexy as* HE *can*) Yeah.

JENNIE

Don't panic and please don't move. I feel like a knight like you should be rewarded for rescuing a damsel in distress.
   (*The lights slowly diminish*)
Ooh, your muscles are so powerful, I just can't control myself, J.J.

ACT I
Scene II

A *few hours later there's a banging at the door.* JENNIE *is asleep,* J.J. *rises up mumbling, the dog is barking again.*

JACOB
Hush, dog, who is it?

MOSE
Me, Mose, open the dough.
   (J.J. *starts toward the door, stops, looks in the direction of his bed, notices that* JENNIE's *head is showing.* HE *goes over and covers her head very quietly and softly*)

JACOB
Just a minute.

MOSE
Man, open the dough.

JACOB
Let me put my pants on.

MOSE
J.J., these cases are heavy, will you open this damn dough.

JACOB
Yeah, yeah, just a minute.
   (*Picking up* JENNIE's *bag and hiding it*)
Coming . . .
   (HE *opens the door*)

MOSE
Damn!
   (MOSE *enters with two cartons of wine*)
Take one of these cases, I told you it was heavy.

JACOB
Okay . . .
   (*Taking the top carton unknowingly* HE *sets it beside* JEN-

NIE's *coat.* MOSE *follows him and rests his case on top of the other case and sits on it*)

MOSE

Whew . . . it's raining hard enough to beat the band. I thought you were drunk.

JACOB

Why you think that?

MOSE

I've been knocking for fifteen minutes.
    (*Taking off his coat and throwing it at the chair*)
Didn't you hear King bark?

JACOB

I must've been tired, I suppose.

MOSE

You must've been drunk.

JACOB

(*Raising his tone slightly*) Why you keep saying that?

MOSE

'Cause I know you, J.J., that's why, when you get drunk it takes all hell to wake you up. The place could burn down and you never know if it wasn't for King over there.
    (*Pointing to* JENNIE)
Give me a drink.

JACOB

It's all gone.

MOSE

All gone?

JACOB

Yeah, all gone.

MOSE

What kind of shit is that? You drank those three bottles of our private stock that Yump gave you, since I've been gone??

JACOB

Yeah.

MOSE

I told you, you was drunk.

JACOB

I wasn't drunk.

MOSE

J.J., one bottle knocks you stone.

JACOB

That's a lie, nigger.

MOSE

It ain't.

JACOB

It tis . . .

MOSE

J.J., I've known you for five years. I should know.
(*Taking off his shoes*)

JACOB

What are you doing that for?

MOSE

What?

JACOB

Taking off your shoes.

MOSE

My feet are wet, that's why.

JACOB

Oh.

MOSE

If you ain't drunk, you sure act like it.

JACOB
Look, I'm tired.

MOSE
Well, go to bed, I'm gonna take one of these jugs from the case and drink it, by that time I should be dried off.

JACOB
No.

MOSE
What do you mean, no?

JACOB
Just what I said.

MOSE
Are you crazy or somethin'? I'm your partner, I'm entitle to one and a half bottle.
    (J.J. *picks up his coat, as* MOSE *begins to tear the carton open, and hands him his coat*)

JACOB
Okay, but go 'cause I'm tired.

MOSE
If you're tired, go to bed.

JACOB
But . . .

MOSE
But what, I ain't never stop you from sleeping befo'.

JACOB
But it's different now.

MOSE
What's different?

JACOB
Everything.

MOSE

You mean 'cause your dog is sleeping with you. I've known
that for years, every time you get drunk and go to sleep, King
crawls right up in your bed and sleeps with you.
   (*Slapping the bottle on its bottom and taking a drink*)
Aaaaaah, but I've never seen him under the covers before.
   (*Taking another drink*)
Is he cold? He must be drunk too, 'cause he would've been
all over me by now. Does that old dog drink, J.J.? Ha ha ha.

JACOB

Listen, Mose, I'm tired, so go to hell on home.

MOSE

Nigger, you sure are peculiar, one minute you're begging me
to stay and drink with ya and the next you're putting me out.
   (*Raising his arms in surrender*)
All right, nigger, I'm going.
   (*Putting on his shoes and coat and starts walking toward
the door*)
I know when I'm not wanted, nigger.
   (*At this moment* JENNIE *stirs, feeling for* J.J.)

JENNIE

J.J., daddy.
   (MOSE *turns*)

MOSE

Who's that?
   (J.J. *pushes* MOSE *toward the door*)

JACOB

I ain't heard nothin'.

MOSE

I could swear I heard a lady's voice.

JACOB

Who's drunk now?

JENNIE
Come closer to me, I'm cold.

MOSE
Nigger . . .
  (*Turning around*)
that is a woman.
  (JENNIE *raises her head up.* MOSE *sees her.* JENNIE *comes out from under the covers and stands on the mattress,* SHE'S *in her slip, and* SHE *still is high*)

JENNIE
Daddy?

MOSE
(*Funning*) Daddy.
  (J.J. *rushes over and tries to lay her down*)
Well, I'll be damn.

JACOB
(*To* MOSE) Hush!
  (JENNIE *starts to kiss* J.J. *frantically*)
Stop that, stop dat!
  (MOSE *returns and lays his coat on the chair*)

MOSE
Well, I'll be damn, they said there was a woman for every man but I'd never believe it.

JACOB
I told you to hush, nigger.

MOSE
You sly, old buzzard, holding out on your buddy, your drinking buddy at that.

JACOB
I wasn't holding out on you.

MOSE
You was.

JACOB

Awwww, man.

(*Going over to the carton and getting himself a bottle and opening it.* HE *starts drinking,* JENNIE *rising up again, extending her arm to* J.J. *for a drink*)

Get back under the covers, Jennie.

MOSE

If you wasn't holding out on me, why didn't you mention it?

JACOB

Mention what?

MOSE

That you was having lady company tonight.

JENNIE

(*Starts toward* J.J. *in her slip*) Give me a taste, J.J.

MOSE

(MOSE *looks her up and down*) Good gawd, here, Miss . . . Miss . . .

(JENNIE *looking around at* MOSE)

JENNIE

Jennie! Mrs. Jennie Louise Harris.

(*Moving toward* MOSE's *jug and taking it, then taking a healthy drink, looking up for consent to kill it*)

MOSE

Kill it, kill it, there's plenty mo' where that come from, right, J.J., ole buddy?

(JACOB *grabs her by the arm and turns her around to face him*)

JACOB

Either you get back in bed, or put some clothes on.

(JENNIE *jerks away*)

JENNIE

I got clothes on.

MOSE
Yeah, she's dressed enough for me, man.

JACOB
Stay out of this, Mose.

MOSE
I ain't got in it . . .
(*Looking* JENNIE *over*)
yet.
(J.J. *picks up her dress and hands it to her*)

JACOB
Put this here dress on.
(*Pleading look in his eyes*)

JENNIE
We've got company, J.J.
(*Throwing it aside, going into her bag and pulling out her red dress,* SHE *holds it up,* SHE's *really feeling proud*)
This is my Sunday go-to-meetings dress, or very very special occasions like this, excuse me, J.J., daddy, and Mister ah . . .

MOSE
Mose Bartholomew Tucker.
(THEY *stare at each other*)

JACOB
Shit, I'm gonna get me some sleep, I got to get up too damn early.
(THEY *answer without looking at* J.J.)

MOSE
Nite, partner.

JENNIE
Nite, daddy.
(*The lights come down slow first on* JENNIE *and* MOSE, *then slowly down on* JACOB *getting in bed*)

ACT I
Scene III

The lights come up slowly, it's a soft color light, on the table with five empty bottles. JENNIE *is sitting on* MOSE's *lap with a jug in her hand, half full.* MOSE *is feeling her up, occasionally* THEY *kiss.*

JENNIE
I want to hear some damn music.
    (*Removing herself from his lap*)

MOSE
Music?

JENNIE
You fuckin' "A" right.
    (SHE *is very drunk*)

MOSE
What kind of shit is that.
    (*Reaching out for her,* HE *is very drunk too*)
Com'mere, bitch.
    (SHE *stumbles away from his reach*)

JENNIE
Don't call me no bitch, nigger, I am a star.

MOSE
Okay, com'mere, star bitch.

JENNIE
Why you say that?

MOSE
Say what?

JENNIE
You know what you said, Floyd.

MOSE

Floyd, I ain't no damn Floyd.

(HE *goes over to her and holds her in his arms*)

My name is Mose Bartholomew Tucker.

(SHE *puts her arms around his neck very tight*)

JENNIE

Yes, Floyd.

(HE *breaks her hold and pushes her down*)

MOSE

I'm no fucking Floyd, bitch.

(SHE *wanders,* SHE *looks around the stage in a bewildered stare. The dog barks a little,* J.J. *turns over still asleep,* HE *answers his dog*)

JACOB

Hush, dog.

(*Very softly* JENNIE *begins singing her song.* MOSE *stumbles over to her, a little ashamed,* HE *sits on the floor with her, touches her gently*)

MOSE

Look, J.J. ain't got no radio, and he ain't got no records for his old phonograph.

(*Very pleased* JENNIE *stumbles over to her bag and pulls out a Billie Holiday record*)

JENNIE

Look . . .

MOSE

(*Mumbling to himself*) Ain't this a bitch, my dick is as hard as a chisel pipe, and she wants to hear music.

(JENNIE *goes over to the record player and puts on her favorite song, "I Gotta Right to Sing the Blues," reaches out to* MOSE, *who is still on the floor*)

May I have this dance?

(MOSE *rises, takes her in his arms and begins to dance.* SHE *sings along with the record, while* MOSE *is dry fucking*)

You have a pretty voice, Jennie.
   (*Running his hands up and down her ass*)
Yes sir, a pretty voice.

JENNIE

I was going to be a singer once.

MOSE

What happen? what changed your mind?
   (*Still running his hands about her body*)

JENNIE

Fate.
   (HE's *cruising her toward the coat bed*)

MOSE

Tell me about it.
   (THEY'RE *at the coat bed, just barely moving,* SHE's *unaware of where* SHE's *at*)
Here, let's lay here, while you tell me about Fate.
   (THEY *lie on the coat bed*)

JENNIE

Fate dammit, fate, fate! Fate! Fate!
   (HE *runs his hands over her thighs*)
Niggar, what you doin'? . . . You mean to say, you don't know what the fuck fate is, niggar???
   (JENNIE *raising her head above* MOSE)

MOSE

Sure I know . . .
   (*Pulling her head back down*)

JENNIE

Ha ha ha, this damn niggar is dumb.

MOSE

Who you calling a niggar, bitch?

JENNIE

I didn't know niggars came that dumb, ha ha ha ha . . .

(HE *slaps her*)
Oh 'cuse me . . . ha ha ha ha ha ha ha . . .

MOSE
Who in the fuck are you laughin' at, bitch?

JENNIE
'Cuse me.
  (*Getting out of the coat bed*)
'Cuse me, Mose Bartholomew who . . . who?

MOSE
Tucker, bitch, TUCKER!

JENNIE
Yeah, yeah, Tucker a bad mathafucker.
  (SHE's *drunk*)

MOSE
Quiet, befo' you wake up J.J. Come back to bed.

JENNIE
You think I'm gonna let a niggar who doesn't know what fate
is fuck me.

MOSE
If you call me a niggar again I'm gonna bust your ass. I might
be dumb, but I ain't no niggar, I'm a negro, and don't you
forget it.
  (*Getting up and getting himself a jug*)
Besides, my grandma was a Cherokee Indian.
  (*Taking a drink*)
Shit, a full-pledge genuine Cherokee, can you say that, you
. . . you, you skunk.
  (SHE *has eased up to* MOSE *and is fondling him, and taking
the jug away*)

JENNIE
No.

MOSE

Well, just don't be throwing stones if you live in a . . . a . . .
a wooden house.

JENNIE

A glass.

(*Taking a healthy drink*)

MOSE

What?

JENNIE

The house is glass.

MOSE

You say what you want, and I say what I want.

JENNIE

But I thought every nig . . . negro knew that. Why the word
"fate" is as familiar to negroes as Jesus, even to a half genuine
Cherokee and a full half negro. I've been saving all year for
that car, and as soon as I was 'bout to make the first down
payment, the kid got sick, or that fine suit, Dorothy gets sick,
or buy a house, open a little business, take a trip, you name
it and fate claims it. Maybe you loved someone once and everything was going along fine and then she spied him, not really
him, but fate, she spied fate. What in the hell is that, Reverend
Johnson, I ask. "My child, that when the hand of God steps
in. Your life is already in the books. The wonders of God are
many, and one mustn't question God's work, for he moves in
mysterious ways." Humph.

(*Taking a good drink*)

That niggar was so mysterious he moved right into my life
and fucked up everything. You see I had everything going
for me: a man, a good man or at least I thought so at the
time, a seventeen-year-old daughter, about to graduate from
school, a promising singing career, I had everything, yeah they
said I sang as good as Billie, or Bessie, I had the fuckin' world
in my hand and in comes that fuckin' Mister Fate and points
his nasty gawdamn finger at my kid's ass, why my kid's ass,

wasn't mine big enough and since he didn't knock, he wanted
to be sure I knew he was there. He was there all right, right
between Doreen's legs. At first I wanted to find a butcher
knife so that I could cut that nigger's dick from stem to stern,
but I couldn't move, I just watch as he pumped his big black
ashy ass up and down, you know he must've had twelve inches
of dick up in her, if he had a inch. I decided to go to the
phone in my bedroom and call the police. I went into my room
and started to dial quietly, but all I could hear was moaning
and groaning, like she was dying. I dropped the phone and
ran back to her room and bust open the door, and that dirty
mathafucker was sucking her pussy, yeah and that black bitch
loving every moment of it. You think they was worried because I'd shown up? No sirree, that bitch had the nerve to say
to me, I was spying on her. I could've killed that little bitch
and would've, if Floyd hadn't stop me. He slapped me and
slapped me, he must've whipped me for fifteen minutes
straight. He shook me, he slapped me. "Jennie," he would say
in between slaps, "it's not her fault, it's not her fault, we fell
in love. . . ." Love, love! What about me, what about me??
I love, I love you both, get out . . . get out! get out!!!!

(MOSE *goes over and caresses her tenderly*)

MOSE

Quiet, you gonna wake J.J.
(*Very tender*)
I know, I know, come and lay down.

(HE *carries her over to the bed and* THEY *lie down.* HE *begins to feel her and kiss her*)

JENNIE

Mose.

MOSE

Keep still, Jennie.
(*Still touching and kissing her*)

JENNIE

Mose.

MOSE
What is it now, dammit?

JENNIE
The floor is too hard.
   (HE *gets up and grabs her arm and pulls her toward the mattress*)
No not there, not where my man's at.

MOSE
Well, get up on the table, bitch, my dick is hard.

JENNIE
No,
   (*Pulling away*)
let's go to your apartment.

MOSE
I ain't got no apartment, I got a room.

JENNIE
With a bed?

MOSE
You damn tootin'.

JENNIE
Well, if you gonna fuck me, it's gonna be in a bed. I ain't
cutting my ass on no cement floor.

MOSE
Well, just hurry up and put on some clothes.
   (SHE *goes over to her clothes and starts dressing*)
Damn hurry up. My dick is as hard as Chinese arithmetic.
   (*Blackout*)

ACT II
Scene I

The lights come up softly on the table where J.J. *is sitting.
There's an empty wine bottle, and a half full one sitting on
the table.* HE's *fussing about* JENNIE *with his dog King,* HE's
drunk. King should bark intermittently in mock reply.

JACOB
Shucks, I don't care if she never comes back. Who in the
hell she thinks she was fooling? Not me!!!! No sir, not one
little bit, 'cause if she thinks that, she got another thought coming. I ain't nobody's fool, never have been and never will be,
just 'cause I felt sorry for her and treated her nice. She think
I'm a fool, do I look like a fool to you, do I?? Huh?
    (King growls softly)
Well I was, that's right, me Jacob Jones, back thirty years ago.
There was only three real Black pimps in America, California
Jack, Downtown Shorty and me. Yeah, we was the top three,
but we all had different games, Jack rules his roost with a long
stick, he'd bust their asses at the drop of a hat, but the hoes
loved his joint. It was so big that they had to suck it, 'cause
if he put his dick in 'em, they was through. I remember one
time at Reefer Jane's joint Downtown Shorty brought a sleeper
in, a little ass niggar who had a joint that hung almost to his
knees. That's right, and Shorty was boasting that his prodigy
was going to put California Jack out of business. Yeah, he was
snorting coke, smoking tea and taking shit, he was charging
hoes fifteen dollars just to look at it, that was nice money back
there then. Now everybody knew Downtown was a head man,
a notorious head man, if he ever put that tongue in your

woman she was his. The nigger was slick too, he offer a hoe twice the going price so that he could get her in bed, just once, especially if she was a good hustler, that's how he got most of his women, by trickin' with 'em. Well, as fate would have it, Jack was in town. Now only the best could get in Reefer Jane's joint. Well, this niggar was running off at the mouth, like he had diarrhea or somethin'. When Jack enter: "What's all this shit I heard about you, Short man, and your prodigy's joint, being as big as mine"? "I was only facting, not cracking, Jack. Chocolate here gots the biggest joint in the world." "Nigger!" Jack said, reaching in his pocket and pulling out a B.R.

(*King growls*)

That's bankroll, stupid, big enough to choke a horse. "Put your money where your mouth's at, niggar, all you niggars that think well of Chocolate, put it on the table!" You should've seen the money hit the table, it must've been . . . easily five grand . . . easily, give or take a few hundred. They measure how long it was, how fat it was, it seem the same no matter how they measure it. Them niggars was really fussing 'bout his is the biggest, no his is, this went on for 'bout fifteen minutes, when Fast Herb came up with the answer. "Let dirty Gertie test them." Now, dirty Gertie was a big blonde bitch who had a hole big enough to put a garbage can inside of her. Yeah those was the days, pussy, women and dope. I probably would've had a business by now, retired even. But I never could hold on to anything. I'd spend it or give it away as soon as I got my hands on it. I always was a sucker for a story. California Jack use to say. "Diamond Jake" that use to be my name back then.

(*King growls*)

"Kindness is a sign of weakness," Downtown Shorty would say. "Never let your right hand know what your left hand's doin'. If you find a broad in the penthouse leave her there, if you find a broad in the basement leave her there, never put a penthouse broad in the basement or a basement broad in the penthouse," and she's just a basement broad to me. I knew she was nothin' the minute I look at her. I had a woman just like her once, she ran off with a bulldagger hog I had. I knew she wasn't shit, a leopard never changes her spots. I knew she was a cat, that's why I didn't let her eat your food.

(*King growls*)

No sirree bob, I gave her what all cats eat, sardines. I don't care if she never comes back.

(*Pause*)

If she did come back I wouldn't let her in.

(*A few minutes pass.* J.J. *continues to drink.* JENNIE *knocks at door. King barks*)

Who is it? Hush, dog, who is it??

JENNIE

Me, J.J. Jennie.

JACOB

What do you want?

JENNIE

I want to get in.

JACOB

(*Jealously*) Mose ain't here.

JENNIE

I know.

JACOB

If you know, then why did you come back?

JENNIE

To see you, I brought you something.

JACOB

What?

JENNIE

Open the door, I'll show it to you . . . J.J., please . . .

JACOB

I'm gonna open, but you can't stay long.

JENNIE

Okay, daddy.
  (HE *opens the door*)

JACOB

J.J.
  (JENNIE *comes in with a bag of groceries and places the bag on the table*)

JENNIE

That's for you.
  (SHE *starts to assemble her belongings, preparing to leave, as* J.J. *rambles through the bag,* SHE *heads for door*)

JACOB

(*Very touched*) Where you goin'?

JENNIE

Didn't you say to leave?

JACOB

Well . . . well, I didn't mean right away.

JENNIE

Thanks.
  (*Putting her bag down and going over to the grocery bag and pulling out the items one by one*)
Look, I got you chops, some butter, some coffee, rice, collard greens, I know all colored folks love greens and some stricker of lean, it gives it taste, bread, oh, and some chop meat for King.
  (*King growls*)

JACOB

(*Ashamed*) Why did you go and do that? 'Sides you had no money last night.

JENNIE

There's no two days alike, J.J. daddy.

(*Going to what appears to be the kitchen, with groceries*)
Oh, did you mop down the house?
    (*Blackout*)

ACT II
Scene II

Later that evening after dinner. THEY *are sitting at the table drinking very sociable.*

JACOB
Tell me one thing.

JENNIE
What, J.J.?

JACOB
How did you learn to cook so?

JENNIE
In Virginia.

JACOB
Is that where you're from?

JENNIE
Um hum.

JACOB
I'm from Virginia.

JENNIE
No.

JACOB
Yes.

JENNIE
What part?

JACOB

Cape Charles, and you?

JENNIE

Norfolk.

JACOB

That was right across the river from me. I use to take the ferry at little creek, when I was a kid and worked around the shipyards. Well, I'll be damn, this sure is a small world.

JENNIE

You can say that again.

JACOB

I knew that cooking was familiar.

JENNIE

We must've passed each other a thousand times.

JACOB

I'm talking about nineteen nineteen.

JENNIE

Oh.
   (*Very dicty*)
I was a baby then.

JACOB

I left that town in twenty-three, I swore I would never return and I didn't either, but many nights I've thought about that town.

JENNIE

Why did you leave, J.J.?

JACOB

I had no choice.

JENNIE

What do you mean? Was the law after you?

JACOB

I suppose they were, I didn't wait around to see. I hightailed it, as fast as I could.

JENNIE

What happened?

JACOB

Nothing important.

JENNIE

Something must've happened, your whole face changed, since we started talking about it. . . . Come on, J.J. tell me what happen. . . . You murder somebody huh, huh? You can trust me, it was murder, wasn't it?

JACOB

If you breathe this to a living soul, I'll kill you.

JENNIE

I won't, I swear.

JACOB

Yeah, it was murder, at least I think it was.

JENNIE

You think it was, you're not sure?

JACOB

Well, I didn't wait around to see. . . . Look, you better not breathe a word of this, you hear?

JENNIE

I hear.

JACOB

Well, one day my sister came home, she was a sight, her dress was torn and dirty, blood all over her clothes, mouth bleeding, her hair was going all which aways, my mother had a fit. "What happen to my baby, oh god," she screamed, "what happen, child?" I was in my room at the time, I was suppose to be at work, but I overslept and didn't want Momma to see me, so I quietly peeped and listened. "Charles Ray," she said. "Charles Ray, you mean Faubus Maddox Ray Boy?" "Yeah, him, him, him!!!!!" "Why did he do this to you?" "He tried to rape me, Momma, I fought him as hard as I could but he kept knocking me down until the last time. I don't remember getting up, my head was dizzy. He kept hitting me in the head and calling me a black nigger bitch. Oh Momma, I'm bleeding inside." "Come, child, let Momma wash you up." For Momma, I suppose sometime in her life she experience that, but for me it was an eye for an eye. I didn't tell Momma I knew, and she didn't tell me what happened. I began to save my money, work overtime when I could, came in only on Sunday, made myself real scarce in town until I had saved about forty dollars. Then one night I waited, by his outhouse, and sure enough about ten o'clock he came strolling out, toward that outhouse. I waited until he was good and comfortable and stuck my butcher knife clean through his chest. As I stuck him I placed my hand over his mouth. I stuck him at least ten times. I didn't go home or nothin'. I left and I never heard or seen my mother and sister since. I suppose Momma is dead by now.

JENNIE

Oh my, you must be very lonely, J.J. . . . then Jacob Jones isn't your real name?

JACOB

No.

JENNIE

It's good enough for me. What's the matter, J.J.?

JACOB

I'm not feeling good.

JENNIE

(*Helping him up and over to the mattress*) Here lie down, get yourself some sleep. I'll wake you up if somebody comes.

JACOB

(*Lying down*) Jennie?

JENNIE

Huh?

JACOB

Would you do me a favor?

JENNIE

Name it!

JACOB

Would you take King out for a walk, I really don't feel too good . . . huh?

JENNIE

Yes . . .
  (*Blackout*)

ACT II
Scene III

As the scene opens TWO MEN *in their early thirties come to buy some wine.* THEY'RE *filthy,* J.J. *is asleep.* JENNIE *opens the door.*

JENNIE

Yes?
  (*Standing at the entrance in her red dress and no shoes*)

BIMBO

Where's Pop?

JENNIE

Pop?

BIMBO

J.J., bitch,
  (*Pushing her aside,* THEY *walk in*)
I wanna buy some sneaky pete.

JENNIE
Both of you?

DIZZY
Yeah, the both of us!

JENNIE
What kind?

BIMBO
What kind? Bitch, do you know who I am? I'm Bimbo, I drinks
swell muscatel, right, Dizzy?

DIZZY
Dig it!
(JENNIE *gets two bottles of wine from the carton*)

BIMBO
We don't want two jugs.

JENNIE
What about your friend?

BIMBO
He came with me, I'm treating.
(JENNIE *hands him one of the bottles and puts the other
one back*)
Sit, man.
(THEY *sit at the table,* HE *opens the jug and deliberately
spills some wine on the floor*)
For the brothers that are no longer with us.

DIZZY
Crazy baby.
(JENNIE *goes over to the phonograph and puts on her Billie
Holiday record softly*)

BIMBO
Yeah, man, we was some bad niggars back in the gang-buster
days. We didn't fear a livin' ass.
(THEY *pass the bottle between them as* THEY *talk*)
We were the baddest things on the West Side.

DIZZY

On the East Side . . .

BIMBO

East Side, them niggars was punks.

DIZZY

Not all of them!

BIMBO

All of them! They wasn't shit, unless they had a group with them, but all the niggars on the West Side could fight.
(*The bottle's empty*)
Give us another one.
(JENNIE *goes over to where they're sitting*)

JENNIE

You ain't paid for the first one yet!

BIMBO

Don't worry about it, put it on my bill.

JENNIE

But I am worrying about it! Another bottle will cost you a dollar and a half.

DIZZY

He said give us another jug, bitch!

JENNIE

I'm not giving up anything until I get paid!
(BIMBO *goes in his pocket and pulls out about ten dollars in ones and slaps them on the table*)

BIMBO

Get to that!!!
(JENNIE *picks up two dollars and brings back a bottle*)
Keep the change, bitch, there's plenty more where that came from.

DIZZY

I wouldn't give her shit.
  (*Opening the bottle*)

JENNIE

Thanks, honey.
  (JENNIE *goes back over to the phonograph*)

BIMBO

One time the Mavaricks caught four of us at the Audabon ball-
room. It was me, Delly, Bat and Crip, they must've had a
hundred niggers with them, they said they was gonna light
our asses up. I ain't gonna lie, my heart was in my mouth, but
Bat and Crip bluffed them by reaching inside their suit jacket
like they had a gun. "Light up," Bat said, and "Get it right
back," said Crip. Them punks frozed, then me and Dilly went
into our act, "Light up, mothafuckers, or split." You know,
them niggers deuce out. That means they punked out.

DIZZY

I know, man.
  (HE's *high*)
I'm a New York boy too. Where do you think I was? In Ala-
bama or somethin'. Shit, you talk like the West Side was the
only gang with heart. As far as I'm concern they wasn't shit!!

BIMBO

What?

DIZZY

You heard me!
  (*Snatching the bottle from* BIMBO)
I'm from the East Side, and I'm not no punk, punk!

BIMBO

(*Putting his hand in his pocket*) Who you calling a punk?

DIZZY

(*Cocking the bottle*) You, nigga!
  (BIMBO *draws his knife*)

BIMBO
I'll cut your mothafucking throat, nigger, for calling me a punk.

DIZZY
You called me one.
  (THEY *stand opposite one another posing*)

BIMBO
I ain't call you nothin'.

DIZZY
You did . . .

BIMBO
Put the bottle down.

DIZZY
Put your knife down.

JENNIE
I don't want that fuckin' shit in here, get out.

BIMBO
Tell him to put my bottle down.

DIZZY
Put your knife up.

JENNIE
I thought yaull was friends.

BIMBO
We are.
  (*Putting his knife away*)
Give me the jug.

DIZZY
Wait, I didn't get me none.
  (THEY *sit down again.* JENNIE *dances slow to Billie Holiday.*
BIMBO *notices her shape*)

BIMBO
Hey, lady, give us another jug.

(SHE *does,* THEY *just sit and drink the whole jug as* JENNIE *continues to dance*)
Hey, lady,
   (THEY'RE *drunk*)
give us another one.
   (HE *holds up the two dollars, so that* JENNIE *can see them,* SHE *does,* SHE *gives them another bottle*)
Keep the change, you want a taste?

JENNIE

Yes.

BIMBO

Get yourself a jug, the treat's on me.
   (*Hands her two more dollars*)
Keep the change.
   (SHE *returns to the phonograph with her bottle and continues her dance, while drinking.* BIMBO *still watches her as* HE *talks*)
'Cause I'm poor, don't mean I'm cheap.
   (*Still watching* JENNIE)

DIZZY

Did I ever tell you about Betty?

BIMBO

(*Not looking away from* JENNIE) No . . .

DIZZY

I could never understand that bitch.

BIMBO

Um . . . hum . . .

DIZZY

Every time we use to see her, we pull a train, sometime it would be twelve at one time and that bitch wouldn't even moan, she just lay there. But the thing I couldn't understand was that she kept coming around every day, she must've had a white liver or somethin'.

BIMBO

Um . . . hum . . .
  (*Going over to* JENNIE)
can I have this dance?

JENNIE

I don't feel like dancing.

BIMBO

Why?

JENNIE

I just don't feel like it, that's why!

BIMBO

Ar . . . come here, bitch.
  (*Pulls her to him,* SHE *struggles*)

JENNIE

Let me go, nigga.
  (DIZZY *rushes over and begins to help* BIMBO)

DIZZY

He ain't gonna hurt you, baby . . .

JENNIE

Let me go gawdammit!!!!!
  (*The sounds make King bark,* J.J. *rises, half drunk as* HE
rushes to her aid)

JACOB

Take your hands off her, nigga!
  (J.J. *grabs* BIMBO, DIZZY *hits him from behind,* HE *goes down
and* DIZZY *stomps him. King is barking,* THEY *drag* JENNIE
over to the mattress and BIMBO *begins to rape her*)

DIZZY

Hurry up, man, hurry up, I want some too.

BIMBO

Wait!
  (*The lights go down slow on them, and* J.J. *who is on the*

floor, *blabbering out of his mind. The* TWO MEN *after a short period of time rush by* J.J. *and out the door.* J.J. *is still blabbering*)

JACOB

King . . . King . . . King . . .

(*King is still barking, the lights come up slightly.* JENNIE *crawls very softly across the room to* J.J., SHE *touches him very gently and kisses him up and down his face, while on her hands and knees. King is still barking*)

King . . .

(JENNIE *is still kissing him*)

King . . . King . . .

JENNIE

(*Turning in the direction of King's room,* SHE *speaks softly*)

Hush, dog.

(*Very softly*)

Hush, dog.

(SHE *turns back to* J.J. *and continues to kiss and lick him tenderly as the lights softly disappear.*

Blackout)

On Being Hit

CLAY GOSS

You see a thing over and over every day. You see it once again and it makes you blink your eyes or do a quick double-take, but nevertheless you keep on breathing. Keep on going about your daily way, wherever it is leading you. No matter how far it is taking your mind away.

And then something registers. Subtly, maybe, at first, but something registers and that is the important element, that it registers within the heart and right between the ear lobes.

As a child, I was almost forced to follow boxing. My father was indeed one of boxing's most avid fans. Wednesdays and Fridays at ten o'clock were his nights to ride the one TV in the house our family "shared." So I watched the fights and slowly came to love the fight game as my father had loved it. Followed it as he so excitedly followed it. Winning with the winners and losing with the losers. Punching and jabbing at the TV set till the sweat would run down my face until one particular night I saw one fighter to the cheers of countless thousands kill another fighter on nationwide TV. Both fighters, of course, were black.

Since that fight (the Benny Paret-Emile Griffith tragedy) I have learned to look at the fighting game a little closer.

Holly, the main character of this play, is named after Holly Mimms, who unknowingly I viewed as a common janitor working in a movie theatre in Washington, D.C. He is dead now, but at one time he was, as we all hope to be (in a sense), the number-one contender for the crown.

Now, there are some of us who will undoubtedly take exception to this number-one contender idea. Only because they have come to either want or expect it all. Expecting more out of life after struggling to transcend the daily "main bouts" we know of as living. Hoping to win that mythical championship and wear that championship crown. They are the relentless sluggers among us. The ones who go for the knockout (many times at the expense of an unprotected chin) at any cost. And I for one am not taking exception with their style. For history is full of *one-punch* knockout sluggers who have gone on to capture the title. Just as it is full of punch-weary and punch-drunk veterans who barely remember their own names.

What I am talking about in this play is something much more. And it is up to the reader or the audience of this play to get to that point or points of understanding. For boxing is a science to some and an art to others. The same can be said of life and war. In fact, the same might be even said of death. Or in the way we come to see ourselves slowly dying.

There is mention of Sugar Ray Robinson in this play. And even though the play is not directly about him or the image that his name instantly brings to one's mind, I can honestly say that in some cosmic kind of way the play is directed toward this champion of champions. For in Sugar Ray we glimpsed it all; the body and soul in coordinated motion.

But in Holly it is all there too. And what isn't there is the secret, as well as the story, of many of our soulful lives.

As Salaam-Alaikum
Clay Goss

On Being Hit

BY CLAY GOSS

SETTING:
Office room (large executive)

CHARACTERS:
HOLLY: *well-built brown-skinned man around forty, janitor*
DUNCAN: *average-built man, same age, janitor*
MR. WILSON: *early fifties, white*

HOLLY
(*Shadowboxing*) You do the best you can, man. Sometimes you get the breaks and sometimes you don't. Then you just die of a kidney ailment one day, that's all.

DUNCAN
(*Mopping floor*) Where at you gonna die, Holly. Huh? Where at and when?

HOLLY
What from? Simple, man. Them punches to the midsection. They got a way of comin' back on you weeks later sometimes. Years later too. Uh huh years later—I should know.
(*Clutches midsection*)
Whew!

DUNCAN
Where at, Holly? I asked you where at. Where at?

HOLLY

Oh, at uh Providence Hospital in a ward section. Providence
Hospital. Smallpox ward . . .

DUNCAN

Smallpox ward, whaat???

HOLLY

Yea, smallpox, man. That's what they used to say was the
matter. Goldie Blumberg, the promoter, said other fighters
turned me down like I had smallpox or somethin'. I was what
you call a spoiler. A spoiler. Ever heard of Willie Troy?

DUNCAN

Willie Troy? Willie? Yea uh, middleweight, right. Back in the
fifties, I think. He was pretty good too. You fought him *too;*
huh.

HOLLY

What you mean *too,* man. I don't have no reason to . . .

DUNCAN

O.K. All right, I was, I was just joking with ya, Holly. Fought
Willie Troy, huh?

HOLLY

Damn right, man. But that wasn't the hurter, man. Now the
thing that hurt me most was that—

DUNCAN

Wait a minute, Holly. Slow down a second. You said you
fought Willie Troy back in the fifties. How . . . how did you
uh make out?

HOLLY

Made out O.K. Pretty good. O.K.

DUNCAN

Come on, Holly. I mean how did you uh do. Did you win the
fight or lose?

HOLLY

I won ninety-five fights, man. Naw, I fought ninety-five fights, you see. Won sixty-four with six draws. Man, I hated draws . . .

DUNCAN

Look, man, I asked you how did you make out? Did you win or lose? What's the matter, did you get knocked out or something?

HOLLY

(*Loud, mad*) Knocked out! I was never knocked out, never! You hear that, Jack, never. Uh—knocked off my feet once though but never—

DUNCAN

Win or lose, Holly. Win or lose? Win or lose?

HOLLY

Lose? Uh
   (*Counts fingers*)
thirty-one fights, I reckon.

DUNCAN

TROY. Willie Troy . . .

HOLLY

Knocked ol' Troy out, Duncan. Knocked the cat out. Old Goldie Blumberg, you know, the promoter, he . . . he said Willie Troy just ran on away from me then. Just was running away from a rematch.
   (*Grinning*)
Grapevine had it out I couldn't punch. Didn't have no punch. That . . . that I was a soft touch.

DUNCAN

Guess Troy didn't think so. Bet he didn't, huh?

HOLLY

Yea, he knew. They all knew soon enough. It was just that I wasn't no slugger.

DUNCAN

A boxer, huh. Like Sugar Ray. Fought six champions. Six championship fights. Man, what you doin' sweeping floors with me then. Jesus Christ, six champion fights.

HOLLY

Naw man, they wasn't no championship fights.

DUNCAN

Whaat. You said you fought six champions—Sugar Ray.

HOLLY

Sugar Ray! Fought him too, Sugar Ray.

DUNCAN

(*Jerking his head as if* HE *hears a sound*) Wait a minute, Holly. Stop that boxing around and hold on to the broom. Think I hear Mr. Wilson comin'. You know he don't like seeing nobody standin' around on the job.
   (HOLLY *stops shadowboxing and grabs broom, starts making sweeping motions.* THEY BOTH *pause, working until the scare has passed*)
Now what was you talking about?

HOLLY

Uh . . . hu . . . uh . . . damn, I really can't remember what I was saying. Uh . . . yea . . . well, my son comes in my room and he ask me for some money. A couple of dollars. He's twenty-one, you know. Takes after his maw, kinda fat. Not too much though. Now his sister . . .

DUNCAN

Naw, you wasn't talking 'bout that. You was saying something 'bout fighting.

HOLLY

Yea, I used to be a fighter. A middleweight. Professional too. After I won the Golden Gloves in '47 turned pro a year later.

DUNCAN

You said you fought Sugar Ray??

HOLLY

You see, Duncan, fight game's a funny business. Like they expects you to go out there and get hurt. All cut up—

DUNCAN

Sugar Ray? Sugar Ray, Holly! Sugar Ray.

HOLLY

Like I was what they called a . . . a . . . counterpuncher. Not a slugger or a boxer but a counterpuncher
    (HE *puts broom back down on desk*)
I didn't call them. They had to call me. And when they did, I had a punch waiting for 'em. A punch right from behind the *counter*. Know what I mean, huh?

DUNCAN

(*Exasperated*) What do you mean, Holly?

HOLLY

Try and hit me, Duncan. Put down your broom and try and hit me. Come on, Duncan. Come on, try and hit me.

DUNCAN

Holly, you must be joking. Old man Wilson hear us up here scuffling about he'll fire us in a second.

HOLLY

(*Dancing around*) Come on, Dunc. Try and hit me. I wanna show you what I mean about a counterpuncher.

DUNCAN

Man, I follow fighting. Don't you think I know what a counterpunch is.

HOLLY

Yea, I know you knows, Duncan. But you ain't never been in the ring with a counterpuncher. Especially not one like me, have you?

DUNCAN

(*Laughing and putting down his mop*) Christ, I must be looney as a bat boxing you here at the job. Well, if we gonna box tonight we might as well do it up right.

(*Imitating an announcer*)

In this corner

(*Points at* HOLLY *who is jumping in place with serious expression on face*)

In this corner with red trunks and white shoes weighing 160 pounds even. HOLLY.

(HOLLY *raises both hands as if to a crowd*)

In the opposite corner, of course, wearing green satin trunks with black patent leather shoes with felt tips weighing in at 160 even, the Great Duncan.

(*Raises hands imitating* HOLLY)

HOLLY

Try and hit me, Duncan. Come on, try and hit me.

DUNCAN

I can't, man. You know that.

HOLLY

Try and hit me, man. Come on now. I'm ready for you now. Come on, Dunc.

DUNCAN

What kind of fighter were you, man. You know I can't hit you yet.

HOLLY

Can't hit me yet? Why not, man. How come. You scared too or something. I scare ya.

DUNCAN

Naw, you don't scare me. It's just that the bell ain't rung yet, that's all.

HOLLY

The bell, what bell you talking 'bout, man. Ain't no bell in here.

DUNCAN

Now, look, I said I'd box you. But only if you ring the bell,
Holly. I mean I got pride, you know I'm a proud boxer, Jack,
you understand!

HOLLY

(*Laughing*) All right, all right, I'll ring the bell. DING! DING!
Now, come on out and get whipped.

(DUNCAN *circles* HOLLY, *waiting for an opening to punch
through. Suddenly* HE *throws a "big right hand" of which*
HOLLY *expertly blocks and throws about six punches at* DUNCAN.
Each punch is accompanied with "POW POW BOOO BOOOM
POW O POW")

Try again, Dunc. Try again.

(DUNCAN *throws another punch—same thing happens*)

Try again, baby. Try me, One Mo Gin.

(*Same thing takes place*)

DUNCAN

(*Amazed at* HOLLY's *speed*) Wheeew, man, you . . . you still
fast as lightning. How old, you man? We must be about the
same age, huh?

HOLLY

I don't know how old you are but I'm forty.

DUNCAN

Forty? You two years older 'n me. Don't seem like it though.
Damn.

HOLLY

No big thing . . . forty. It's how you feel inside that counts.
Try and hit me again, O.K.?

DUNCAN

O.K. One more time and that's it.

(HE *throws punch at* HOLLY. *Same thing takes place. Only
this time* HOLLY *throws flurries of six punches each saying the
names*)

HOLLY

Paddy Young, Spider Webb, Mile Sabage, Johnny Bratter, Ernie Durrando, Ray Robinson, RAY ROBINSON. RAY ROBINSON!

(*Furious punches.* DUNCAN *has to stop him from punching out so hard and wild at the very atmosphere surrounding him*)

DUNCAN

Whoa now, Holly. Calm down, man. Be cool now. You gotta think about this job now. I don't mind you messing around none or nothing but you gonna make us both lose our jobs. What you got against Ray Robinson, man. Wow. You was scaring me there for a while punching out like that. Huh, Holly? Holly, what ya got against Sugar Ray? You said ya fought him once.

HOLLY

Yea, that's right one. I uh lost a close decision to him in '51. Real close. Real close.

DUNCAN

Blew your mind huh, losing to Sugar . . .

HOLLY

Losing. Man I won . . . I only lost . . . losing! The cat, Sugar Ray was about the meanest coolest cat there was, Dunc. Wasn't no excuse losing to him. People still dug me and all. 'Cept that . . . that!

DUNCAN

Yea . . . yea!?

HOLLY

'Cept that . . . you see, Duncan, the fight game's a funny business.

DUNCAN

You said that before now.

HOLLY

Well, it is a funny business. It was down in Miami. The fight was. Me and Sugar Ray Robinson. The great Sugar Ray Robinson against me. I . . . I was kinda nervous before the fight but not that much. I knew myself, see . . .

DUNCAN

Knew yourself? What has that got to do with it?

HOLLY

You just can't go into a ring with somebody like Ray Robinson without knowing who you are, understand. 'Cause you know who he is, dig it. And you know what he can do to ya. Real quick too. He don't waste no time playing around. Ca Pow that's the show.

DUNCAN

Yea, yea go on, go on. The fight, the fight!

HOLLY

Well . . . I was in good shape. Reflexes sharp as a tack nail. Surprised myself that night. Fought real good. Real good. Lost a close decision. Real close decision.

DUNCAN

Yea, well . . . you know . . . that's the way it goes, you know. Win a few, lose a few. You fought good anyway.

HOLLY

But that wasn't the hurter, man. That wasn't the hurter. After the announcer gave out the decision Sugar came over to me and told me I gave 'em a hell of a fight. Hell of a battle. That's the way he was, all class. All class. New York, New York. You know.

DUNCAN

The hurter, man. What was the hurter?

HOLLY

The hurter? Yes. The hurter was that the word got out about my fight game.

DUNCAN

That grapevine you was talking earlier about . . .

HOLLY

The grapevine, yea. That's what they called it too, the grape-vine. Word was out that I wasn't no soft touch but a dangerous fighter.

DUNCAN

That bad, huh . . .

HOLLY

It . . . it became so bad there were days I thought I'd never get another fight. That bad.
(*Unexpectedly* HE *takes off his shirt and undershirt*)

DUNCAN

Holly, are you drunk or somethin'? Now what you go take off your shirt for?

HOLLY

I was considered a spoiler.

DUNCAN

Put your damn shirt back on. The matter wit you? You funny or something?

HOLLY

You ain't laughing, are you? Anyway, what's wrong with taking my shirt off? Lest it bothers you.

DUNCAN

Lest it bothers me. Why you take your shirt off, Holly? If you keep acting crazy I might have to call Wilson up here myself. Wow!

HOLLY

The hurter, man. Like this was me. My body. All I had.

DUNCAN

Still don't mean you gotta undress in here in front of me. Startin' to wonder about you, now.

HOLLY

Just 'cause I show you my chest I funny, huh. I showed this
chest ninety-five times in the ring. Didn't nobody think nothing. Where was your chest then? Where was it? Was . . . was
Sugar Ray gay, man just 'cause he showed himself, huh? Was
Sugar Ray gay?

DUNCAN

Was Sugar Ray gay! Holly, you feeling all right, man? Was
Sugar Ray gay!

HOLLY

He had beautiful legs, didn't he? Didn't he?

DUNCAN

Look here, Holly. I think we better get back to working. Was
Sugar . . .

HOLLY

Well, they was. That's what my wife said after the fight. She
said he had beautiful legs.

DUNCAN

That's your wife's problem, Jack. Don't mean I got to say it.
Or you. Now get to work.

HOLLY

All right, all right, I was just making fun, that's all. Just making
a joke. That's all. Forget it, O.K. Forget it.

DUNCAN

All right, I'll, uh, forget it. Come on now, let's finish up this
job, solid.

HOLLY

Be with you in a second, Dunc; first I got to make it to the
bathroom for a second.
(*Picks up shirt, undershirt*)
My kidneys, you understand. Nineteen years in the ring.
(*When* HOLLY *leaves to go to the bathroom,* DUNCAN *is just
standing up there sweeping the floor and* HE's *whistling. Then*

HE *hears the noise and* MR. WILSON *comes in and* DUNCAN *tries to ignore him acting like* HE's *really doing work.* HE *speeds up his sweeping*)

MR. WILSON

How you doin', Duncan?

DUNCAN

How you doing. Pretty nice night, huh.

WILSON

Hey, Duncan, how about that Holly, huh. Died on us, huh. Guess he just didn't want to come in to work any more.

DUNCAN

(*Being cool*) Yea that was something—that was something.

WILSON

(*Taking newspaper from back pocket*) That's something about Holly, a number-one contender. It says here in his obituary.
(*Unfolds it*)
It says here in this here obituary that . . . that Holly fought in the ring for nineteen years. Nineteen years he fought without gettin' a crack at the big money. At the championship. Know what, Duncan, well, I use to ask the man . . . I'd say, "Hey, Holly, your luck just wasn't with you back in them prize fighting days."
(HE *laughs*)
All Holly'd do was shrug my question off and keep on gettin' on up. Know what I mean? That's the way he was. Never got a break but he just kept on gettin' on up. Kept on living, I guess. Says here he died from his kidneys.

DUNCAN

(*Still sweeping*) Just like he said he would!

MR. WILSON

Providence Hospital. General Ward. I . . . I could tell he had lost some weight lately. Humph! Nineteen years of being hit. Nineteen years of gettin' smashed in the face without getting the one punch over. Duncan, you know he told me one night. He told me one night that he was in the encyclopedia.

(HE *laughs*)

The boxing encyclopedia. Brought it in to work to . . . to prove it to me. Wonder how much money he made in the ring off of ninety-five fights. Wonder where it went. Hell, I was payin' him $1.86 an hour. Less than you, Dunc.

(HE *laughs*)

Yea, less than you.

(WILSON *walks out of room.*

DUNCAN *freezes, facing audience.* HOLLY *has walked back onstage fumbling with his zipper. Finally closing it*)

HOLLY

You know, Dunc. The fun part about boxing was the press pictures. The women loved 'em, know what I mean. The photographer would take three poses. First was one with your hands up on guard like this. The second one was a close-up of just the side of your face like. The third one, now that's the one I liked the best.

(*Lights dimming*)

The third one was a close-up of the front of your face smiling.

(HOLLY *smiles broadly*)

Just smiling.

(*Hands up in exultation to the sky. Lights out*)

If It's Black, Then It Relates to Black People

CHARLES F. "OYAMO" GORDON

There are things that Black people are going through, problems that we have, things that we have to get together ourselves and work on. And we're trying to find solutions to things. We're trying to build a nation. We're trying to do everything. And we're confused about a lot of things. But we're trying to free ourselves.

And the life that playwriting comes from is part of that effort to be free. The playwright is attempting to free himself and his people in whatever way he can. But the playwright by himself cannot be freer than the people.

I try to work toward the accomplishment of the ideal of freedom through writing plays which seek to eliminate the many confusions that hinder Black people. And I deal with questions that are crucial to Blacks.

I'd like to see forty million Black people see my plays. And anybody else who wants to see them too. Whoever wants to do them can because they are all Black plays. And you have to have Black directors, actors, etc. And if the right people do them, they can be a hit. No matter what you talk about it relates to everything else. If it's Black, it relates to Black people.

(From a conversation with
CHARLES F. "OYAMO" GORDON,
Fall '72)

His First Step

BY OYAMO

His First Step was presented on a bill of one-acts, *The Corner*, presented by the Public Theater in Spring of 1972. *His First Step* was directed by Kris Keiser. Settings by Marsha L. Eck; lighting by Ian Calderon.

THE CAST:

PRITCHARD	Michael Coleman
COUNTRY	Ilunga Adell
MARY	Yolanda Karr
SAM	Cornelius Suares
PEEAIR	Adolph Ceaser

Scene I

It is late October in Harlem. Two YOUNG MEN *stand on a tenement stoop near 112th Street and First Avenue.* THEY *are looking down beneath them, listening to the passionate meowing of two cats.*

PRITCHARD
You think she gon' let 'im have it?

COUNTRY
She just trying to show how precious her pussy is. Das how cats fuck, man.

PRITCHARD

(*Looking up and laughing*) She betta go on give it up 'fore ole tom scratch her ass.

COUNTRY

Nawh, man. Ole tom don't wanna blow dat pussy. 'Sides, she 'sposed ta ack like dat, hard ta git. Ole tom can dig it betta then. Shit, ole tom the one likely ta git scratched. It's a natural law dat . . .

PRITCHARD

(*Combing his hair*) Damn, Country, you know all 'bout how cats fuck. You musta been down there on her 'fore ole tom got there. No wonda she don' wanna give up dat.

COUNTRY

(*Laughing at himself*) Man, das da way it is. No lie. Why you so hard on me, brotha Pritchard?
(THEY *both turn away from the cats*)

PRITCHARD

(*Laughing*) Ah don't mean to be hard, Country. Swear ah don't; we tight. But you sound like you got a doctor's degree in cat fuckin'.

COUNTRY

Shit, that kinda shit does happen. I rememba dis dude from college, he . . .

PRITCHARD

Damn, Country, you neva tole me you went to college. Ah thought we was working together three months.

COUNTRY

Well, ah did. Anyway, dis white boy . . .

PRITCHARD

(*Looking at his watch and thinking aloud*) Where da fuck is Sam? I need dat shit . . . um sorry, Country. Go 'head.

COUNTRY

Anyway, dis dude . . .

PRITCHARD

(*Patting his hair carefully into place*) You didn't say what college it was. New York Jew?
  (*Laughs by himself*)

COUNTRY

Naw, man, Red Junction University.

PRITCHARD

(*Cracking up*) Red Junction, eh?

COUNTRY

(*Laughing himself*) Aw, man, dere you go again.

PRITCHARD

Um sorry, Country—but where in the fuck is Red Junction?

COUNTRY

South Dakota.

PRITCHARD

(*Cracking up*) Oh yeah, I heard of dat place. Dat's in Turkey, ain't it?

COUNTRY

(*In obvious feigned hurt*) Damn, Pritchard.

PRITCHARD

(*Placing a hand on* COUNTRY'S *shoulder and speaking in mock innocence*) Um only kiddin', Country. Ah ain't dumb as ah ack. Even know some of dem college boy words too.

COUNTRY

(*Looking around*) Looka here, Pritchard, umo have to split if Sam don't get here soon.

PRITCHARD

Relax, man. He said he'd be here at eight and it's only eight-thirty. What you wanna do? Go home and watch the late show?
  (*Making gesture of realization*)
Ah, wait a minute. You must be gittin' drugged with me talkin'

'bout your alma mater. Um sorry, Country. You just got to understand I don't mean no harm. Um tryin' ta git back to college myself. In music, you know. Yaw have a music department?

COUNTRY

Yeah. You usta go ta college? Where?

PRITCHARD

Actually, ah quit high school, but ah got a diploma in da Navy. Dey sent me on for further schoolin' and ah picked up two years of college training. You think ah could git inta dis music department at the Junction?

COUNTRY

Yeah, ah guess so. What you gon' do?

PRITCHARD

Maybe ah kin git a name for mahself singin' in a music department. You know, git me a chance to git in on some heavy dollas. Ah mean ah wanna learn how ta read music 'n shit, but ah really wanna just sing. Like dig on this:

(PRITCHARD *goes into a thing on "I Want to Testify" by the Parliaments.* HE *accompanies himself by making the sounds with his mouth of the instrumental background.* HE *also dances as* HE *sings. After a couple of verses* HE *speaks*)

So dig, Country, um laughin' but, you know, ah could function heavy at the Junction.

(*Laughing*)

No harm, Country, no harm.

COUNTRY

Yeah, das what your grandfather told me when you took me to yo house.

PRITCHARD

He did? I don't rememba.

COUNTRY

You went to git some more beer.

PRITCHARD

Old gramps talkin' 'bout me behind mah back, eh? What'd he say?

COUNTRY

He said you always usta do things to people when you was a kid, but he said you neva meant no harm. Said you liked to fool folks, mess wid 'em all the time.

PRITCHARD

(*Smiling proudly*) He did, Country? Did he say that? I mean, really?

COUNTRY

That's what he said.

PRITCHARD

(*Stops smiling and looks straight in* COUNTRY's *eyes*) You lyin', Country. Ah know mah gramps talked 'bout me like a dog.

COUNTRY

Man, I done tole you what he said. Why he got to call you a dog? And why I wanna lie?

PRITCHARD

(*Satisfied*) It's true. I know you ain't lyin'. Man, I usta sing and do impersonations and all dat shit when I was a kid. Dig, I usta dial numbers from the phone book and pretend I was calling from the city morgue to report a death in the family. Talk about upsettin' some crackers. Mostly, I usta call up and sing though.

COUNTRY

Damn, you musta been a mufucka, but your gramps didn't say nothin' bad.

PRITCHARD

But you don't know my gramps. He sharp as a razor, but he paranoid. That dude got 'im plenty coins stacked up some-where in dat house. Got all dat money preaching on the radio, and he think everybody tryin' ta steal from him. He slick. Da only things in da house dat ain't got no locks on 'em is my bedroom door and my grandma's pussy. Gramps don't put nothin' in them two places. Just cause he found a lock busted one time, he think I tried to fine his money. Shit, I ain't the only one live in dat house. Coulda been my grandmother. Wuddin nothin' in dat closet anyway but some old double-breasted suits from 1930. Pawnshop wouldn't even take dat shit.

COUNTRY
What time is it?

PRITCHARD
Damn, man, da sky ain't gon' fall 'fore you git home. Relax. Dig, you didn't finish telling me 'bout dat dude at your college.

COUNTRY
What dude?

PRITCHARD
Dat white dude who used to fuck cats for yaw.

COUNTRY
Oh. Naw, man, he didn't fuck cats for us.

PRITCHARD
Well, for who then?

COUNTRY
(*Irritated*) Da dude didn't fuck no cats at all.

PRITCHARD
(*Realizing* COUNTRY's *irritation*) Um only trying to git it straight. What da white boy fuck if he didn't fuck cats? His roommates?

COUNTRY
It didn't have nothin' ta do with fuckin' cats. I don't know 'bout his roommate ta tell da truth.

PRITCHARD

That's probably what he was doin'. I knew a lotta white boys like dat in da Navy. Usta catch them paddies pluukkin' each other. We'd beat da shit out 'em 'fore they could get unhooked.

COUNTRY

(*Sighing heavily*) All ah know is dat dis dude wrote a long play 'bout a man who fucked hogs.

PRITCHARD

(*After a brief silence*) Ah don't think umo git to Red Junction.

COUNTRY

(*Sighing again*) Naw, Pritchard, ah guess not. Looka here, umo have to split.

PRITCHARD

(*Looking down the block*) Hole tight, Country. Here come Mary down da block.

COUNTRY

(*Looking*) Ah don't know no Mary.

PRITCHARD

Ah'll introduce you. Got some good pussy. You got to learn to relax.

(*Laughing loudly to himself*)

Talk 'bout bein' relaxed. You eva see dem old Step'n Fetchit movies? Man, dat dude sure know how to relax. Laziest mutha-fucka I eva seen. Dig, here he go . . .

(PRITCHARD *does an impersonation of Step in motion and words.*

As HE *does so,* MARY *walks up to the stoop and watches.* HE *is conscious of her presence.* PRITCHARD *finishes his impersonation amid his own laughter.* COUNTRY *looks down at the cats*)

Mary, whas happnin', sweethot?

MARY

(*Climbing to the stoop*) Nothin' but some bills and some work. How are things with you, Melvin?

PRITCHARD

Ain't nothin' to it, baby. Ah thought you was tending bar at Slim's tanight.

MARY

I am, but I came by to tell you something good.

PRITCHARD

(*Playfully hitting* COUNTRY's *arm as if telling him to dig this*) Ah been waitin' ta hear somethin' good from you for a long time. What made you change you mind?

MARY

What IS you talkin' 'bout?

PRITCHARD

Dat good somethin' you got for me.

MARY

Shit!

PRITCHARD

Whas a matta, baby?

MARY

Ain't nothin' the matta now, and ain't nothin' gon' be the matta.

PRITCHARD

Damn, you ack like . . .

MARY

Look, Melvin, I just came by to tell you 'bout a talent scout from a record company.

PRITCHARD

(*Getting angry*) Wait a minute, Mary. Ah know you ain't talkin' 'bout dat dude from Motown. Um lahble ta punch him in da eye. Dat muthafucka come runnin' ta me 'bout they was tired of fuckin' with the Supremes. Said they thought ah was betta, had mo' appeal to the public than the Supremes. They had me sing three songs on tape. Dug me right away. Dat dude called up Detroit as soon as he heard mah tapes. Tole me he'd call me next week 'bout signin' a contract. Mutha-fucka ain't called yet and dat was a year ago. Shit, they still got the tapes. I don't like havin' no game run on me. I'll choke dat dude if I see him again.

MARY

That is a shame, Melvin, but I ain't talkin' 'bout the same fella.

PRITCHARD

(*Losing his anger*) Um glad ta hear that. Oh, Mary, you hear dat new thing by Aretha?

MARY

You mean "Satisfaction"?

PRITCHARD

Naw, it's dis one:
    (HE *begins singing "Respect." HE accompanies himself with background and dancing. After the first verse*):

MARY

Melvin, um sorry, but I got to get to work.
    (PRITCHARD *stops*)
This man's name is Peeair. He stay over there on Sixteenth, the other side of Lenox.

PRITCHARD

Dat's near da Temple, ain't it?

MARY

(*Rummaging in her purse*) Look, ah'll write it down for you 'cause ah got to leave; um late now.

PRITCHARD

Mary, dig this:
    (*Starts to sing "My Girl" by the Temptations.* COUNTRY *lights a joint*)

MARY

(*Quickly scribbles and puts the paper in* PRITCHARD's *hand*)
Here, I got to go. Be sure and check it out—it could be a break.

PRITCHARD

(*Sticking paper in his pocket*) Hole tight, Mary. You gon' run off widout meetin' Country?

MARY

Country? Whose Country?

PRITCHARD

(*Pointing at* COUNTRY) Mah man. Country, dis is Mary. Mary, Country.

COUNTRY

(*Taking her hand awkwardly*) How you doin'?

MARY

(*Slowly taking his hand*) I'm fine. I don't mean to be nosy, but is that reefer you got?

COUNTRY

Yeah.

PRITCHARD

Yeah, old Country love ta smoke 'im some reefa.

MARY

Lemme see it?

(COUNTRY *hands it to her.* SHE *looks at it carefully. Then smells it*)

I know this gon' sound bad, but I got to ask ya.

COUNTRY

It's cool.

MARY

Now tell me da truth, we can still be friends no matta what you say. Do you eat pussy?

COUNTRY

(*Incredulously confused*) Ah shit, what kinda question is dat?

PRITCHARD

It's an honest question.

MARY
You gon' give me a honest answer?

COUNTRY
(*Hunting a cigarette*) Damn!

MARY
All you got to do is say yes or no.

COUNTRY
No.

MARY
No, you don't eat pussy, right?

COUNTRY
Right.
(MARY *looks carefully at him for a moment, then smokes the joint*)

PRITCHARD
It's all right, Country, Mary just don't like ta smoke afta people who eat pussy.

COUNTRY
(*Recovering his confidence*) Yeah, ain't nothin' wrong wid dat.

MARY
(*Sniffing small breaths*) Um sorry, but I had ta ask ya.

COUNTRY
It's all right.
(*The cats become louder*)

MARY
(*Between sniffs*) Them cats must be havin' a gang war down there.

PRITCHARD
They jus' fuckin'.

MARY
Fuckin'? Where is they?

COUNTRY

(*Pointing*) Right down there next to da garbage pile.

MARY

(*Leaning over to see better*) WhoooooooooooooEEEE! Ole tom got his tongue hangin' out. Know he don't wanna stop.

PRITCHARD

(*Tapping* COUNTRY *and looking at* MARY's *ass*) Kinda make you wish you was doin' it too, don't it?

MARY

(*Straightening up*) Shit! Don't want no ole tom nigga fuckin' me and then runnin' back to roam the alleys while ah got ta run afta some otha tom nigga who done stole mah welfare check.

COUNTRY

Ah kin dig where das at. Beautiful.

PRITCHARD

(*Unappreciative*) Looka here, Mary, you didn't finish tellin' me 'bout Peeair.

MARY

Ah tole you all ah know.

PRITCHARD

Square bidness?

MARY

(*Handing a roach to* COUNTRY) The onliest thing the fella tole me was that Peeair works for Ebony Records.

PRITCHARD

Ebony Records?
    (*In mock West Indian*)
Damn, dat's a big company. Got plenty dough.

MARY

(*Starting to leave*) Okay now, ah'll see you later.

PRITCHARD

Ah know you got to go, but kin ah ask you one mo' question
'fore you go?

MARY

(*Edging down the stoop steps*) Drop by the bar tonight and
ask me then.

PRITCHARD

Damn, ah ain't gon' be anywhere 'roun' da bar tonight.

MARY

You kin stop by and let me know what happened. Look, Melvin, ah got to go; it's almost nine.

PRITCHARD

You ain't got time to answer one question? You wrong.

MARY

Well, good lord, what you wanna ask me?

PRITCHARD

Dis dude Peeair tell you to come git me?

MARY

Peeair? I jus' tole you ah don't know the man. A fella at the
bar told me 'bout 'im.

PRITCHARD

Well, who is dis cat?

MARY

He's a friend of mine; you wouldn't know him.

PRITCHARD

Whas his name?

MARY

You don't know him, Melvin.

PRITCHARD

I might. Come on, whas his name?

MARY

Damn! Muthafucka!

PRITCHARD

(*Laughing and speaking to* COUNTRY) Aw, she warm now.

MARY

(*Sighing heavily*) Melvin, I got to go. Come by my house tonight if somethin' good happens. I get off at two.

PRITCHARD

Be there at two-thirty.

(SAM *walks to the stoop with his FM portable radio playing.* HE *stands there nodding heavily*)

MARY

(*Walking down the block*) How ya doin', Sam?

(*To* PRITCHARD)

Don't forget to do your best. You don't know, this might be your first step.

(*To* COUNTRY)

Nice meetin' ya, Country.

PRITCHARD

Lata, sweethot, see ya tonight.

MARY

I hope so.

(*After* MARY *is gone*)

PRITCHARD

(*To* SAM) Ah see you copped. You got mah shit?

SAM

(*Floating*) You ack like umo steal yo' shit.

PRITCHARD

Damn, Country, dis nigga git paranoid when he git high.

(COUNTRY *watches both of them*)

SAM

Naw, you jest ack like umo steal yo' shit.

PRITCHARD

Jus' gimme mah shit so ah can get together. 'Sides, mah man here gittin' nervous.

(*To* COUNTRY)

Be back ina minute, Country.

(SAM *slips* PRITCHARD *a packet and* PRITCHARD *disappears into the doorway.* SAM *remains nodding.* COUNTRY *lights another joint and tries to belong to what's happening.* SAM *begins scatting to some jazz* [*maybe Trane*]. COUNTRY *tries to appear more high than* HE *actually is. At hearing the scatting,* COUNTRY *softly taps one of his big feet.* SAM *notices the foot and stares at it.* HE *turns off the radio*)

SAM

Say, brotha man, where you from?

COUNTRY

South Dakota.

SAM

(*Stands nodding silently for a few comprehending moments*) What kinda shit you cop?

COUNTRY

(*Too calmly*) Saaaaaay wwwhat?

SAM

Whooooowee! You musta had some good shit. Where you cop?

COUNTRY

Oh . . . ah . . . from mah man.

SAM

Yeah?

COUNTRY

Yeah.

SAM

Ah see you lay reefer on top of yo' shit. Ah usta, but reefer make me sick now.

COUNTRY

Well . . . ah . . . dig . . . ah ain't had no shit; ah just smokes me some reefer.

SAM

Reefer?

COUNTRY

Yeah.

SAM

Ain't nothin' wrong wid dat. Fact, ah wish ah could git high wid some reefer stead of dis shit.

COUNTRY

(*Understanding*) Yeah, I dig.

SAM

(*Extending his hand*) Mah name is Sam.

COUNTRY

Country, brother.

SAM

You musta hada hod daddy gi' you a name like dat.

COUNTRY

Pritchard gimme dis shit. 'Bout Country.

SAM

He knew yo' daddy?

COUNTRY

Naw, man, ah met da dude 'bout three months ago when ah first got here.

SAM

How in da fuck you come to meet 'im in da middle of eight million people?

COUNTRY

We work in the same stock department in Macy's.

SAM

Mah man got 'im a gig wid some big dollas. How in da fuck he talk dat man inta makin' him stock manager I don't know.

COUNTRY

Naw, man, we just stock boys.

SAM

Oh yeah? Swear fo' god, he lie lika mufucka all da time. Tole me dey made 'im stock manager over da clothing department.

COUNTRY

(*Realizing what he has done*) Sometimes dey let 'im take over, like . . . like when da man got ta split.

SAM

Damn, many times dat mufucka been in dat dope program at Bellevue, he don't neva stop lyin'. Shit, he might be da man. He might be blowing our case right now while we stannin' out here talkin'.

COUNTRY

Well . . . you know . . .

SAM

Say, ah got a nice radio here, FM stereo, almos' brand new, still got numbers 'n shit on it. Cos' $135 brand new. Gimme $30.

COUNTRY

Ah don' need a radio, brother, thank you.
(*The cats become quite loud.* COUNTRY *leans over the rail to look at them*)

SAM

Who in da fuck is dat?

COUNTRY

Some cats fuckin' each otha.

SAM

(*Floats over to look*) Damn, mus' be some good pussy 'way dey layin' in all dat garbage.

COUNTRY

Guess so.

SAM

Now, if brotha rat come, he lahble to run off tom and git dat pussy hisself.

COUNTRY

(*Laughing*) Yeah, ole tom know he kin fine 'im some mo' pussy.

(SAM *turns on his radio.* PRITCHARD *returns from fucking himself with a needle.* HE *speaks in the aftermath of the rush*)

PRITCHARD

Man, you must git freak behind cat fuckin'.

COUNTRY

Wow, you sho do come down hod on me.

PRITCHARD

Country, ah seldom comes down.

SAM

Dat sho ain't no lie.

PRITCHARD

Ah ain't in da habit of lying.

(SAM *listens to that last statement and goes into a heavy nod.* PRITCHARD *looks at him with obvious disgust*)

Damn, dis mufucka is most uncool.

COUNTRY

Pritchard, ah got ta split.

PRITCHARD

Damn, ain't you gon' run 'round here on Sixteenth and see Peeair wid me?

COUNTRY

Ah got some things ah wanna read tonight.

PRITCHARD

Ain't gon' take but a hour, and you got da rest of da night.

COUNTRY

Ah been puttin' it off for so long.

PRITCHARD

So anotha hour ain't really gon' matta.

COUNTRY

Puttin' it off for "anotha hour" is why um so far behind.

PRITCHARD

Behind? Behind in what?

COUNTRY

The things ah wanna read.

PRITCHARD

Damn, man, ah thought we was tight.

COUNTRY

Damn, man, dat ain't got nothin' ta do with it.

PRITCHARD

What if dis man start talkin' 'bout contracts? Dat muthafucka might cheat me.

COUNTRY

Aww, man . . .

PRITCHARD

What if he makes me compromise the whole race?

COUNTRY

Aww, man . . .

PRITCHARD

What if he make me forget uma nigga and got me singing like TOM JONES?

COUNTRY

He can't do none of that if your mind is strong.

PRITCHARD

(*Desperate, almost screaming*) But what if he can? He got all the bucks, you know? And ah want me some bucks too. Why I got ta stay poor?

COUNTRY

Okay, Pritchard, okay, man. But less split now.

PRITCHARD

Um wid you, Country. You gon' hang wid us, Sam?

SAM

(*Coming out of a nod*) Beautiful.

PRITCHARD

Naw, on second thought, you betta not. Dat man wonda where da fuck um at if he see you goin' through dem changes. Lata.
    (*As* COUNTRY *and* PRITCHARD *walk off*)
Ah know what umo sing for dis dude. Dig dis:
    (HE *starts to sing "The Tracks of My Tears" by the Miracles.* SAM *is left there nodding quietly for a few moments. Then there is a sudden explosion of meows and hissing.* SAM *leans over the side of the stoop and looks*)

SAM

Pussy was good, wuddin it, tom?
    (*Lights*)

Scene II

    (*A small, dim, vastly overcrowded room.* PEEAIR *is closing the door behind* PRITCHARD *and* COUNTRY)

PEEAIR

(*Walking around in front of them and looking at them carefully*) Please, please, take your coats off.

(*To* PRITCHARD)
You said your name is Melvin Pritchard?
(*Entering a coughing fit*)

PRITCHARD
(*Getting out of his coat*) Yes.

PEEAIR
(*Recovering from his fit*) Please do forgive me. I've had this
dreadful cough for the longest.
(*To* COUNTRY)
And you, sir, are called—Country?

COUNTRY
Uhhuh.

PEEAIR
(*Going to a small refrigerator*) Please, please be seated. And
do forgive the untidiness. I'm staying here until I find more
suitable accommodations. Country? Forgive me, but is that
your familial title?

COUNTRY
(*Finding a seat near the bed*) Well, actually . . .

PRITCHARD
That's his most familiar title. The fellas at our office gave him
that name.

PEEAIR
(*Getting his last two bottles of beer*) You'll have to excuse
these mean refreshments. It's all I seem to have at the moment.
Country—that is a—ah—different kind of name. I imagine you
must have difficulty at the banks.

COUNTRY
Naw, den ah use mah real name, Nathaniel Bloodwater.

PRITCHARD
(*Laughing*) You can see why we at the office prefer "Country."

PEEAIR

(*Setting a tray with two bottles and two glasses near* PRITCH-ARD) Is Country a messenger in your office, Mr. Pritchard?

COUNTRY

Well, actually . . .

PRITCHARD

(*Speaking rapidly as* HE *gets up*) He has a more important position with us. By the way, you, of course, can call me Melvin.

PEEAIR

(*Standing close to* PRITCHARD) Thank you, Melvin.

PRITCHARD

I know you're a busy man, so I'll come right to the point.

PEEAIR

Excellent.
    (*Stifling a cough*)

PRITCHARD

I understand you're looking for singers.

PEEAIR

(*Going to his bed and putting on an elaborate bathrobe*) Before we begin you two enjoy your beer.
    (*Picking up his attache case*)
I feel I should refreshen myself.
    (PEEAIR *coughs uncontrollably as* HE *goes to the toilet down the hall*)

COUNTRY

(*Putting down his beer*) Dat dude a faggot.

PRITCHARD

(*In a frantic whisper*) Damn, Country, he might be listenin'. Be cool. Sometimes, dey be listenin' in ta see what you like behind dey backs. Dey don't want no mo' singas who gon' mess up like Otis Redding.

COUNTRY
(*Pouring his beer*) Shit, dis muthafucka . . .

PRITCHARD
(*Putting his hands on* COUNTRY's *shoulders*) Please, Country, dis may be mah chance to make a name for mahself and git inta some a dat long dough. Ah could help a whole lots of brothas if I was rich. Don't blow it for me, man, please. Dis is fa da whole race. It's only the first step.

COUNTRY
(*Sighing heavily*) All right, Pritchard. Ain't gon' blow nothin' fa ya.
(PEEAIR *enters before* PRITCHARD *removes his hands*)

PEEAIR
(*Walking to the bed*) I do hope I'm not inconveniencing you.
(*Taking off his robe*)
This illness is terribly unpleasant, but it IS a pleasure to have you with me.

PRITCHARD
Likewise for us.
(*Rubbing his hands together*)
I have some songs prepared for the audition.

PEEAIR
(*Sitting on the bed*) Oh that won't be necessary. I have plenty of music right here.

PRITCHARD
That's fine, but I have a habit I picked up recently of singing popular tunes, and . . .

PEEAIR
Yes, of course. I've all the latest popular music.
(*Picking up his case*)
Please, please, come look at my collection.

PRITCHARD

(*Crossing the room*) Well, of course, I can sing anything. Anything!

PEEAIR

(*Coughing and fumbling with the case latch*) Yes, yes, I have some splendid selections.

PRITCHARD

(*Reaching for the case*) Here, I'll help.

(*The case opens unexpectedly and out falls several pieces of sheet music and a half-empty pint bottle of muscatel.* PRITCHARD *gathers the sheet music.* COUNTRY *retrieves the bottle and slowly hands it back to* PEEAIR)

PEEAIR

(*Sticking the bottle back into and closing the case*) Oh, do forgive me. This illness has made me so clumsy at times.

PRITCHARD

Yeah, a bad cough can do that.

PEEAIR

I knew you'd understand. Come, have you found any selections you would care to render?

PRITCHARD

(*Flipping the sheets*) Oh, I see what kind of music this is. I haven't done this kind of material since my high school glee club.

PEEAIR

I see. Perhaps you wish to sing something else?

PRITCHARD

Certainly. This is not to say that I don't care for your selections.

PEEAIR

Yes, yes, of course, do not worry.

PRITCHARD

Here's a popular tune that Country likes to hear me sing:
  (PRITCHARD *begins to sing "My Girl"*)

PEEAIR

Please, please.

PRITCHARD

Too fast for you, wasn't it. Here, I'll slow it down a bit.

PEEAIR

No, no, no. What is that other noise you make with your
mouth?

PRITCHARD

That's just the background. It helps my singing to hear the
rhythm section.

PEEAIR

But you mustn't do that.

PRITCHARD

Okay, here, see how you like this one:
  (PRITCHARD *begins to sing "The Way You Do the Things
You Do"*)

PEEAIR

(*Coughing*) No, no, not here, wait one moment. Those things,
that noise, that movement.

PRITCHARD

Well, what do you want me to sing then?

PEEAIR

Anything you like.

PRITCHARD

That's what ah been tryin' ta do.

PEEAIR

But all that noise in the background and that senseless movement is so amateurish.

PRITCHARD

You mean the bass? I can cut that out. I'll just do the drums.

PEEAIR

You may "cut out" the drums as well. And that movement—really now I . . .

PRITCHARD

I don't understand. You ask me to sing, I have to sing this way, this is the way I sing.

PEEAIR

Yes, I understand, but Mr. Slobberstein at Ebony Recordings might not understand.

COUNTRY

Da Jew wid da money?

PEEAIR

Yes, if you prefer, "da Jew wid da money."
(*To* PRITCHARD)
And now if you care to continue.

PRITCHARD

I'll try to think of something you'll like.

PEEAIR

It's not what I like; it's what Mr. Slobberstein prefers.

PRITCHARD

Well, maybe you should let me sing to Mr. Slobberstein.

PEEAIR

I'm certain he wouldn't want to hear you.

PRITCHARD

What you mean?

PEEAIR

(*Getting up*) I mean it's not the way we work at Ebony Recordings.
(*Going to* PRITCHARD)

Please, please, do not get excited. It is not good for your voice.
(*Touching* PRITCHARD's *neck*)

PRITCHARD
(*Recoiling*) Um all right.

PEEAIR
You're so tense in the neck. Perhaps a gentle massage . . .

PRITCHARD
Muthafucka!
(PRITCHARD *pushes* PEEAIR *in the face and knocks him down behind the bed.* PEEAIR *is half coughing, half moaning.* PRITCHARD *kicks and stomps at him until* PEEAIR *is silent.* COUNTRY *watches silently*)

COUNTRY
Don't kill da muthafucka. Ah don't wanna be goin' ta no jail fo' anybody.

PRITCHARD
(*Looking down at* PEEAIR) He ain't dead.

COUNTRY
(*Getting coat*) Let's split.

PRITCHARD
You think he might call da fuzz?

COUNTRY
(*Buttoning up*) He don't know us from shit, and da police don't know he exist. Get your coat, man.

PRITCHARD
Ain't no hurry. We da only ones know what happened.

COUNTRY
(*Starting for the door*) Ah ain't arguing.

PRITCHARD
(*Getting coat*) Okay, wait, Country. Lemme git mah coat. Don't open da door till ah git on mah coat.

COUNTRY

(*Pausing at door*) Okay, quick.

PRITCHARD

(*Grabbing anything of value*) Might as well take somethin'
to git me some mo' shit.

COUNTRY

Goddamn, Pritchard, git yo' fuckin' coat an' less git out dis
place!

PRITCHARD

Um comin', Country. Don't be so scary. Swear fo' god you gon'
blow if you don't stop bein' nervous.

COUNTRY

Collect what you want fast.

PRITCHARD

Sure, Country.
   (*Collecting various things and mostly talking to himself*)
Muthafucka got jus' what he deserves. Jive faggot!
   (*Walking to* COUNTRY)
Country, ah know um fucked up, but 'least ah know I'm nigga.
Jive Tom! Less go!
   (THEY *exit*)
   (*Black*)

Uh, Uh; But How Do It Free Us?

SONIA SANCHEZ

The reason that I decided to become a playwright is about the same reason I decided to become a poet. That is, one day I sat down and decided to write a play. I write plays, I guess, because I can't say what I want to say in a poem. I have to stretch it out into a play. And a play is a special kind of writing in that it has a lot of dialogue in it. And the dialogue tries to convey messages to people as to what is. *The Bronx Is Next* is the first play that I did. Then I wrote a play called *Dirty Hearts*. Then a play called *Sister Son/Ji*, then *Malcolm Man Don't Live Here No More*. And then *Uh, Uh; But How Do It Free Us?* And I'd say they're all similar plays; however, they're all different plays in that the two most important words in "playwright" is write plays. Meaning that you try to show what is right and what is to be played right.

I'm trying to say that when I did *The Bronx Is Next* I was talking about Harlem and the tenements in Harlem. How people live in Harlem. It was my opinion at the time and it still is that those same tenements need to be burned down. As a consequence in the play I have, I guess, what you'd probably call the militants, in the terminology of America, I have some men who decided to move Black people out of Harlem and burn down the tenements.

The Bronx Is Next was the first part of what I call a trilogy where you would have the second part of the play be people making a trip either South or to the Midwest. In between there I haven't done it except for parts in my mind.

At the time I knew that a lot of Black people were dying in the cities. I watched us die. I watched some of us make it as such, meaning that some of us survived. But the majority of Black children, Black young people were dying, being killed in the city called New York and at the time that I did *The Bronx Is Next* I thought that one way we could eliminate this dying was for us to leave the city. I knew all of us would not.

You see, some of us need to get back to the land. You know, from whence we came. Some of us need to touch earth, you know, and get—because we've all come from earth—we need to return to earth which really nourished us. Because the city, the tenements, the stone-cold brick buildings where we are stuffed on top of each other like mice are destructive. When you walk down Seventh Avenue and Lenox Avenue and Eighth Avenue in New York City we can say this is all beautiful, this is us, but this devil in this country has made us become almost animals and then he's packed us in buildings like animals. And when I did *The Bronx Is Next,* it was on that level, like we've got to leave.

Now in the play, if you remember, not everyone wanted to leave. But it seems to me at some point in order to like move away from this madness, some of us will have to leave the big cities like New York City just to live and become in a sense human beings. Because living the way we live tends to make us inhumane, tends to make us animals.

I'm not saying that I agree with that premise now, at this time. But at the time that I wrote the play that was the point of making it, in quotes, a trilogy, and starting out the trek.

I wasn't going to call it the trek, but the movement South or the movement to the Midwest. I thought that would involve the kind of trials and tribulations which in my mind might be unraveled along the way. There were problems among the leaders, the people that led them. There are all kinds of this kind of interplay. It was going to be a longer play than *The Bronx Is Next.*

Each succeeding play was going to be longer than the previous. And then eventually the people would settle someplace, wherever they settled with all those problems that they were going to have. I felt these things very strongly because I was raised in a tenement in New York City. So one understands exactly what happens. The constant dealing with roaches in dingy apartments and too small places and a room that faces a wall. I suppose that's why I wrote a lot. Because if you have a bedroom with the only window in the bedroom facing a wall outside, your imagination is always running rampant. You've got to do something behind that wall.

Because once you stuck your head out the window, garbage hit you in the head coming from the windows above yours. So I guess at the time I wrote because I had ideas, if not ideology; I had ideas or opinions about things being Black in this country. So *The Bronx Is Next* was one of them.

No Black woman even like nowadays tells you things you're familiar with, like Black women have problems. In a family situation, I'm talking about a classic, if you understand what I'm saying, a classic Black woman figure. Showing her not just surviving, yet surviving, not just being but being, but also not just being a slave but you know still being a slave, not just being a whole but just the Black woman in all her majesty. The Black woman in all her non-majesty as well. The Black woman surviving yet not surviving but being. If that makes any kind of sense.

(*From a conversation with*
Sonia Sanchez,
Fall '72)

Uh, Uh; But How Do It Free Us?

BY SONIA SANCHEZ

CHARACTERS:

GROUP I:

> (*Brother is stretched out across the bed and sisters are seated on outer side of bed. One sister is reading*)
> MALIK: *twenty years old, dressed in traditional clothes*
> WALEESHA: *twenty-one years old, pregnant, sitting on the left side of the bed*
> NEFERTIA: *eighteen years old, in traditional dress, sitting on the right side of the bed, reading a book*

GROUP II:

> (*Four brothers, one devil, sitting on five/white/rocking/ horses. A sister/whore and white whore stand on either side with whips*)
> SISTER WHORE: *about twenty-five years old in tight/mini/ dress/long/knee/boots, black stockings and an expensive red/colored wig on her head*
> WHITE WHORE: *about twenty-four years old in purple/see/- through/shirt and bell-bottom pants. Has on boots and blond hair*
> THREE BROTHERS AND ONE WHITE MAN: *ranging in ages twenty-six to thirty-four, dressed in bell bottoms, cowboy hats, big ties and jewelry*
> BROTHER: *about thirty-eight years old, dressed in dashiki with tiki and African hat*

GROUP III:

(*A screen separates a sister and a devil/woman [white woman]. On the sister's side of the screen are African masks and she sits on an African stool; there are suitcases on the floor. A table with phone. On the devil/woman's side is pop art, a table with phone and phonograph, and a butterfly chair, where she lounges. The brother sits on pillows in the middle of the floor. In front of the pillows is a table with liquor*)

BROTHER: *about thirty-four years old, has on two/toned suit, one side is brown suede with a big yellow flower in the center. One side is an orange dashiki with a brown/embroidered map of Africa, wears a talisman, tight/brown/ suede/pants and sandals, shades and a floppy/suede hat*

SISTER: *about thirty-two years old, big natural, dressed in long dress*

DEVIL./WOMAN: *about thirty-three years old, plain-looking, light brown hair, dressed simply but richly*

DANCERS:

(*Two brothers and two sisters, stretched out on the floor observing the three groups*)

SETTING:

(*The lights are low at the beginning, just light enough to see the arrangement of the* ACTORS *in the three groups. The* DANCERS *are stretched out in front of the group as if waiting. . . . As each group speaks the light is directed on them and the* DANCERS *move conspicuously/inconspicuously in front of them and watch and listen. When the talking ceases, the* DANCERS *begin their talking*)

TIME: *Now*

(*The light moves to* GROUP I)

WALEESHA

Are you goin' out again tonight, Malik?

MALIK

Yeah. Got a lot a people to see tonight 'bout the play we doing;
then we have a rehearsal. Why, what's the matter?
(*Raises up from the bed and looks in her direction*)

WALEESHA

Oh. I just wondered if you were gonna be home or not.
(*Stands up, stretches; we see* SHE's *about seven or eight
months pregnant*)
I just thought you might want to go to a show or something.
Felt like doin' something this evening. I guess I'll knit.
(*Picks up her knitting and for a few minutes the quiet sound
of needles pierces the ears*)
Are you going also, Nefertia?

NEFERTIA

(*Looks up from her book*) Uh, huh. We're rehearsing again
tonight. But the play is real baddddd. And Malik is the best.
He's beautiful, Waleesha. You should see how the others just
stop when he's onstage and just listen to him. It's like the
brother who wrote the play was writing it just for Malik.

MALIK

(*Turns toward Nefertia*) Do you really think so? I mean, I
don't really feel that I have the necessary fire or depth for
the second act. I mean, I say the words, but they don't feel
true inside. You know what I mean? It . . . sometimes I think
an older dude should play the part.

NEFERTIA

It sounds fine to me. You are just a perfectionist, Malik. Always
pushing yourself. You are a brilliant man. The part is you.

MALIK

(*Gets up and walks around the room and stops in front of a
long/mirror, turns and swaggers slightly*) Do you really think
so?

NEFERTIA

Man. You simply too much in it. Don't you remember when

they were giving out parts they kept looking at you. I knew then that it was going to be yours. Remember how you thought at first that they hadn't cast you for anything. I saw you get uptight when some of the better roles were given. I knew then. Mannnnnn, I knew then that the part was yours. That my Malik had gotten the best, the main part of the play and was gon' to tear it up, be mean. The meanest.

(*Is laughing at the end*)

WALEESHA

Are you in the play also, Nefertia? I mean, now that you are three months pregnant it might be too much for you. Goin' to school and all.

NEFERTIA

Girl, no. I ain't tired at all.

(*Stands up and walks across the room slowly*)

And, no one knows I'm pregnant yet. I haven't told them a word. As long as I'm small they won't know and have to be concerned.

WALEESHA

But, sister, you should tell everyone, after all, it is an occasion for rejoicing. Is it not so, my husband?

(MALIK *is looking at himself in the mirror*)

Malik, I said is it not so that Nefertia's pregnancy should be a time of rejoicing?

MALIK

(*Turns around*) Yeah, and she don't even look pregnant, does she? I remember when you were three months pregnant, Waleesha, you were biggggggg. The doctor had to put you on a diet at three months.

(*Laughs*)

Do you remember?

WALEESHA

(*Stops knitting*) Yes. I ate a lot during those early months. It was around that time that Nefertia first moved in with us. Remember?

(Begins knitting again, and the sound of the needles click-ing is heavy)

MALIK

Yeah. I remember. Well, I'm gonna split now.
   (Goes to closet and gets his jacket)

NEFERTIA

Wait a minute. I'll get my coat, too.

MALIK

No. I have a couple of stops to make. I'll be moving too fast for you. You come on later to the theatre. I'll meet you there.

WALEESHA

Do you want somethin' to eat before you go?

MALIK

Naw, I'll be eating where I'm goin'. Hey, I need a couple of dollars. Nefertia, did your school check come?

NEFERTIA

Yes. But I didn't git a chance to cash it. And I have only two dollars.

MALIK

That'll do.
   (Walks over and takes two dollars)
See y'all later.
   (Exits)

WALEESHA

Yes. I was huge, wasn't I, when I wuz three months. No, it was really four months. Don't youuuu remember, Nefertia?

NEFERTIA

Uh huh.
   (Reading again)

WALEESHA

Yes, he is right. I was really big. Don't you think so, Nefertia?

NEFERTIA

(*Without looking up*) Uh huh.

WALEESHA

(*Raises her voice slightly*) Say something besides uh huh. I'm just trying to have some kind of conversation.

NEFERTIA

(*Without looking up*) No, you ain't. You just trying to start an argument. You know it. I know it. We both know it. That's why I don't answer ya.

WALEESHA

An argument? An argument 'bout what, Nefertia? What do we have to argue about?

NEFERTIA

(*Finally looks up*) 'Bout me. That's what. 'Bout Malik and me. That's what. You mad cuz I'm the second wife. You still mad at me, sister, and you know it.

WALEESHA

Why should I be mad at you? Just tell me why, Nefertia. Malik brought you here—you were his choice. His decision. And since I love him I have to abide by his choice, no matter how unwise it may be.
(*Stands up*)
I guess I'll fix something to eat now.
(*Stretches*)
Ah. This warrior is kicking me hard. He's gon' be bad cuz he's bad already. Ah. He's moving again.
(*Puts hands on stomach*)
You want to feel little Maliki, Nefertia? You want to hear him running around this house of mine, playing his warrior games?

NEFERTIA

What I want to feel yo/stomach for? No. I got to finish this reading for tomorrow's class.

WALEESHA

(*Gets a can of beans and begins to open it. Begins to speak softly*) One thing's for sure, though. When I have my warrior the burden will be on you. Oh, yes. When I have my sweet Maliki, you'll be big and fat like me and you

(*Great laughs*)

will have a longgggggg nine months. Just you wait, just you wait . . .

NEFERTIA

You a bitch, you know, Waleesha. You and yo quiet/sneaky ways. How you know fo sure you gon' have a male/child? And what if it's a girl? Huh? What if it's a girl/child? And so what if you do have a male/child? I can have one too. Or even if I have a girl, Malik will love her just like he loves me now. Just like he loved me befo I came here to this house. He used to tell me about, you. You and yo/knitting and going to the movies. And hardly ever interested in him, he said. He said you never saw him, never. He said you never read anything, not even a newspaper. We love each other becuz we have everything in common. Theatre, school, poetry. Ours is not just physical love, he says. It's mental, too. So it's you who don't really stand a chance here. I might have been chosen second, but he told me I saved him from you and yo/non/interest in anything.

(*During the above,* WALEESHA *has warmed the beans and is making a salad.*

NEFERTIA *moves over to her, still talking*)

Yes, Waleesha, I saved him from the boredom that is you. You dig? I am the second choice, but first in his heart. You dig it, sistuh?

WALEESHA

(*Sits down and begins to eat, and just before eating, looks up and slowly smiles*) Just you wait and see, sister. Just you wait and see . . .

(*Light fades and moves to* DANCERS. *One* MALE DANCER *stays stretched out watching. Moving to see better.* DANCERS: MALE

DANCER *walks across stage. Two* SISTER DANCERS *sitting down on imaginary chairs,* ONE *knitting, the* OTHER *reading. When* HE *passes the* KNITTING SISTER, HE *beckons to her and* SHE *gets up and follows him, knitting. Then, looking at him, knitting.* MALE DANCER *passes the* SECOND SISTER *reading. Stops. Turns around, escorts the* FIRST KNITTING SISTER *back to other side of stage, constantly straining his neck to see* OTHER SISTER. HE *turns the* KNITTING SISTER *around, back to him and audience.* SHE *stands mutely, knitting.* MALE DANCER *turns, jumps up and down joyously, walks, stops. Look in make-believe mirror. Flexes left leg, then the right leg. Combs his natural. Turns quickly around to look at the* KNITTING SISITER. HE *sits down next to* READING SISTER. *Begins to read with her. Starts to rap.* SHE *looks up. Listens. He raps more. And still rapping,* HE *removes her book. Touches her body, still rapping. Holds her as they dance a love dance. When* SHE *becomes mesmerized,* HE *takes her and puts her next to the* KNITTING SISTER. HE *lines them up behind him and begins to walk around the stage, stopping at a mirror to preen.* HE *returns to get the other two* SISTERS, *the* KNITTING SISTER *behind him and the* READING SISTER *behind the* KNITTING SISTER. *The* READING SISTER *keeps trying to move in front of the* KNITTING SISTER *but* SHE *is blocked each time. And the* MALE DANCER *never looks around. As the* MALE DANCER *walks,* HE *keeps turning his head as* HE *sees some other sisters, beckons, like as to "I'll see you later" look, spruces up. Stops at mirror again and does a preening dance. The* SECOND MALE DANCER *on the floor laughs, rolls over the floor and laughs. Laughs. Laughs.*

Light moves to GROUP II. ALL MEN *riding their horses*)

FIRST BROTHER

This horse is good.

SECOND BROTHER

The best ever.

THIRD BROTHER

Yeah. Giddap, you goddamn horse. Faster. You too slow today.

Gots to ride my horse a little higher today. Gots to go to the
moooonnn. Soooonnnn. Boommmmm. Boommmmm.

(*Laughs*)

WHITE DUDE

It's good being out that joint. It's gooood being free again.
After two years. It's good being out. Ain't it, men?

BROTHER MAN

Yeah, mannnn. That place was a M.F. Eight years there. Amid
everything. But I'm out now. And the first thing I said I wuz
gon' do wuz to get the biggest fix in the world. It wuz gon'
be so big that I would be the world. You diggit. I would be
the world. Cuz, man, I got the biggest hustle in the whole
wide world today. I found Blackness in the joint, you dig,
and I wrote a book and everything I write is licked up by
everyone. The Blk/prison/writer is a hero. All thanks is due
to Malcolm/man, Eldridge/man for making this all so simple.
Man, I got it made after all these thirty-eight years of little
hustles, little busts. I got it made. All praises is due to Blackness.

FIRST BROTHER

Hey, you Black/bitch. Git over here and do yo/job. What you
gittin' paid for? You broken down whore. Git over here and
pree-form. Right now. You ain't gittin' paid to stand around.

SECOND BROTHER

Yeah, make it over here, tootie suitie or we'll remove y'all.
Cuz we some bad ones right here. We the new breed, ain't
we, man.

(*This section is spoken fast. A climax of sorts. At the con-
clusion* THEY *return to their pleasant light/high*)

THIRD BROTHER

The new Black man raging in the land. We the organized/
gangster/Blk/man. We mean. We do what's to be done. We
dealing. We the new Blk/mafia. We dealing.

FIRST BROTHER

Dealing? Man, do we deal. Look around ya and you see us.
Dealing from city to city. Making money, bread. Controlling
an entire Blk/community.

SECOND BROTHER

Yeah. We keep coming up four aces and the only thing beat
four aces is a flush.

THIRD BROTHER

And if that shows, y'all knows toilets is for flushes!
(*Laughs*)

FIRST BROTHER

We badddddd.

SECOND BROTHER

BadddddddER than bad.

THIRD BROTHER

Baddddddder than a dude's bad breath.

FIRST BROTHER

We meannnnn.

SECOND BROTHER

Meaner than MEANNN.

THIRD BROTHER

Meaner than a dude whose corn you done stepped on.

FIRST BROTHER

We Blk/mafia/men.

SECOND BROTHER

Blk/on/Blk/mafia men.

THIRD BROTHER

Blacker than Blk/mafia/men. Bother us and you'll see!

WHITE MAN

Come here, you.

(*Beckons to* WHITE WHORE)
Come here now. I want you to beat me again while I'm riding.

WHITE WHORE

No. I ain't coming this time. The last time you hurt me. You paying me to beat you. O.K. That's it. Nothing else. I won't do anything else.
(*Turns to* BROTHER MAN)
You said only the beating, nothing more, since y'all already had your lady.
(*Points to the horse*)
You promised. The last time he was awful. What's wrong with him? Do he hate women or something?

WHITE MAN

What you calling me, whore? You trying to call me something, you think something wrong with me? I got my stable together already. Out one week and I got three bitches breathing their desire over me already. They humpin' for me. Bring me all their money. They can do more than you can anyday, you anemic-looking witch.

BROTHER MAN

(*Laughs softly*) Take it slow, man. She just a little scared of you. You did take her through some deep changes. We had to pull you off her. Now, didn't we?

WHITE MAN

She weak. She weak like all women. Don't need them, though. Got my girl. Cumon, girl. Let's go. Let's you and me git a thing going. I want to feel you in my guts. Warming my insides. Making me feel good. Warm. Secure. Manly. Gots to git that again. C'mon over here, you purple bitch. Help me to come. Hit me, hurt me. Turn me inside out with pain. C'mon you dead-lookin' whore.
(WHITE WHORE *moves over slowly. Begins to beat him softly.* HE *screams. Harder. Beats him harder. And on the last hit,* HE *grabs the whip and pulls her toward him.* SHE *screams.*

WHITE MAN *gets off the horse. His movement is like a slow memory of death)*
What you doin' beating me, Momma? I didn't do anything. Really, I didn't say no dirty/bad/words, Momma. Please don't beat me. Please pull up my pants, Momma. You get so carried away you hit me all over.

WHITE WHORE
There he goes again. Git him away from me. He's crazy.

BLACK WHORE
Help her, you dudes. He crazier than you think. He gon' kill her.
(Moves to help and is blocked by BROTHER MAN*)*

WHITE WHORE
Help me. Don't let him hit me again.
(Tries to run away but is caught in the WHITE DUDE'S *massive arms)*
I didn't mean to hit you. Please excuse me. Let me go now. I really have to go. Don't hit me again.

WHITE MAN
(Oblivious to all that has happened) Momma. Why you always hitting me. I am good. I ain't gon' turn out bad. There ain't no evil spirits inside me. Momma, don't hit me. I'm just seven years old. I wasn't doing nothing. Dottie and I were just playing house. OWWWW. Momma, I'm bleeding. Don't hit me so hard. I'll never play house again. Help me. Somebody help me. Daddy, come back and help me. Help me.
(Sobs)

WHITE WHORE
(Is on her knees now and her cries mingle with the WHITE MAN's *cries)* Help me.
(Sobs)
Help me, somebody, help me, help me.

BROTHER MAN
(Still on horse) They a sorry sight, you know.

FIRST BROTHER

Why you always letting him hang around here, man?

SECOND BROTHER

Yeah. It's one thing to do the biz—another to socialize with the dude. I mean, brother/man, he be weird.

THIRD BROTHER

You know when we wuz in the joint they caught him being somebody's "kid"—so what good is he anyway?

BROTHER MAN

I don't know. Perhaps you right. He's always hanging around. I guess I feel sorry for him in a way. I owe him something. When I first got out the joint, he saw me through till I could move around—got my thing straight. Look at the po/sorry/bastard. With a mama complex or something. Guess I should stop this madness.

(*Turns and looks at* BLACK WHORE)

What you think over there, Blk/whore? Should I stop it now?

(*Moves over and puts* WHITE DUDE *back on horse. Talking softly to* WHITE DUDE. *Hands whip to* WHITE WHORE. WHITE WHORE *slides on away to the* THIRD BLACK DUDE *who helps her*)

BLACK WHORE

Y'all some crazy dudes, but ya paying me so that's all I'm gon' say.

BROTHER MAN

(*Moving toward* BLACK WHORE) What's yo name, girl?

BLACK WHORE

Ain't got no name. Lost my name when I was eleven years old. I became just a body then so I forgot my name. Don't nobody want to know a Black woman's name anyway. You gon' take me home with ya to keep? Put me in your pocket to hold/touch when you need some warmth? No? Well, since you ain't, then there ain't no reason to tell ya my name. All ya need to know is on my face and body. If you can read a map you can read me.

BROTHER MAN

Yeah. Well, it's well traveled. But don't get smart with us. You are what you are cuz you wants to be. Don't go telling us nothing 'bout some dude turning you on when you was young. Every whore in the world says the same thing. Can't no dude in the world make you want to turn a trick less you inclined to do so. But y'all always blaming us. Blk/men for your whoring whore. You a whore cuz you wants to be, now ain't that so?

BLACK WHORE

Uh huh.

FIRST BROTHER

Is that all you gots to say is uh huh?

BLACK WHORE

Uh huh. Amen. And yassuh, boss.

SECOND BROTHER

You a smart whore, ain't ya?

THIRD BROTHER

(*Still helping the* WHITE WHORE) Too smart, if you ask me. Never could stand no smart Black women anyhow. Always opening they mouths.

BROTHER MAN

Come over here, Black Whore.

BLACK WHORE

Yeah. I'm coming. I'm coming to receive my payment as usual on time, on schedule. For showing you just a little of yourselves whenever you see me.

BROTHER MAN

Get down on all fours.

BLACK WHORE

Yassuh, boss.

FIRST BROTHER

Man. Let me get down from my horse and git her.

BROTHER MAN

No, she's mine.

(*Puts a collar on her neck and climbs on her back and begins to ride her as* HE *was riding the wooden horses*)
What kind of a day is it today, Black Whore?

BLACK WHORE

How in the hell I'm spoze to know, man, since I've been in here with ya crazy dudes all day.

BROTHER MAN

(*Pulls collar hard till* BLACK WHORE *cries out*) Would you say the sun is shining?

BLACK WHORE

(*Quickly, sensing danger*) Yes, it is. The sun is shining.

BROTHER MAN

How is that so when I wore my raincoat in here today? Are you suggesting I'm crazy or something for wearing my raincoat, Black Whore? You think you know better than me, Black/woman/whore?

BLACK WHORE

I mean the sun was shining for a while but it started to rain. Now it's raining. It's steady raining outside.

BROTHER MAN

(*Smiles*) Is it still raining, Black Whore?

BLACK WHORE

Yessir. Mr. Brother Man. It's raining.

BROTHER MAN

Still raining? I can't believe that for this time of year. Take me over to the window so I can see if it's raining or not. Giddap now, blk/horse. Giddap. I know you ain't gon' take me higher cuz only the white horse can do that. Hey, stop here for a minute. Them dudes got some coke that look goooood. Gots to git some of that now.

(BLACK WHORE *takes him slowly over to the three* BLACK DUDES *and the* WHITE DUDE)
Is it any good?

FIRST BROTHER
I'm ten feet tall and gittin' taller.

SECOND BROTHER
I am god. I am god. I am god.

THIRD BROTHER
Get me a woman. No, get me five women. I need five women to satisfy what I see in my mind. Send out for some more women. Ya hear me?

WHITE DUDE
I rule the universe. I am the universe. The universe revolves around me. I am the universe. I am a man. A man. A man. Can't no one surpass me. I am a man. The man. A man. The man.

BROTHER MAN
This stuff must be good. Give me some. Now
(*Smiles a long smile*)
here's some for you, Black Whore. I know you just itching for some. Here, have some of mine.

BLACK WHORE
(*Reaches for it hesitantly, then takes it greedily. Becomes more relaxed*) Thank you, Brother Man.

BROTHER MAN
Think nothing of it, Black Whore. Now, let us continue our trip toward weatherland.
(*Laughs*)
Whew. That stuff is baddddd. Whoa. Blk/whore.
(*Turns*)
Man, is that any of our stuff? It is. That too good for the nig-

gers outside. They don't need that stuff at all. Whew! That's
goooood, lady. Awright. Giddap, Black Whore. We got a destiny with the weather.

BLACK WHORE

(*Softly, mumblingly*) Our destiny is over, my man. We're yes-
terday.

BROTHER MAN

(*Stops the* BLACK WHORE) Whoa! What you say, whore? What
you mumbling, ain't you satisfied? Didn't I just give ya some
coke? Now, didn't I? I mean, ain't ya satisfied? Are you just
the typical Black/woman? Always complaining, never satisfied. Always bitching about something. What's wrong, you want
some more coke, don't ya? Yeah, that's it. C'mon. Ima gonna
see to it that you personally get more coke.

(*Turns*)

Hey, you dudes, c'mon off and get some more coke for the
lady here. I mean, let's share it with this no-name whore here.
Why she could be your sister. Maybe somebody's momma?
Hey, whore, is you somebody's momma? Huh? You somebody's
momma? You got a kid?

(*Pulls collar tightly*)

Answer me, bitch. I'm talking to you. The new Blk/man in
America. The successful Blk/man in America. Answer me now.

BLACK WHORE

Yes. I have a kid.

BROTHER MAN

You a mother. It figures, though. You all have one kid or
something living with some old woman or something and you
visit there on holidays and bring presents and hugs and kisses
and promises of an earlier visit, right?

BLACK WHORE

That's right.

FIRST BROTHER

Hey, how you know that, man? That sounds like my ole lady.

I didn't know what she was 'til someone told me 'bout her. I always thought she was a teacher or something.

SECOND BROTHER

She was a teacher all right, man. She was steady teaching dudes all they needed to know to git by. She still humping, man?

FIRST BROTHER

Man, she died last year. O.D. When I got in the bizness, I had one of my boys run her some good stuff. Guess it was too much for her. They found her in her room, sleeping like a baby. In fact, when I saw her laid out she looked like I remembered her to be when I was little and thought she was a queen. A beautiful queen.

BROTHER MAN

They saying today that Blk/women are queens. Did y'all know that? Have you heard any of that stuff, Blk/whore?

BLACK WHORE

Yeah. Some of the younger dudes talk to me sometimes. Say I should stop this stuff. They say I'm a queen, the mother of the universe. A beautiful Blk/woman/queen.

BROTHER MAN

Do you believe it?

BLACK WHORE

No. I know I ain't no queen. Look at me. I'm a whore. I know it. It just that they young. They see Blk/women differently. They say I'm not responsible for what I am. They say . . .
    (*Stops*)

BROTHER MAN

Don't stop. Continue on.

BLACK WHORE

Aww, it ain't nothing but a lot of talk.

BROTHER MAN

Some call it rhetoric. Go on, finish it. I want to hear who is responsible.

BLACK WHORE

They say—it ain't me saying it, now, they say that we're the way we are because the men, the dudes, the brothers our age couldn't see us as anything else except whores, suz they couldn't see theyselves as anything else except pimps or numbers runners or junkies or pushers, or even . . .

(*Stops*)

BROTHER MAN

Don't stop now. Hey, y'all. C'mon over here, y'all are missing a education. Git your behinds over here and listen to our Blk/whore. She gon' rap on what's wrong with us all. Continue now. Or even—

BLACK WHORE

Awwww, man. It ain't me. I'm just repeating what they done told me. It ain't my words.

BROTHER MAN

Continue, I said.

BLACK WHORE

Or even the Blk/gangsters who go round thinking they baddddd. All they doing is repeating themselves out loud. Cuz they still hurting, killing, selling dope to our people, and they don't know that instead of having a little bit of the planet, that the planet earth is ours. All ours just waiting to be taken over.

BROTHER MAN

You believe that, girl?

BLACK WHORE

No. Course not. Just some young punks rapping hard.

BROTHER MAN

Would you like to believe it, girl? I mean, would you like to

be a queen of the universe, c'mon on. Get up off ya knees.
Ya, a queen. Hey, White Whore, bring the fur coat out the
closet and some makeup. Hurry up. We got a queen here,
waiting to be fixed up.

(EVERYONE *moves around the* BLACK WHORE, *fixing her
up till* THEY *step back and see her dressed up*)

Everyone bow. No. Altogether. On the count of three. Every-
one bow and say yo/majesty, one, two, three, yo/majesty.
C'mon. Louder than that. One. Two. Three, yo/majesty. Yeah.
That's better now, yo/majesty. Walk around and view your
subjects. Walk around and see what's your kingdom's about.
Go ahead, now, we ain't gon' hurt you any, go on now.

(*The* BLACK WHORE *begins to walk shakily.* SHE's *obviously
scared. But as* SHE *walks,* SHE *relaxes, and as* SHE *passes by
the second time, her face changes and her body seems taller.*
SHE *looks queenly, like a latter day Lady Day looked on TV,
nervous and unsure but queenly*)

WHITE DUDE

Stop it. What is this sheeeeet. Who she think she is anyway?
If anyone's gon' be queen of the universe around here, it's gon'
be me.

(*Goes to closet, puts on coat, high-heel shoes, wig, earrings.
Turns around slowly and walks sensuously toward the* GROUP)

Here now. Look at me. I'm your queen of the universe.

(*Begins to switch all around the room. The* DUDES *begin
to laugh. Loudly clap*)

See, I'm the real queen. I am the universe. And I'm a queen,
too. I'm the queen of the universe. Look at me, everybody.
Don't look at her. She's Black. I'm white. The rightful queen.
Look at me, everybody. Your queen for today, for tomorrow,
forever. The only queen for America. You get your queen
some coke right now.

(WHITE WHORE *brings some coke from one of the* DUDES)

And don't you forget that I'm the queen, you hear? Get back
over there, you purple witch you.

(*Takes his coke*)

BROTHER MAN

All right, we have two contestants for the prize of "queen of the universe." Here they are, America. Look at them. Hear ye, hear ye. All you dudes, c'mon over here. You, too, White Whore. We're having a contest to find out which one is the true queen of the universe. The decision of us the judges will be final. All right, the contest begins. Begin your walk, all you would-be queens.

(*The* TWO QUEENS *walk around the room. As* THEY *move, the* BLACK WHORE *becomes more regal and silent and the switching sounds and sighs of the* WHITE DUDE *become shrill. As* THEY *make a final turn, the* WHITE DUDE *moves in front of the* BLACK WHORE *and blocks her path.* SHE *moves aside and* HE *moves in front of her.* SHE *moves aside and* HE *moves in front of her again.* SHE *moves aside and* HE *moves in front of her and as* SHE *moves* HE *punches her in the stomach and face.* SHE *falls to the floor. And the* WHITE/DUDE/QUEEN *continues his walk and each time* HE *passes the* BLK/WHORE HE *kicks her*)

WHITE DUDE

It is obvious that I'm the queen. Is that right?

BROTHER MAN

Without a doubt. You've proved the point, man. The only queens in the world are white. And probably men. It's a good lesson for sorry whores who listen to young dudes rapping 'bout nothing, cuz me and my men are the time. It's the 1970s, and don't ya forget it. The decade of the hustles. The hustlers. The decade of easy/good/long/bread if you willing to take chances. We know who we are. We take off banks now. Run the whole dope operation in the Black communities. We run it and we run it well.

(*Turns to the* THREE BROTHERS)
Where y'all going to tomorrow?

FIRST BROTHER

Detroit, man. A big shipment tomorrow.

SECOND BROTHER

Chicago. Got a meeting going with some Black cops who'll make sure things stay cool.

THIRD BROTHER

Louisville. Having a little trouble with one of the lieutenants there. Nothing too serious. If need be, he goes.

BROTHER MAN

C'mon. Let's take off one more time before we split. Queens. Not in my time. Get off the floor, Blk/whore. C'mon, do yo/ preordained/work.

(MEN *get on their horses and wait. The* WHORES *come over and begin to beat/hit them with a rhythm and* THEY *ride their horses. Quietly staring out at the audience,* EACH ONE *involved with his own orgiastic dreams.*

Light moves to the DANCERS. DANCERS: MALE DANCER *is obviously a* LITTLE BOY. *Looks lost. Alone. Moving around stage. Looks up and sees a "*MAMMA*"* FEMALE DANCER. *Runs toward her but* SHE *knocks him down.* HE *runs toward her again, but* SHE *knocks him down.* HE *runs toward her again, but* SHE *knocks him down. Keeps going, begins to play with other* FEMALE DANCER. SHE'S *a* LITTLE GIRL. *Playing house—mama and daddy.* SHE *hugs him.* HE *hugs her. The* MAMMA FEMALE *walks past. Pulls them apart. Begins a thrashing, killing dance, and leaves the* YOUNG BOY *sitting alone. Within himself. And as* HE *sits,* HE *grows older. Becomes a* MAN. *And a "*LITTLE GIRL*" female dancer, about eleven years old, passes by him, and* HE *watches her. Sees* SHE *is being stalked by an* OLDER MALE DANCER. HE *watches, fascinated by it all. The two* DANCERS [LITTLE GIRL/ OLDER MAN] *return now together.* SHE *is following. The* OLDER MALE DANCER *comes over to* MALE DANCER [*sitting down*] *and offers him the* YOUNG GIRL. *The three* DANCERS *dance a new/ orgiastic/blue-bird-blue-bird through my window dance and the* LITTLE GIRL DANCER *goes mad and becomes a* WOMAN *and we'll never know the exact moment her childhood ends. The three* DANCERS *move down the street and the two* MALE DANCERS *turn the* YOUNG CHILD WOMAN DANCER *over to another*

FEMALE DANCER *who begins to console her caressingly. The two* MALE DANCERS *move off together and shyly begin to touch each other. Discordant music is heard!*

Light fades and moves to GROUP III.

GROUP III: *The* BROTHER *slowly moves from the pillows.* HE *has a disturbed look on his face.* HE *mixes himself a long drink, turns around and looks at the two* WOMEN *in each separate room.* THEY *are both reading.* HE *shakes his head, turns, and finishes his drink.* HE *picks up a red/blk/green pillow and goes to the* SISTER *side first, and* HE *must stand or sit always with the dashiki side showing and never show the other side while visiting the* SISTER)

SISTER

(*Walks to the* BROTHER) Well, I'm here. I finally made it. Three thousand miles from cold NYC to you and San Francisco.

BROTHER

Uh huh. I thought once that you wouldn't but you did. You a strong sister.

SISTER

I have to be, man. You a strong brother and you ain't got no time for nobody who's weak.

BROTHER

Uh huh.

SISTER

What's wrong, honey? You seem distant. Is something wrong?

BROTHER

No. Well, not wrong, but I have to go out tonight. To see this dude about something. Ain't sure I'm gon' git back tonight. And this yo/second night in town. Just wanted to be with you every night since you've finally come to me.

SISTER

Business is business, my man. I still have a lot of unpacking to do. The movement comes before you and, me, love/making all. When you have to TCB you have to.

(SHE *moves away from him and begins to busy herself*)

Now you git stepping and if you git a chance, call me. I'll be okay. Man, don't look so sad. We've got a whole lifetime of touching, loving, ahead of us.

BROTHER

I just want you to know, lady. You'll never regret coming out here to me. I'll take good care of you. Your family still mad about your coming?

SISTER

And how. They said you just can't pick up and go three thousand miles to a man you've only known six months. My father said, he needs to shave off that big beard of his. He looks like Castro. And what does he do? When I told them, you were in school getting your master's, they wanted to know then how would you support me. I told them that the new/Blk/woman didn't worry about a man taking care of her. She and her man work together. If he had no job she worked and let him do the work of organizing the people. Since the money came from the oppressor, it didn't matter who made it. My mother stared at me in disbelief. Well, girl, she said, the new/Blk/woman, as you call her, is a first-class fool and had better git that part 'bout support straight right away cuz any Blk/man who don't think he has to support you will eventually begin to think you a fool, too, for letting him get away with it. You gon' end up in a heap of trouble. And it went on and on like that every day till I left. My mother finally told me that it would have been better if I hadn't read all those books. She finally hugged me and said if I got into trouble to call her right away cuz wuzn't no—what's that he calls himself?—I said, revolutionary Black man—well, wasn't no revolutionary Black man gon' hurt her one and only daughter with no foreign talk. She said we Blk/women been fighting a long time just to get Blk/men to take care of us now you and yo/kind gon' to take us back.

Girl, I think we older women needs to talk to y'all 'bout something called common sense. Then we hugged again and that's all.

(*Goes to* BROTHER *and hugs him and becomes playful*)

Then I jumped on a plane, no wagon train for this sister, and California here I wuz. And you were at the airport with a rose, one lone red rose. And I thought, man, that's beautiful. I'm going to press that rose in the first book you sent me. Do you remember?

BROTHER

Yeah. It was Fanon's *Studies in a Dying Colonialism,* wasn't it?

SISTER

Uh huh.

BROTHER

Well, baby. I gots to split, but bizness is calling me tonight. I'll try to call you. If I don't, I'll send some sisters over to bring you out to the school tomorrow. All right?

(*Kisses her and picks up the red/blk/green pillow and leaves*)

SISTER

(*For a moment* SHE *stands as if waiting, then begins quick movements. Goes over to one of the suitcases and begins to unpack.* BROTHER *returns to the middle of stage and puts the red/blk/green pillow down. Crosses to table, pours himself another drink, turns, peers to the right, picks up a red velvet pillow and enters the* WHITE WOMAN's *apartment*)

BROTHER

Greetings from afar. Your boy/wonder has returned.

WHITE WOMAN

How was your trip down the peninsula?

BROTHER

Not bad. We'll talk about that later, but now some food and

drink for one who has traveled so far to partake of your charms.

(*Slightly drunk*)

WHITE WOMAN

(*Smiling but serious*) Ah, my man, you are most definitely mad. And didn't you promise me that you would cut down on your drinking? You got blotto, no. Now what is it you say . . . ?

BROTHER

Wasted, my love.

WHITE WOMAN

Yes. You got wasted night before last. I had to put you to bed. That's no good. How are we going to change this diseased world if you're drunk?

BROTHER

I know. You know it's just these recent happenings. Like you know, it's hard to leave you sometimes, and you know I'll have my new family starting next week. It's just so hard. You see, she doesn't know anything about you. She could never understand you and me and her and me at the same time, you being white and all.

WHITE WOMAN

Now, my man, it's your decision to make.

(*Gets up and fixes two drinks*)

If it's too much we can stop seeing each other. I'm not here to destroy you or make you feel guilty. I love you, my man, and whatever decision you make I'll abide by.

(*Hands drink to* BROTHER)

But since you're moving up in the movement out here, you do need a Blk/woman image. She's cute looking. Small. Compact, with a good/growing/awareness of what's to be done. You made a good choice and she obviously adores you. I saw how she was watching you in New York. You are her life. So she'll be dedicated to you and you need a Blk/woman who will dedicate her life to you, for you are becoming a very im-

portant man out here. But people are noticing that you don't
have a Blk/woman.

BROTHER

You're a rare woman, you know. Not many women would
share their man the way you do. You know, I wuz coming here
tonight to say that we had to stop seeing each other. That
since she's coming next week it wouldn't be fair to both of
you, that you both would be cheated in some way. But you've
made it so simple. Since we understand, we can keep this just
between us. And she'll never know.

(*Hands empty glass to* WHITE WOMAN)
How's about another one of those goodie good drinks you fix
for your VIP's, huh? Then some good dinner for a hard-
working revolutionary.

(BROTHER *sits on pillow*)

WHITE WOMAN

(*Moves over to* BROTHER *and sits down next to him*) After we
eat, could we go to the club and see John Handy? I haven't
seen him since your birthday. Let's go out tonight. Make it a
grand celebration since my wandering warrior has returned
from the peninsulan wars.

BROTHER

Girl, I'm tired. Just wants to sleep for a coupla days.

(*Turns and sees her face*)
But . . . all right. I tell ya not for long. Just for one set. Now
go fix my food. RAT NOW! Y'all hear? This nigger is ready to
grease out loud.

(WHITE WOMAN *gets up and moves behind the screen. The*
BROTHER *goes over to phone and dials a number. We see the*
SISTER *stretched out on the floor and* SHE *picks up the phone*
on the first ring)

BROTHER

How you doing, baby? Were you sleeping?

SISTER

No. Just dreaming, 'bout you and me, and us, 'bout our yet

unborn children waiting for us. To be born. Just thinking good things 'bout us, man. 'Bout what will be cuz we, this new Blk/man Blk/woman will finally put to rest the thoughts that we can't/don't git along. It wuz good news, man, just like you good news for me.

BROTHER

Yeah. I feel the same way 'bout you. You beautiful people and I'm happy you here. We got a whole lot of work to do and to do it with someone like you should be a gasssss. Look, baby, this meeting is taking longer than I thought. I won't be able to get back over to ya. I gots a lot of talking to do this night so you close yo/eyes and continue to dream 'bout me. Us. Our future, just continue to dream 'bout us. Don't let nothing interfere with that. Yo/dreams of us. Me and you. As long as we're together in yo/dreams we will BE. Remember that, baby. Just remember that. Don't you ever forget that you my woman. My Black woman. The woman I'ma gonna show to the world. My choice for the world to see.

SISTER

I love you, man. I love only you. Been waiting for you for a long time and now that we together time had better git stepping cuz it's you and me now and nothing's gon' git in our way.

BROTHER

Git some sleep now, baby. I'll see you tomorrow. Later on.
    (BROTHER *hangs up and moves behind the screen.*
    SISTER *hangs up, gets up and happiness is on her face.* SHE *does a quick spin and lets out a loud laugh. Stretches out on floor and goes to sleep. At the same time, you see the* BROTHER *and* WHITE WOMAN *dancing past. Talking. Laughing*)

WHITE WOMAN

And I thought you had forgotten my birthday.

BROTHER

(*Smiles*) I thought you thought that. I just didn't mention it to you because I wasn't sure if I would be able to buy you what

I wanted to. I solved it all, however. I wrote a bad check that's so full of rubber it'll bounce from here to the Golden Gate Bridge.

WHITE WOMAN

(*Laughs*) You're incorrigible.

(*Moves away from him and hands him a letter*)

Here you are. On time as usual, my man. Now, don't you do that again.

BROTHER

(*Doesn't raise his hand to accept the letter. Turns away and flops down in the chair*) I ain't gon' take no more of yo/money, girl. I'll/we'll, she and I will have to make it on her check and the school check. It was all right befo but no mo. Not now. It wouldn't seem right.

WHITE WOMAN

Ahhhhh, my man. That's what I love about you. Your values. You know you two can't get along on the money you're both making, that part-time teaching job she has can't/won't really help. I mean the money is rightfully yours. I told you that a long time ago, it's the money that my father got by un-derpaying Black people for years. It's rightfully yours. It should go to a Black man twisting and turning to be someone. Twisting and turning to survive it all.

(*Moves to table and puts the check down. Pours two drinks*)

It's really amusing. The estate sends me all this money and I give it to you and you travel around. Talk. Organize. Get people to change the world so no more men like my father will exist. If my mother only knew she would have one very real attack instead of one of her many fake ones.

(*Hands* BROTHER *a drink*)

BROTHER

Yeah. It just seems weird taking care of her with your checks.

WHITE WOMAN

But, baby, she deserves it, too. After all, she's Black and she works hard, too. She's a sort of inspiration to Black women.

BROTHER

(*Taking a sip*) Don't you . . . well, don't you envy her or hate her at all? She comes down hard on white women, you know.

WHITE WOMAN

Yes, she does. But I understand her bitterness, loneliness. She's had a very hard life. Not many people would have survived it. No. I don't hate her. After all, she says a lot of truth.

(*Crosses over and sits down in front of* BROTHER)

A lot of white women do love Blk/men. She feels threatened by this.

(*Kisses him, then takes down her hair. Lets it flow on him, his face, as* HE *stretches out and pulls her on top of him*)

BROTHER

I don't know what I'd do without you, baby. You good to me.

WHITE WOMAN

Don't try to. Everything is as it should be. I can share you any time as long as you always turn up here. Drunk or sober. You hear?

(*Holds his head as* SHE *talks*)

You are mine, my man. I found life, a reason for living, when I found you. I live from the light you bring me. When you stand up to talk and I hear you telling your brothers and sisters what we've discussed, I feel all warm inside. I see me up there on stage and it's so goood.

BROTHER

Come here, you, and say it's so goooood again.

WHITE WOMAN

(*Moves on him and covers his face with her hair*) It's so gooooooooood, my man.

(*Light moves to the* BLACK WOMAN's *side,* SHE's *on the floor, exercising. Her rhythm on the floor corresponds to the sounds coming from the* WHITE WOMAN's *side. When* SHE's *finished,* SHE *relaxes at the same time the* WHITE WOMAN *and* BLACK MAN *separate and rest alongside each other.* BLACK WOMAN *stands up and you see* SHE's *pregnant. Early stages of pregnancy. Holds up a beautiful long dress and puts it on a hanger. Turns when* SHE *hears the door open*)

SISTER

Hey. What's happening? Look at this dress. I made it this morning.
  (*Holds it up to her body*)
How do you like it?

BROTHER

You'll be tough, baby. Are you speaking tonight?

SISTER

Yes, at the cultural center. It should be a good crowd. Imagine having five crazy poets onstage together. The Black Experience indeed! It's gon' be smoking tonight. I just did a new poem tonight for the sisters at San Francisco State. It's called "To All Sisters." Listen to it.
  (*As the* SISTER *reads the poem, the* BROTHER's *face and body tense. When* SHE *finishes,* HE *sits down*)

BROTHER

You coming down kinda hard, ain't you, baby?

SISTER

Hard. Can't nobody be too hard on a devil/woman. She's the same as the devil/man, ain't she? One of the sisters came into my office today saying her old man has won. He said that it was a political move. So she asked him what's political about a devil/woman since she thought we were talking about all white people, not just white men. She said he looked at her and said you don't know what's happening. That the only way he as a Black man could maneuver would be to have a well/to/do/white chick in his corner. Man, she's all torn up so when I come home I wrote this poem. That's why it's got to be baddddddd—baddddddddder than bad so we can put that white woman in her proper perspective, you dig? Tell me, man, what's happening with Greg, huh? Frances is a beautiful sister. Loyal, hard-working. What is on his mind, man?

BROTHER

(*Looks up. Worried*) How in the hell should I know? I don't
know what's on that nigger's mind. It's his business, not ours.
    (*Stands up*)
Look, baby. I got a whole lot on my mind. Johnny and I are
leaving tomorrow night for Mexico to hook up with some revolutionaries down there so I ain't got no time to figure out the
workings of some dude's mind.

SISTER

Oh, I'm sorry, man, but you know what's happening here. It
was just on my mind and I had to spit it out. Had to. Sometimes this is just so unreal. I mean, sisters really working hard
at being true Black women. Really hard. And then some dude
takes them out, so far out to lunch that they might never come
back. Couldn't you speak to him, mannn?

BROTHER

(*Impatient*) Yeah. When I come back I'll talk to him, O.K.?
Now miss do-good lady, would you please pack me a bag before you go out?

SISTER

(*A worried look*) You not coming with me tonight? Oh no.
But you promised, mannnnnnnn. Our last night together, you
promised it would be our night. You'll be gone a whole week.

BROTHER

Too tired, baby. Had meetings all day with the people here
who are to hook us up in Mexico.

SISTER

(*Sulking*) I know, but you promised.

BROTHER

So what? What you sulking 'bout? So I promised. I'm here,
ain't I? I ain't goin' no place tonight. When you come back
I'll be here waiting for you. I just don't feel like hearing no
poets up on a stage talking bad.

(*Smiles*)
It's just hard for me, you know, to see you up there on stage
gittin' all that applause. Makes me begin to wonder why you
chose me. After all, I'm not really famous yet. I'm working on
it. But you, everybody knows you so . . .

SISTER

Ah, man. I understand now. It's alright. Look, I'll leave as soon
as I read. So I can come home to you, man, to one who has
chosen me from afar.
(*The bell rings*)
There they are. I'll run on downstairs. They'll bring me home.
You get some rest, mannn, cuz when I come back . . .
(*Smiles*)

BROTHER

Do it to them, baby. See you soon.
(BROTHER *fixes drink and picks up the phone.* HE *hesitates.
A worried look on his face. Dials the phone. Phone rings. On
the* WHITE WOMAN'S *side the phone rings and rings and rings
and* SHE *looks up and continues to read.* BROTHER *puts down
the receiver and dials again. The phone rings and rings and
the* WHITE WOMAN *gets up and fixes herself a drink. Puts some
music on and picks up the phone and dials.* BROTHER *jumps for
the phone*)

WHITE WOMAN

Greetings, my man. How are you? Thought I'd take a chance
and call you there.

BROTHER

Uh huh. Where are you? I've been trying to get you all night.

WHITE WOMAN

Why, I'm home. I've been here all night. Thinking about you.

BROTHER

I've been calling you all night. And the phone just rang and
rang. Where you been?

WHITE WOMAN

I told you. No place, just here. You must have dialed a wrong number.

BROTHER

Bitch. What you take me for, a fool?

WHITE WOMAN

(*Coldly*) Impregnating women is a criteria for revolution?

BROTHER

You think Black babies ain't part of the change?

WHITE WOMAN

How are we going to have time for a baby? There's no place for children now. I thought you had better sense than that. There's too much work to be done to stop and have a baby. Too much hard work to be done. That baby will tie you down, my mannn. You been together six months and she's pregnant already.

BROTHER

Just leave her out of this. She's happy about the baby. Just leave her out of this.
   (*Coldly*)
If you worried about supporting us all, just stop worrying. When I return from Mexico, I'm gon' git a part/time/job to tide us over. Don't you worry about us at all. Look. I better hang up. Got some packing to do tonight. I'll call you from Mexico.
   (*There's no answer*)
Are you there? Hey. What's wrong?

WHITE WOMAN

I'm crying.

BROTHER

Why? I've been away before.

WHITE WOMAN

I'm crying because for the first time I was being a bitch. I was jealous of her. She's carrying your child inside her. She's tied to you forever. You can leave anytime you want to. You just need . . . want . . . me for my money. That's all you want me for is my money.

(*Begins to scream. Cry*)

BROTHER

Stop that now. Get yourself together and stop! Hear me? Do you hear me? Answer me. Do you hear me?

(WHITE WOMAN *sits crying by the phone. Listens to him calling her. Lights a cigarette and listens.* SHE *stops crying and sits silently*)

Answer me. Do you hear me? Are you all right? Speak to me. Answer me. Are you all right? Don't do anything silly now, you still got those sleeping tablets in your house? Answer me. Do you hear me? Do you still have those sleeping tablets in your house? Hey, answer me!

(BROTHER *hangs up phone, takes a drink, walks back and forth. Drinking. Thinking.* WHITE WOMAN *takes a drink. Walks back and forth. Finally stretches out on the floor and waits.* BROTHER *leaves the* SISTER's *house and enters the* WHITE WOMAN's *house, sees her on the floor and tries to wake her up.* SHE's *motionless*)

Hey, lady. Wake up. Are you all right? Hey, lady. C'mon now. I'm sorry for making you cry. Did you take anything, huh? I'm sorry it took me so long to get here. Couldn't get a cab. I finally had to walk/run here. Are you all right, baby? My baby.

(*Puts her hand in his lap and kinda croons the words "my baby" over and over again like a chant*)

My baby. You gon' be all right. You not gon' leave me. Your mannn. We're together forever. I am committed to you, lady. Don't nobody mean to me what you mean to me. C'mon, baby, you gonna be all right. I'm yo/mannnn. Nothing can change that, you know. So what if she's having a baby. It's something she wanted. I guess it fulfills her as a Black woman, but it didn't bother you and me, baby. Not us. We were together before she came and we'll stay together. Why, lady, you've made me all that I am. I'm almost finished with school because of you. I can travel whenever I want to because of you. I dress well because of you. I never want for money because of you. I'm a man because you've allowed me to be a man. Say you all right, baby.

(*Moves her head back and forth*)

C'mon, baby, speak to me.

WHITE WOMAN

(*Speaks dully*) Where am I?

BROTHER

Ah. Thank God, here with me. What did you take, lady?

WHITE WOMAN

(*Slowly*) I took some sleeping tablets with a glass of scotch.

BROTHER

Lady. What you do that for? You had no reason to do that. What would I do if something happened to you? How would I make it without you? I neeed you, lady. Don't scare me like that.

WHITE WOMAN

(*Slowly*) I just felt so lonely. So all alone. And I thought, he'll leave me one day.

(*Tries to sit up and* BROTHER *helps her*)

He'll leave me one day just with the memory of three years together. Just with the sound of my door opening and shutting. He'll leave me and I'll dry up without his light. Without his sun. And I didn't want to see that day, my mannn. Do you understand? Don't be mad with me. You called me a bitch and I knew you were mad at me and I am a bitch . . .

BROTHER

No, not you. You're my life. I was just mad at you because you weren't home on my last night.

WHITE WOMAN

I was home, my love. I was just trying to make you jealous. Forgive me, my mannn. Forgive this foolish honky/woman. Devil/woman as yo/Black/woman calls me.

BROTHER

Hush now. And don't call yo/self those names.

WHITE WOMAN

But I am a honky. A devil. Am I not? Isn't she talking about me, mannn?

BROTHER

No, she ain't. Not about you. You exceptional, lady. There ain't nobody like you. You no honky, or devil or none of those names. You're my woman. You understand that? If she has to call names and identify whites by certain names that's her business. But you and I know it's not you she's talking about. You're the most humane person in the world.

WHITE WOMAN

Ah, man. Say you love me.

BROTHER

I love you.

WHITE WOMAN

Say you're all mine.

BROTHER

I'm all yours, all yours.

WHITE WOMAN

And you'll need me always.

BROTHER

I'll need you always.

WHITE WOMAN

(*Stretches back out and puts her head in his lap*) Stay the night with me, man.

BROTHER

I can't. I promised . . .

WHITE WOMAN

Say you'll stay the night with me until I go to sleep. Please. It's your last night. If you stay I'll be able to get myself straight. Please.

BROTHER

All right, baby. Let me call home. O.K.?

(WHITE WOMAN *gets up. Slowly. And moves behind the screen.* BROTHER *goes to the phone and dials and the phone rings at the same time the* BLACK WOMAN *enters her apartment.* SHE *picks up the phone*)

Hey. You just get in? How was the reading?

SISTER

Oh, fine. Mannn. Where are you?

BROTHER

I got a call from one of the organizers of the trip. Something came up, I can't talk about it on the phone. Look. I should be home soon. Would you start packing my clothes for me? I'll be there soon.

SISTER

But—but—but—why?

BROTHER

Now, no questions. Just do as you're told. And we'll talk when I get there. Later.

(*Hangs up the phone.*

SISTER *stands with the phone in her hand. Finally hangs it up. Moves and takes three suitcases out and opens them and methodically begins to pack each one of them. Slowly. Crooning a low mournful song. Maybe "Sometimes I Feel Like a Motherless Child."* BROTHER *is fixing himself a drink when*

WHITE WOMAN *comes from behind the screen.* SHE *has on a natural wig and a long dress*)

WHITE WOMAN
Well, how do I look?

BROTHER
Fine. Just fine, lady. You lookin' good.

WHITE WOMAN
I wanted to surprise you. Do I have that natural look she's always talking about?

BROTHER
Yes, you do.

WHITE WOMAN
Come here, my man.
(BROTHER *moves to her and kisses her*)
Who do you love?

BROTHER
You, lady.

WHITE WOMAN
And who am I?

BROTHER
My woman.

WHITE WOMAN
And thou should have no other woman besides me. For I am all that you need. I can be all that you want.
(*Spins away from him*)
I can be natural when you need naturalness.
(*Takes off wig*)
Or I can be me when you want me. I am all things for you.
(*Moves back to him excitedly*)
I know, let's get married. Right here, tonight. Let us marry one another to each other.

BROTHER

Aw, lady, I don't know, that sounds, well, I don't know.

WHITE WOMAN

What's wrong with vowing to each other to love eternally?
You didn't mean what you said, evidently.

BROTHER

No. It just seems unnecessary. But if you want to, why not?

WHITE WOMAN

Good. You go over to that side and I'll walk from this side.
We'll kneel together and say our vows.

BROTHER

What should I say?

WHITE WOMAN

Just say what I say. All right?
(BOTH *move to a separate part of the room and walk toward
each other. Meet. And kneel, facing the audience*)

WHITE WOMAN

We have come to declare our love. This white woman and
Black man. We have come to speak out loud our love so that
the night will hear us and know.
(*Turns to* BROTHER)
I love you, Black man.

BROTHER

(*Turns to* WHITE WOMAN) I love you, White woman.

WHITE WOMAN

And the words are spoken. And what can take back the words
which represent the feelings, time and place and the words
will travel throughout the land and make this universe stop
and listen because I have said I love you Black man and his
reply was love. The words have been spoken. And we are.
Now. We have spoken in the night but the morning light will
know. For the night and the morning are one. As we are one
and our love shall be eternal.

BROTHER
And our love shall be eternal.

WHITE WOMAN
For you are the light. The energy. The sun. And I receive
your light and live. And grow stronger each day. For you are
my light, otherwise I shall dwell in darkness. And together
we are the universe. Light and darkness, strength and weakness. One and two.
   (*Turns to* BROTHER)
Say we are one.

BROTHER
We are one.

WHITE WOMAN
You are the light and I am your darkness.

BROTHER
I am yo/light and you are my darkness.

WHITE WOMAN
We need each other to be.

BROTHER
We would be lost without each other.

WHITE WOMAN
And the universe has joined us together, and the universe
will curse those who try to deny us, the universe will pour
out her anger on those who would separate the darkness from
the sun for naturalness is the order of the day.
   (*Takes from her pocket two onyxes. Hands one to* BROTHER,
puts one around his neck)
I bring you eternal darkness.

BROTHER
I bring you eternal light.

BROTHER/WHITE WOMAN
We are one.
As the morning and night are one.

As life and death are one.
We are one.
(THEY *stand as* THEY *say the above*)

WHITE WOMAN
(*Almost hysterically*) All those who move to destroy this will
be damned. Shall be damned. You are warned. My focus will
destroy you.
(*Laughs a rasping laugh*)
Now, my husband of one minute. Let us rest for a while. We
need to rest. It's been a long night, hasn't it, my man.

BROTHER
Yes. My wife of one and a half minutes. Let us rest for I gots
to split and pack for the trip today. C'mon, lady, let's rest for
a while.
(BROTHER *and* WHITE WOMAN *stretch out,* SHE *on top of him,
and light fades.*
The SISTER *is sitting on the stool. Three bags are packed.*
SHE *waits. The* BROTHER *enters the room hurriedly.* HE *looks
somewhat tired. Disheveled. Obviously worried*)

SISTER
Who is she? I just want to know who she is.

BROTHER
What are you talkin' 'bout?

SISTER
(*Rises*) Who is she, mannn? Just tell me who she is. What she
is. What she is that she can get you to stay out till 6 A.M. in
the morning. Who is she, mannnnn?

BROTHER
I don't know what you're talking about.

SISTER
I'ma talking about you, mannn. I'ma talking about you leaving
me here alone on our last night together. I'ma talking about
you not coming to the poetry reading, I'ma talking about me

anxious to get home rushing up the stairs to you. To the silence of a room, to a telephone call that told me nothing, I'ma
talking about lies and more lies, I'ma talking about us, mannn.
(*Moves up to his face*)
Who is she, man? Is she prettier than me? Is she blacker than
me? Is she taller than me? Does she make love better to
you than me? I just want to know who she is.

BROTHER
(*Coolly*) You're hysterical. Why don't you calm down. Just
shut up and calm down. I told you where I was. I was taking
care of some business.

SISTER
(*Moving away with back to audience*) With whom?

BROTHER
With someone who is organizing the trip.

SISTER
What's her name?

BROTHER
It's a he.

SISTER
What's his name?

BROTHER
What's his name? Girl, what's yo/problem. I told you from
the git so that when I'm on business it's private. When I'm on
business in the movement it's very private. And don't be asking
me. I'll tell you what I want you to know. No mo, now stop
this nonsense and help me pack. I'm gon' be late for my plane.
(SISTER *turns and runs over to him and hits him—the slap is
loud and there is a momentary silence.*
Backs away)
Don't do that again, you hear me? What you tryin' to start.
You want me to beat you up so you can show everybody what

a no/good/nigger I am? Is that what you want? Lookie
here, baby.

(*Moves to her*)

Lookie here, girl, I had to leave. It was urgent business. I
don't like telling you everything cuz it could be dangerous for
you and . . .

SISTER

You're lying. I know it. I feel it inside that you're lying. You
got another woman. I know it. Tell me who she is, man? Is
she younger than me? Is her stomach flatter than mine?

(*Turning around*)

What's wrong with me now? You don't like my getting big
with the baby? Is that it? Why mannnnn, why another woman,
when you told me I was all that you needed. That yo/life
was complete now that you had a Black woman. Were they
all lies too? Just a six-month year-old lie. Not even a year-
old lie. Just a six/month/year-old lie. Well. That's it. I'm leaving. My bags are packed. I'm going back home.

BROTHER

Just like that.

(*Has moved over and poured himself a drink*)

You just gonna pack up and leave. Go back to mommy and
daddy so they can say/remind you every day with I told you
so, I told you he was a no/good/nigger. I told you he meant
you no good, him with that big Castro beard. I told you so.
I told you so. And I thought you were a mature Black woman.
Ready for the unknown. Ready for the fight, ready to run
at the first sign of trouble. You gon' go home cuz you can't
figure it all out. You don't have all the right answers.

SISTER

(*Hesitates slightly*) But this isn't the first time you've done
this. This is just the first time it's been so blatant. I've gotten
so many phone calls from you explaining why you couldn't
come this way that I began to think you and that telephone
were one. I am a Black woman, but that don't mean I should
be a fool. To you being a Black woman means I should take

all the crap you can think of and any extra crap just hanging loose. That ain't right, man, and you know it too.

BROTHER

Well. Let's stop this now. You unpack yo/clothes. I need one of the suitcases for my trip.

SISTER

I'm going, I'm leaving you.

BROTHER

You ain't going no place.

SISTER

I'm going back to New York.

BROTHER

(*Moves to suitcases and opens them, begins to throw her clothes out of cases*) You ain't going nowhere now. You are officially unpacked. So just sit down and keep quiet since you acting like such a fool.

(SHE *stands up and* HE *pushes her back down on the stool*) Stay seated and keep quiet. I got too much on my mind to listen to this foolishness.

SISTER

That's the way my life is now. Scattered just like those clothes on the floor. And I'm pregnant too. What a trick bag I'm in. It's funny, you know. Don't you think it's funny, mannnn? And we ain't even legally married.

BROTHER

You sound like one of those TV/soap operas
(*Sings a Hearts and Flowers song*)
"Tune in tomorrow and see how our dear sister turns out. When last we left her her life was scattered out on the floor like leftover stale potato chips, pregnant, alone, unmarried, standing with her face to the sun. What more could happen to our courageous heroine? Tune in tomorrow and find out." SHEEEEET. Everytime one of you bourgie bloods decide

to become Black you act like people owe you something. Well, I've been Black ALL my life. Done struggled all my life in Louisville. My mother and all her different men. All my brothers and sisters with different daddies. Girl, you don't know what hard times is all about. Just because you decided to wade into Blackness and you found the water steaming not from the sweat of yo/brothers and sisters, you gon' turn around and go back to N.Y.C. you bourgie/Black/bitch. Who do you think you are? Just because you're well known you think you an exception. You get what all the other Black/women of yo/ time gon' git. Stand up.

(SISTER *doesn't move*, SHE's *thinking quietly*. HE *moves over and pulls her up*)

I said stand up. Who do you think you are? Just because they applaud you for some words, some poems, you say, you still gon' git what every Blk/woman's getting, you ain't no different from them at all. This is 1967. Don't you forget that. Let me help you remember who you are.

(*Slaps the right side of her face*)

You a Black woman bitch.

(*Slaps the left side of her face*)

You the same as every Black woman.

(*Slaps the right side of her face*)

You were born to cry in the night.

(*Slaps the left side of her face*)

You ain't no different from any Black woman.

(*Slaps the right side of her face*)

You're my mother, and my mother's mother every Blk/man's mother I've ever seen.

(*Slaps the left side of her face*)

You like all Blk/women, ain't no difference.

(*Then he kisses her. Long and hard*)

Now. Pack my bag like I told you to. I got just a few minutes to make the plane.

(SISTER *picks up one bag and begins to pack the bag in silence*)

Anything special you want from Mexico.

SISTER

Nothing.

BROTHER

Well. I'll choose you something nice. Hey. Maybe if Johnny and I save on some of our expenses, maybe by Friday we could send for you. How about a weekend in Mexico with yo/old/man? How would you like that?

SISTER

Yes. I'd like to be someplace with MY old man.

BROTHER

I'll see if I can work it out. Maybe with a few calls here and there I can work it out.
(*Fingers the onyx as* HE *talks*)
Yes. Maybe it can be done.

SISTER

You know, I didn't think too much about it night before last. But I had this dream. It seems that we went to the hospital together. It was time for the baby and I had two babies, one white and one Black. I kept saying the white one wasn't mine. The hospital nurses and doctors kept smiling. No, it's yours. They said in fact we almost missed it. Thought it was the after/birth until we looked and saw this baby. It's yours. I screamed, but it's deformed. It's deformed. It's ugly. I don't want it. And their grinning faces grew bigger and bigger as they said two for one. We've got two babies for you. You can't have one without the other. That's the way it goes in this hospital. Take the two babies or none at all. I remember they were laughing as they left my room.
(*Hands suitcase to the* BROTHER *and stands up*)

BROTHER

It's just a dream. Nothing to it. Some dreams are just weird. That's all. But sometimes, baby, you try to live too Blackly. Like giving up yo/wine and not smoking and no more pork.

Girl, it don't matter what we eat as long as we do it to this man. As long as we upset his system it don't matter what we eat.

SISTER

But we are what we eat, mannnnn. And drinking is slow death. And smoking. No mo cigarettes. No mo weed for me. It's all wrong. How can we change things doing it the same way he's doing it. How can we be different being like him. Look. When some of us in New York first got our naturals people said they weren't important—that they didn't make no difference. But they have made a difference, you know. We've made people change their minds about the beauty of their hair.

BROTHER

Aw right. I know. I know. Another time we'll argue this out. It's time for this ole dude to make it on outa here. I'll call you tonight from the hotel. Okay? And stop looking so lost. So sad. I still love you in spite of your foolishness. I forgive you. C'mon and give me a kiss.

SISTER

(*Moves toward the* BROTHER *and kisses him*) Goodbye, mannnnnnnn.

BROTHER

Maybe I'll see you on Friday night.
(*Exits*)

SISTER

(*Stands for a while and stares. Then turns around and begins to pick up her clothes. She puts them in the two bags. Then she moves/walks around the room, stopping first one place then another*) There must be a place for me somewhere. Let me continue walking. Ah. Here's a corner for me.
(*Gets on her knees, begins to pray hesitantly*)
Oh Lord. Help me, this poor Blk/woman/sinner sitting here.

Help me out of this misery. I know I have done wrong and all, but help me, dear Lord, help me, yo/poor servant here in the wilderness of California, help me . . .

(*Begins to laugh*)

Help me to . . .

(*Bursts out laughing*)

Girl, ain't no Lord gon' help you, at least not one that we've been taught to pray to, git off your knees. You look like some fool asking for help from one who ain't never helped Black people do anything 'cept stay on their knees. But you do need some kind of help. You made a mistake and you don't know what to do about it. What about yo/child? What about yo/child rushing out of the darkness of yo/womb into light. You've got to give him light. Not madness. But light. What you gon' do, Black girl?

(SISTER *goes over and picks up the two bags and starts out. Sits down and begins to unpack. Slowly*)

How can I go home with this big stomach? How can I? I'll forget it, that's what I'll do. I'll forget it happened and wait for him to change. He'll get over whatever she is. He'll change. He'll stop drinking. And smoking. He'll understand why a Black man must be faithful to his woman, so she'll stop the madness of our mothers repeating itself out loud. He just needs time. I just got to rock myself in Blackness, insulate my soul with righteousness and that will sustain us both. Gots to. Yeah.

(*Begins to rock back and forth*)

Gots to rock myself in Blackness. In sweet, sweet Blackness, cuz I am the new Black woman. I will help the change to come. Just gots to rock myself in Blackness in the knowledge of womanly Blackness and I shall be.

(*Begins to sing a tune as* SHE *continues to rock*)

I'm a Black woman,
gon' get Blacker than the nite
become one with my man.
I'm a Black woman
mother of the sun,

Gon' become one with my man
and get Blacker.
    Yeah. Yeah.
    (*Continues to rock*)
Gots to rock myself in Blackness
Gots to rock myself in Blackness
Gots to rock myself in Blackness
    (*Light fades to* DANCERS.

MALE DANCER *turns and faces the audience. The two* FEMALE DANCERS, *one with black mask on, the other with white mask, sit in back—one to the right and one to the left.* MALE DANCER *stands. Walks around and drinks a drink. Turns and looks at* BOTH *of them, tosses a coin to see which one* HE'LL *visit.* HE *walks a hip/walk to the* FEMALE DANCER *wearing the black mask, holds out his hand. Kisses her and leaves hiply. Goes to* FEMALE DANCER *with the white mask on and* THEY *circle each other.* THEY'RE *apparently equals.* THEY *dance.* HE *leads. Then* SHE *leads.* HE *leads then* SHE *leads.* HE *leads then* SHE *leads.* HE *finally gives up and* SHE *heads the dance. The* MALE DANCER *returns to the* FEMALE DANCER *with black mask and her stomach is now big, and as* THEY *dance* THEY *can't touch till finally* THEY'RE *dancing without touching each other.* HE *returns to the* FEMALE DANCER *with the white mask.* HE *finds her stretched out lifeless on the floor.* HE *tries to wake her up—*HE *drags her back and forth trying to wake her up. When* HE *fails* HE *sits and waits, and waits.* SHE *turns.* SHE *twists her body snakelike and slides up to him and curls herself round him.* HE *is hypnotized and* HE *begins to follow her snakelike on the floor, moving in and out finally touching.* THEY *stick out their tongues and kiss and the* FEMALE DANCER *with white mask becomes lifeless again. The* MALE DANCER'S *body becomes like the sun warming her till* SHE *begins to stir again and* THEY *dance a sensuous dance. When the* MALE DANCER *returns to the* FEMALE DANCER *with black mask on* HE *is shaking. Chilled, tired to the bone.* SHE *greets him discordantly. Moving around, dissatisfied. And* HE *is so tired that* HE *begins to shake. The slow movement from the feet to his shoulders and* HE *knocks* *her down as* HE *spins with each quiver of his body.* HE *picks up his bag and moves slowly out, body twitching from the cold that* HE *feels. The* FEMALE DANCER *with black mask on rolls across the floor, trying to find a comforting place. Gets on her knees and prays. First one place then another until* SHE *can clasp her hands no longer. And* SHE *laughs. Her body laughs and* SHE *becomes still. Finally* SHE *rises and straightens out her black mask. Her long dress, her natural. And* SHE *begins to march at first in a tired manner, but as* SHE *passes,* SHE *becomes upright in her Blackness and* SHE *smiles, slightly.*

Stage darkens.

There is no beginning or end)

On Black Terror

RICHARD WESLEY

I wrote *Black Terror* because of certain things that I saw in the political climate of 1969–70. I had noticed that the rhetoric of the late sixties was going off in a direction that was not beneficial at all to Black people. The late 1960s saw the concept of revolutionary suicide, urban kamikaze, rather than concrete political theories that would ultimately lead to the survival of our people in this society.

So, I decided to write a play in which certain ideologies would be given, given a chance to be aired onstage, and the people, Black people, could come and see the play and observe these ideologies, and try to take from what they saw onstage an idea or a hint as to what they had to do as a people in order to free themselves of this rhetoric and move on to another method of action.

I guess I was about as successful as an artist can hope to be—and art in America, as a very wise brother once said to me—"is not really appreciated." America, basically, is an anti-intellectual country, and art in America is looked upon as some sort of freakish activity of weird people whose ideas and opinions really aren't listened to or valued. Artists in America are looked upon only to entertain and not to try to tell you anything.

So, there were a few people who came to see *Black Terror*, who seemed to benefit from it, at least from what they said to me, while there were many others who just viewed it as another play.

With few exceptions Black playwriting is stagnating. I'll be frank. I feel that there are not enough writers who are trying to move beyond the tired, worn-out theories of traditional drama. There's still some writing for street theatre. Others are still doing rituals which were almost left behind almost two years ago. Others are or have degenerated into a form of exploitation; either they're exploiting the revolution or they're exploiting legitimate anger by Black people in the form of revolutionary movies and musicals, musicals that really don't say anything except repeat old philosophies and ideas that writers such as Imamu Baraka had enunciated years ago.

I draw my strongest inspiration from the work of a few playwrights: writers such as J. E. Gaines, Clay Goss, Martie Charles, Ed Bullins and writers who initially influenced me, like Imamu Baraka and to some extent, Ronald Milner.

Black theatre tries to deal with reality, tries to motivate people to change, tries to inform people of problems that are among them, tries to confront, create conversations among Black people and the society that oppresses them.

White theatre is lost in fantasy. Its playwrights are forced to compromise any progressive impulses they may have to making money to benefit a producer, to benefit a director, to benefit any number of anonymous white people known as backers who put these plays on for their own reasons and cause theatre to be mired down in dead classics, avant-garde bullshit and mediocrity.

Right now, I think the most important thing that all young playwrights can do, myself included, is to read, to get a working knowledge of history, so that they can better understand some of the things that are happening now, and better understand the future, and also to avoid getting themselves caught up in philosophies that have absolutely no flexibility.

(From a conversation with
RICHARD WESLEY,
Fall '72)

Black Terror

A revolutionary adventure story

BY RICHARD WESLEY

BROTHERS AND SISTERS
INVOLVED IN THE STRUGGLE:

ANTAR: *Late twenties or early thirties. College education. Strong, well-muscled and stern. Relatively quiet. Speaks in soft tones. Aloof. Not given to boisterousness.*

AHMED: *Somewhat younger. Full of fire. Could be a good leader if he would calm down and check things out.*

KEUSI: *Full name, Keusi Kifo ("Black Death"). He is in his mid-to-late twenties and is a war vet. He is always a man who knows whereof he speaks.*

M'BALIA: *Named for M'Balia Camara, a Black woman who is known in Africa as a woman whose death was one of the sparks of the Guinean drive for independence from France. The sister is strong, determined and a devoted revolutionary. She is not unfeminine, but displays her womanness only when she feels it suits her.*

GERONIMO: *A fiery revolutionary. Leader of the local chapter of the American Liberation Front. Quick-tempered; a flair for the dramatic. At times he seems almost unreal.*

CHAUNCEY RADCLIFFE: *Middle-aged. A moderate Black man who thinks he is doing the right thing.*

OTHERS: *Three Brothers, a Sister, other members of the Black Terrorists, and white-sounding voices coming in over the radio.*

The setting will alternate between the Terrorist headquarters, a tenement apartment, and the home of Dr. Chauncey Radcliffe.

TIME: *The very near future, given the nature of American society.*

The New York production of *Black Terror* opened at the Public Theater in Fall of 1972. The production was directed by Nathan George. Lighting by Buddy Butler; sets by Marjorie Kellogg.

THE CAST:

KEUSI	Gylan Kain
M'BALIA	Susan Batson
ANTAR	Paul Benjamin
AHMED	Kirk Young
GERONIMO	Don Blakely
RADCLIFFE	Earl Sydnor
DANCER	Dolores Vanison
PRIESTESS	Freda Vanderpool
BROTHERS AND SISTERS	Preston Bradley
INVOLVED IN THE	Niger Akoni
STRUGGLE	James Buckley
	Sylvia Soares

MUSICIANS:

Babafemi Akinlana
Ralph Dorsey
Ladji Camara

Scene I

Blood red lights on a dark chamber. A number of young, Black REVOLUTIONARIES *are gathered to perform a ceremony. Drums are playing. The* WOMEN *sing in eerie, high-pitched voices; the* MEN *make grunting and moaning sounds that blend in with the voices of the* WOMEN. BODIES *are swaying. Dancing. The smell of incense is in the air. A fire burns at an altar.* ANTAR *stands in front of the altar. The music, singing and dances build to a frenzy until* ANTAR *bids silence.* AHMED, *standing nearby, steps forward, raises clenched fist:*

AHMED
We are the Black Terrorists, sworn to the liberation of our people.

ALL
May we never lose sight of our duty.

AHMED
We seek the death of those who oppress us.

ALL
May our vengeance be as swift as lightning.

AHMED
We are the Black Terrorists, sworn to uphold the dignity of our African bloodline.

ALL
May we suffer death before disgrace to our ancestors.

AHMED
We live by the will of the Supreme Black Spirit to create a world of peace and beauty after the revolution.

ALL
May the blood of our oppressors never cease to flow until that world is realized.

AHMED

We are the Black Terrorists, sworn to die for the liberation of our people.

ALL

The oppressor of our people must die! We shall kill him where he works, we shall kill him as he sleeps, we shall kill him wherever he is. He must know of the wrath that befalls those who consider themselves above the laws of God and humanity. His death will free our nation! His death will free the world! AAAAAAAAAAAAAIIIIIIIIIIIIIIEEEEEEEEEEEEEE!!!!!!!!!

(*Drums. Wild dancing.* WOMEN *dancing.* MEN *shuffling in place. Shouting and screaming. Chants are heard. Silence as* ANTAR *raises his hands*)

ANTAR

Bring in the candidate.

(*Two young* TERRORISTS *escort* KEUSI *to the altar. Drum is heard softly in background.* KEUSI *kneels before* ANTAR *and altar*)

Ndugu Keusi Kifo, you kneel before me having been chosen by vote to carry out a mission of assassination against the most vicious and ruthless enemy of the people in this area.

Your target is Police Commissioner Charles Savage, organizer of the mad-dog Night Rangers of the police department. He is an avowed enemy of the revolution and he is therefore an oppressor. He must die.

ALL

(*Chant*)

Lasima Tuchinde Mbilishaka!
Lasima Tuchinde Mbilishaka!
Lasima Tuchinde Mbilishaka!

(M'BALIA *will come forward from the assembly and kneel at the altar before* KEUSI.

Sing)

Spirits of our forefathers
Come forth
Reach into our hearts

And remove the fear
Reach into our minds
And remove the doubt
Release the anger in our souls
And give us strength
To do
What must
Be done.
    (*Chant*)
Sifa Ote Mtu Weusi
Sifa Ote Mtu Weusi
Sifa Ote Mtu Weusi

ANTAR

Dada M'Balia, you kneel before me, having volunteered to
team with Ndugu Keusi in the execution of this mission. Your
past performances in action have proven you to be an out-
standing revolutionary and an expert terrorist. Your knowledge and experience will prove to be the perfect complement
to Ndugu Keusi's own revolutionary talents.

(*The* OTHERS *will sing the lines below as* ANTAR *is given a
large knife by* AHMED. HE *places the knife in a fire on the altar
to purify it.* ANTAR *holds the knife aloft. Drums grow louder,
then subside.* ANTAR *takes* KEUSI'S *arm and makes an inci-
sion, then does the same with* M'BALIA.

Meanwhile, the OTHERS *are singing*):

ALL

(*Sing*)
Spirits of the Black Nation
Come.
Take hold of your servants
Guide our lives
Make us strong
Place steel in the marrow of our bones
Grant us inner peace
To fulfill our terrible missions.

(*Chant*)
Lasima Tuchinde Mbilishaka
Lasima Tuchinde Mbilishaka
Lasima Tuchinde Mbilishaka

ANTAR

Ndugu Keusi and Dada M'Balia, the two of you have been joined together by blood. Until this mission is complete or until I terminate this mission, you will guard each other with your lives.

(AHMED *steps forward with an array of weapons on a dark red pillow*)
You will assume secret identities and live within the community and await the opportune moment to carry out your orders.

(*Hands weapons to* KEUSI)
These are your weapons. You will use them well, my brother. What say you both?

KEUSI and M'BALIA

(*In an incantation*)
Spirit Guardians of the dark regions
Hear my cry
Let not my will falter
Let not my desire fall
With all my strength
Let me defeat my enemy
With all my soul
Let me defeat my enemy
Let me see to the will of
The Black Nation
Show me
No mercy
Should I fail my
Sacred oath.

AHMED

(*Steps forward, raises clenched fist*) We are the Black Terrorists, sworn to the liberation of our people.

ALL

May we never lose sight of our duty.

AHMED

We seek the death of those who oppress us.

ALL

May our vengeance be as swift as lightning.
AAAAAAAAAAIIIIIIIIIIEEEEEEEEEEEE!!!!!!!!
(*Drum, music, dancing as* KEUSI *and* M'BALIA *exit.
Lights go down*)

Scene II

*Lights up on a room in a tenement apartment. Very little
furniture. Large rug on the floor.* KEUSI, M'BALIA *and* AHMED
sit on large cushions.

AHMED

All right, listen up. Ndugu Keusi, your target has a set pat-
tern of behavior. He plays golf at the Golden Triangle every
weekend from 11 A.M. to 5 P.M. He showers, then leaves the
golf course promptly at 6:45 P.M. He always takes the parkway
back to the city.

KEUSI

He travel alone?

AHMED

Always. Now, about twenty-five miles south of the city, the
parkway has this big curve in it that goes through this valley.
There are a lot of trees, high grass and shrubbery. He usually
hits that curve around 7:15. And he drives in the left lane.

KEUSI

What kinda car do he drive?

AHMED

(*Piqued*) Man, didn't you study the briefing notes on the
target?

KEUSI

Yeah, well, I don't remember seeing anything in it about the kinda car he got.

AHMED

It was in there, man. Dammit, man. Get yourself together. You blow this mission—

KEUSI

(*Annoyed*) Just tell me what kinda car he drive. I don't need no lecture.

AHMED

You better watch your mouth, man. You still only an initiate. One word from me and your ass'll be crawling in the dirt.

KEUSI

I'm sorry, man. Nervous, I guess.

AHMED

Don't be sorry, just keep in mind your position when you talk to someone who got rank over you. Now, in view of the fact that you ain't studied, I gotta take time out to get up off a whole lotta insignificant information. The target drives a 1965 Buick LeSabre; four door; blue. License plate number NPD-911.

(KEUSI *writes info down*)

KEUSI

Got it. Thanks, man.

AHMED

(*Ignoring him*) It's important that you be on the right-hand slope of the valley at 7:15 to get the best shot at the target. The high grass will hide you. We figure once the oppressor is hit his car will veer out of control and crash. In the confusion, you can make a sure getaway. Be sure you can find the ejected shell and take it with you. We don't want no clues left behind, at all.

KEUSI

Aw, man, now how the hell am I gonna find an ejected shell
in all that grass?

AHMED

Look, stop questioning your orders and do like you're told.
All the FBI gotta do is find a shell, or some other seemingly
insignificant shit, and the next thing you know they'll be banging on our door.

KEUSI

They ain't gonna find us behind no goddamn shell.

AHMED

Stop questioning your orders and do like you told.

KEUSI

Yeah. Okay, I'm sorry. You got anything else to tell me?

AHMED

No. That's it. The rest is in your notes.

KEUSI

Yeah, okay, I got a question. This shit sound too risky. Have
y'all got an alternate plan?

AHMED

Yeah, but it's more difficult 'cause you got to eliminate your
target in front of his home. The target is pretty much of a
loner. He's a bachelor, so he lives alone in his house. He got
very few real close friends and seldom gets visitors. His house
is at 631 Peachtree Drive, near Talmadge Avenue. He works
a sixteen-hour day and usually gets home about 9:30 at night.
Usually all the lights in his house go out around 11:30, so we
figure that must be about the time he goes to bed. Observa-
tion shows that he usually gets outa his house by 7:30 A.M.
The best time, then, to eliminate him is between 9:30 at night
and 7:30 in the morning. There's a park across the street from
where he lives. Lotsa trees and good cover. Ideal for a mission
like yours.

KEUSI

Yeah, I like that. A park. Nighttime. Good cover. Hell, yeah, I like that idea. I'll probably do the job at Savage's house rather than on that stupid highway. Shit, why not?

AHMED

Where you eliminate your target doesn't matter. The idea is to execute your mission cleanly, efficiently and without the possibility of detection. Complete your assignment by the end of the week.

KEUSI

It'll be done.

AHMED

(*To* M'BALIA) Have you any suggestions or amendments, my sister?

M'BALIA

No. Y'all the men. I trust your ideas.

AHMED

Okay, then it's all set. Good. I've got to leave, 'cause Antar and I got things to discuss.

(ALL *rise.* THEY *move to door*)

A word of caution, Ndugu Keusi Kifo. Your mouth is too big, man. You got the makings of a damn good revolutionary, but you try to think too much. You know? Don't think. Let your leaders do the thinking. That's their job. Your job is to do or die. Remember that. Okay?

(KEUSI *smiles and nods.* AHMED *and* KEUSI *shake hands. Then* AHMED *embraces and kisses* M'BALIA *on both cheeks*)

Good luck to you both.

KEUSI

Yeah, man, thanks.

M'BALIA

Asante, Ndugu Ahmed.

AHMED

Kwaheri.

KEUSI

Later.

M'BALIA

Kwaheri, Ndugu Ahmed.

(AHMED *exits*)

KEUSI

Jive-ass, motherfucker. I wouldn't follow him across the god-damn street.

(M'BALIA *looks at him very hard*)

Well, it's all set. That's good.

M'BALIA

I'd better go and clean your weapon.

KEUSI

Hold it a minute. I'm not so sure I wanna use that rifle.

M'BALIA

(*Harshly*) What do you propose to use then? A knife? Your hands? You could fail if you try those methods. The revolution can't afford any failures, Ndugu Kifo.

KEUSI

I'm hip to that, M'Balia, but look at it from this angle: Out on the parkway, if I got to take aim and fire in all that high grass, how the hell am I gonna know where the spent shell falls? I could be up there for days looking for some goddamn shell just so the FBI don't have too many clues. I could get caught up there looking for that shell. And that park across from where Savage lives. It's in a white neighborhood. I'm gonna have a helluva time even gettin' into that area. Then fire a high-powered rifle. The sound of the shot is gonna bring people. Someone's bound to see me running. Of course, I could put cushioning and wire mesh around the barrel and chamber of the gun to muffle the sound of the shot, but then there's the problem of the gun flash. Suppose I need more than one shot—highly unlikely as good as I am, but possible anyway—suppose I need more than one shot, people are bound to see the gun flash. It's warm out, there gonna be people all over the place. Then, 'cause I shouldn't question orders, I gotta crawl around in the dark lookin' for some stupid-ass shell. After I do that, I gotta worry about gettin' my Black behind outa there with cops crawlin' all over the place lookin' for the sniper who offed the pig. Naw, there got to be an easier way. I don't wanna wind up a martyr on my first mission.

M'BALIA

We know it is risky, Ndugu Keusi, but you should realize that the success of your mission overrides any consideration of the success of your escape. You should not expect to survive the revolution. As an initiate to the Black Terrorists that realization will be some time in coming. But as you become more of a part of us, you will accept that point of view as a reality.

KEUSI

I don't accept the inevitability of a revolutionary death. Understand? He who assassinates and gets away shall live to assassinate another day—if he's clever. And I intend to be clever. I ain't hardly suicidal.

M'BALIA

No one asked you to be. You have an assignment to carry out. You will not shirk your duty.

KEUSI

I ain't shirkin' no duty. I'm just tellin' you that to kill this man there must be a simpler way just as efficient as a gun that won't give me the problems I mentioned before. I know I'll think of something. Just give me some time. Commissioner Savage will not see the weekend. Imagine, he's walkin' around thinking about his golf game this weekend not knowing that there's a nigger right now thinking of offing him before he even gets one stroke in. Life is funny like that. One minute everything is cool, the next minute, CRASH!!!! Just like that it's all over. Too bad. I almost feel sorry for that old bastard.

(M'BALIA *looks at him incredulously*)
Yeah, I kinda feel sorry for his ass, you know.

M'BALIA

(*Firmly*) Don't. Your target is the oppressor. He is not a man, he is the enemy. He is the devil, the beast. Your target is zero. Compassion is an emotion that is wasted on him. When you eliminate your target, you are destroying a non-man. You are killing a no-thing. The oppressor's life is zero. The death of your target will mean life for the revolution. You should remember that. Reduce your enemy from humanity to zero. Once you have done that in your mind, such emotions as compassion seek to have relevancy, and pulling the trigger becomes easier and easier. Ultimately you can kill with the same nonchalance as brushing your hair.

KEUSI

You really believe that?

M'BALIA

Of course. I'm a revolutionary. The total extermination of the enemy is my goal. After you've been with us awhile, you'll come to adopt this point of view as well.

KEUSI

Yeah, uh-huh, well I recognize my duty to fight and maybe die for the revolution, but I ain't never been able to see killin' in a machinelike fashion. I'm a man, not a machine.

M'BALIA

You refuse to understand. Compassion is beyond the emotional range of the true terrorist. We say that the only true emotion in the revolution is revolutionary fervor.

KEUSI

I can see that my education is going to be a long and hard one.

(M'BALIA *looks at him but says nothing*)
Hey, I'll tell you one thing, though: That info that Ahmed had on Savage was very meticulous. Whoever was assigned to

check him out sure did a good job. Looks like they got his shit down pat.

> M'BALIA

I watched the target. I worked as a maid in his house for a coupla months. I got to know him pretty well. He tried to get me to sleep with him a couple of times, but I kept refusing, so he fired me and got someone else. But by that time we had most of the information we needed. When I think about it, though, I should have slept with him. It would have been so easy to execute him then. One of the other sisters did it. I understand it works very well.

> KEUSI

I don't see why y'all need a female assassin's unit in the first place.

> M'BALIA

Manpower needs dictated it. There just weren't enough brothers to do all that needed doing.

> KEUSI

Yeah, but could you as a woman, a giver of life, teach a doctrine of terror and death to your children?

> M'BALIA

I'll never know. I'm an assassin and we're not among those women who're allowed to have a husband and children. Our tasks are too dangerous and they require our full allegiance and dedication to what we do. Besides, our duty overshadows any considerations of love and/or motherhood.

> KEUSI

But you will have a man and kids someday, won't you?

> M'BALIA

I've devoted my life to the revolution. A man and children are luxuries a woman can afford when there's peace. We're at war and I haven't the time to even think of such things. And don't be getting any ideas. Just because I have a womb, don't think I'm that eager to put something in it. I won't be judged by my sex. I'm a revolutionary before I'm a woman.

(KEUSI *and* M'BALIA *look at each other.* KEUSI *is bemused and* M'BALIA *is dead serious.* SHE *starts out. A sly smile comes over* KEUSI's *face*)

KEUSI

M'Balia?
(SHE *turns*)
Are you for real? Y'all really can take sex or leave it?

M'BALIA

(*Trying to deal with* KEUSI's *insolence*) Well . . . every now and then some of us still have the need, Keusi. After all, it *is* a natural human function, you know.

KEUSI

(*Smiling*) Yes, I know.

M'BALIA

(*Insulted*) Don't be vulgar.

KEUSI

M'Balia, you got a man?

M'BALIA

(*Bitingly*) No. I haven't found one who interests me.

KEUSI

You sure?
(KEUSI *looks at her.* M'BALIA *avoids his eyes and the question*)

M'BALIA

I'll go clean your weapon. You should rest. You have important work to do.

KEUSI

Yeah, okay,
(*Sarcastically*)
"Mommy."

(Angry, M'BALIA *exits in a huff)*
Ain't this a bitch?
(KEUSI *laughs to himself and lights up a joint.*
Lights go down)

Scene III

Lights up on ANTAR *and* AHMED *seated in the headquarters of the Black Terrorists.*

ANTAR

You know, once we eliminate the oppressor Savage, we will have to be prepared for some very hectic times. Many of us will probably be killed.

AHMED

Yeah, I know. Well, we all have to die sometime. I guess going out with the blood of the oppressor on our hands is the best way for the true revolutionary to die.

ANTAR

Once Savage has been eliminated, we must prepare ourselves for full-scale reprisals. The oppressors will scour the entire Black community until they find us, and when they do, I guess it'll be a fight to the death.

AHMED

I know it'll be a fight to the death, 'cause I ain't hardly gonna go to jail behind destroying some oppressor.

ANTAR

Assassinating that oppressor will probably mean that another, more beastly oppressor will take his place. He will unleash the Night Rangers and that could signal the beginning of the next phase of the revolution: open all-out warfare between the Black community and the local forces of the oppressor. I just hope we are prepared.

AHMED

We're ready as ever. The Night Rangers will have one helluva
time gettin' in here and if they do, they'll have less than half
the men they started with, no matter how many men they
send at us. The revolutionary example we set will inspire revolutionaries all over the world.

ANTAR

That's the greatest honor any revolutionary can have. The
death cries of the enemy can serve as our dirge.

AHMED

Dig it.

ANTAR

It's good to know that, as a leader, I am surrounded by
brothers of such courage. I know that none of you will let me
down when the time comes.

AHMED

All of us except maybe that new brother.

ANTAR

Which one?

AHMED

Keusi Kifo.

ANTAR

What's the matter? Don't you trust him?

AHMED

I wouldn't go so far as to say that. But I am kinda worried
about where his head is at.

ANTAR

You don't think he's the man, do you?

AHMED

No, we've had him followed and we've checked as thoroughly
as we could on his background. He's clean as far as we can

tell. Our spies in police headquarters said that they couldn't find nothin' on him, but they still keepin' they ears open. Kifo's a veteran of the Vietnam war and he's a weapons expert and was also a sniper. Much decorated and alla that shit. The brother who recommended him is one of our most trusted revolutionaries. No, I don't think he's the man. That's not the kind of vibration I get from him.

ANTAR

Well, then what's the trouble?

AHMED

I was with him a little while ago. He's a very incorrect brother. No discipline, no revolutionary fervor; just a very uncool nigger who acts as though what we're involved in is just an advanced stage of gang-banging.

ANTAR

I guess it's a carry-over from his war experiences. You should remember that, unlike most of us, Kifo has fought and killed for a number of years while in Vietnam. This is all old hat to him. I think we should be patient and try to coax him along gently.

AHMED

Yeah, well, I went to check on his efficiency report an' that report ain't that good. I told you before that I didn't think he shoulda been selected for this mission. Just 'cause he got a good military record that don't mean that that's enough. Hey, man, listen to this report: "Too compassionate . . . given to feeling sorry for his targets . . . hangs on to such emotions as pity and mercy . . . doesn't realize that such emotions are beyond the range of the true revolutionary." Antar, any brother who got any kind of political knowledge knows that our situation in this country is the result of inhuman treatment that has in turn dehumanized us. We are outside humanity because inhuman beasts have forced us there. Now they threaten us because we seek to return to humanity. But the beast blocks our path. We got to use inhuman means to defeat inhumanity. See, Keusi Kifo won't acknowledge that fact and I feel that in the long run he gonna be a detriment to the organization.

ANTAR

I see. Ahmed, I think your suspicions have some validity, but on the other hand, the War Council decided unanimously on Ndugu Keusi, with you, of course, abstaining. It's too late to call everything off, now. The wheels of death for the oppressor are rolling and no one can stop them.

My own opinion is that you exaggerate just a little. Kifo is certainly no troublemaker. Recognize that you've already decided that he is not the man and you've determined that he is a good killer. His loyalty, at this point, is not in doubt. So what you should understand, then, is that his lack of discipline and fervor are but the characteristics of a great many new members of this cadre. His fire is much like yours when you first came to us.

AHMED

But I understood the seriousness of what we did and what we had to do. Therefore I took the revolution seriously. I don't think Ndugu Keusi does and that's the shit that's botherin' me.

(*A young* TERRORIST *bursts in, salutes and addresses* ANTAR)

YOUNG BROTHER

Excuse me, Mkuu Antar, but Geronimo of the American Liberation Front is outside. He's been shot in the shoulder and he's all beat up lookin'.

ANTAR

How the hell . . .
(*To the* YOUNG BROTHER)
Bring him in here soon as you can.

YOUNG BROTHER

(*Saluting*) Ndio, Mkuu Antar.
(*Exits in a hurry*)

AHMED

Great, now Geronimo's ass is lit up. Who's gonna be next? We gonna have to put an end to this shit, man. Kifo better not fuck up. I'll put fire to his ass if he do.

ANTAR

(*Softly*) Take it easy, man.

(*Two* BROTHERS *bring in* GERONIMO. HE *is wearing a brightly colored headband, Apache-style moccasins laced up to his knees, and wears an army fatigue jacket. A* SISTER, *who remains silent and in the "background," enters and begins to dress* GERONIMO's *wound*)

SISTER

Please try to relax, my brother. This is going to hurt a bit.

GERONIMO

(*Ignoring the* SISTER; *to no one in particular*) Those white motherfuckers!! Goddamn spiritless, devil-eyed dogs! Aw, man!! Oh man!! Goddamn!!!

ANTAR

(*Calmly*) Geronimo, be cool. Calm down.

GERONIMO

The pigs man, the pigs!!! They put all my best shit to sleep!!

AHMED

Geronimo, damn, man, make some sense.

GERONIMO

The Night Rangers destroyed my headquarters, man. They took weapons, records, smoke, everything. Three of my men are dead, more of my warriors are wounded or in hiding, and I'm here all shot up.

SISTER

Geronimo, I'll have to ask you not to move so much. I can't fix your bandages right if you keep movin' like you do.

GERONIMO

(*Ignoring the request*) The bullet went clean through my

shoulder, man. I ain't never been shot before. It hurt like hell, but it was wild. Ow! Goddamn, watch it, sister!

SISTER

I'm sorry, my brother, but I told you before it was gonna hurt.

GERONIMO

Yeah, well, okay, sister. But don't let it hurt too much.

AHMED

You gonna tell us what happened, man?

GERONIMO

Yeah, okay. This was extremely well planned and coordinated. They killed Ramon, my Chief of Security, Victor, my Chief of Culture, and Juney-bugs, my Chief of Propaganda. I think the Night Rangers probably got all my records. If they do then they got the who's who of every chapter in the country. They got a list of all my known contacts and a list of the white boys who was payin' my expenses when I gave speeches at colleges and shit like that. Man, the pigs got the American Liberation Front by the balls.

AHMED

I guess y'all have had it, brother. You better make preparations to go underground and split.

GERONIMO

Hell no! That punk Commissioner Savage pulled off this shit and I want his ass! He's responsible for the deaths of three of the baddest brothers who ever lived. I shaped and molded those cats myself. Victor, Ramon and Juney-bugs was smokers, man; very righteous revolutionaries. Good sharp minds. They learned well and followed orders to the letter. Damn, man, they was *revolutionaries!* Man, I shudda died with them. They were the best, man. You know?

ANTAR

You still haven't told us what's happened.

GERONIMO

(*Angry; excited*) Hey, man! Goddamn! I told you, the pigs vamped on us!

AHMED

How? I thought y'all had some security.

GERONIMO

We figured we did. We had these five Marxist white boys covering for us.

AHMED

White boys?! Aw, *man!!* Geronimo, was you crazy?!

GERONIMO

Well, hey, man, we thought they was different.

AHMED

See, man, we told you about that alliance shit in the first place.

GERONIMO

We thought they was bad, man. You know, these cats been blowin' up the Bank of America, draft offices, Dupont Chemical property, goin' on days of rage and shit, and quotin' Marx better than the Russians. You know, these cats was those crazy motherfuckers who called themselves "The Narodnikis." Hey, man, we thought we had some dynamite dudes with us . . . and the pink pussies punked out!!! The pigs musta moved fast 'cause the first thing we knew Finkel and Schmidt came bustin' thru the door headin' for the escape tunnel shouting, "Pigs outside! Pigs outside! Let's get the hell outa here!" They hit the tunnel shaft and we didn't see them no more.

ANTAR

We told you a long time ago about alliances with those white radicals. They are either suicidal in outlook or thrill-seekers who have no real stomach for true revolution. I thought that a lesson had been learned by all of you alliance-prone brothers after the way Bobby got used in Chicago a couple of years ago.

AHMED

The only place for white boys in the struggle is *outside* the struggle.

GERONIMO

Yeah, I realize that, now. They all the same, all those white radicals. All they can do is sell woof tickets and hide behind Black revolutionaries' coattails, waitin' for us to tell them what to do next. They stand around wavin' Viet Cong flags and shit, and spittin' at pigs. But soon as they start gettin' they heads cracked by some pigs, they start cryin' and shouting.
(*Very effeminate*)
"Oh my god, what's happening. But we're the kids! We're the kids!" They got no heart, man. No heart, at all. They don't understand revolution. Not really. So fuck 'em! They all pussies! The faggots, they oughta drop they pants and spread they "cheeks." That's all they good for, anyway.
(*Calms down a bit. Tries to pull himself together*)

SISTER

Brother, you gonna have ta try to control yourself. I can't do nothin' for your shoulder if you remain in your overexcited state.

GERONIMO

(*Breathing hard; looks at the* SISTER *a moment. Face grows hard*) Aw, later for my shoulder. My men lyin' dead, wounded and scattered all over the fuckin' city. And you botherin' me about a stupid-ass flesh wound! Fuck my shoulder. Woman, get away from me, I ain't asked you for your advice!!
(*Hurt, the* SISTER *quietly bows her head and starts to leave.* AHMED *looks hard at* GERONIMO *who does not notice him.* HE *seems almost in another world. Realizing* HE *has been rash,* GERONIMO *takes the* SISTER's *arm*)
Wait, hold it, sister. Please stay. I'm sorry. You doin' a good job. Please . . . I'm sorry.
(GERONIMO *kisses the* SISTER *on the cheek*)
Finish what you were doin'. I'll try to be cool.

(*The* SISTER *looks at* ANTAR *who nods approvingly;* SHE *smiles slightly at* GERONIMO *and resumes dressing his wound. It takes only a few seconds and* SHE *has finished. Having done that* SHE *moves to a quiet corner of the room where* SHE *remains*) That's a good job, my sister. You do your work well.

SISTER

Asante, Ndugu Geronimo.

GERONIMO

(*Smiles*) Hey, man, that's a beautiful sister. I almost forget what I been through when I look at her. You know?

(*The* SISTER *smiles*)

But I can't forget. Nothin' can ever make me forget. Nothin'll make me forget what went when those pigs staged they massacre. But we made them pay. We made them pay!

(GERONIMO *becomes exhilarated as* HE *relates the following details*)

Me, Ramon and three other brothers was on the windows. Juney-bugs was downstairs guardin' the door. Everybody else scattered at every other available position. We put the steel shutters up. Then I put a sister on the phone callin' up the Black radio station, so she could tell the shit as it was happenin'. I didn't want the pigs floodin' the airwaves with their version of battle. We had to be ready for those motherfuckers on every level. These pigs was the Night Rangers an' we knew they was better armed than the 101st Airborne, so we wasn't takin' no chances. Then these two pigs tried to dynamite the door open. Ramon leaned out the window an' fired twice: Bam! Bam! Two pigs fell for the revolution! AAAAAAAAIIIIIIIEEEEEEEE!!!!!! Then, I heard a loud crunch an' I saw Ramon's face turn into a charred lump of blood. Ramon! Ramon! Oh, man, goddamn . . . But we held 'em, man. The chumps threw everything they could at us an' we held 'em off. Then there was an explosion an' screams an' the place was fillin' up with smoke. They finally managed to dynamite the door open. The explosion busted Juney-bugs all

up. He couldn't move, man. The brother didn't have a chance.
But that didn't stop Juney-bugs. He had a piece in each hand.
The first four pigs thru the door died. Juney was settin' a beautiful revolutionary example: four pigs lyin' dead at his feet, two
more lyin' wounded in the doorway cryin' for they mamas
an' they gods. Juney-bugs just kept on firin' into that cloud
of smoke an' not one pig dared to move from behind the cars
an' shit they was hidin' behind.

An', man, there was bullets zingin' all past my head, people
screamin', guns an' shit, an' I was feelin' . . . I was feelin' . . .
damn about nothin'. I could feel the spirits of all the great
revolutionaries with me. Man, it was like I was feelin' mystical
an' shit. An' then, with everything blowin' up all around me,
I saw the spirit of death laughin' at me. He raised a clenched
fist. An' I raised a clenched fist an' shouted, "Right on, motherfucker!!!" an' laughed back. I swear to God, man, an' I'm
ashamed to admit it, but I loved it! I LOVED IT! We was
heavin' the righteous wrath of the people on the pigs.

(*Hysterical laughter*)

HAHAHAHAHAHAHAHAHAHAHAHAHAHAHAHA!!!!!
Another explosion an' there was only seven of us left alive
by this time. I could hear the pigs comin' up the stairs an'
I knew that Juney-bugs musta been killed. It was time to get
outa there. We got the sistuhs out first. . . . Then, man, the
craziest thing: Victor knelt down beside Ramon's body an'
he put his hand in his blood, an' he started tremblin' an'
screamin' an' actin' wild an' shit. He charged the pigs, firin'
as he went. No! No! Nooooooo!!! . . . It was just me, now.
I ran inside the main room an' bolted the door shut. I could
hear the pigs tryin' to bust it down. I set the room on fire.
Couldn't afford to let the pigs get nothin'. Then someone shot
thru the door an' I got hit. I started to fall, but I held on. I
knew if the pigs found me alive, they'd kill me on the spot.
I started to crawl to the tunnel. The room was burnin' when
I left, but I'm sure the devils musta been able to put the fire
out an' get those files.

AHMED

You shudda had summa those sisters destroyin' those files the minute the first shot was fired.

GERONIMO

They was all upstairs on the third floor when the shit started. An' they was asleep. When the shit started, it was started. Either you shot or got shot. There was no time to worry about files.

ANTAR

You should have taken time, Geronimo. Now, the whole Front's gotta go underground or maybe even disband. The FBI's gonna be bustin' ass right and left.

GERONIMO

My only hope is that the fire I set took care of business. That's all I got to say on the matter, so don't be bustin' my ass about no goddamn files.

(*Mood changes. Body sags a bit*)

Oh, man, those three brothers. Oh, man, they was so beautiful. Blazin' away even as they fell. Ramon, with his face blown off, lay on the floor still holdin' his piece. Even in death he was settin' a perfect revolutionary example. Man, why do dynamite brothers like those three cats always have to be the ones to get offed?

ANTAR

They have attained the ultimate freedom in this oppressive condition Black people live in, Geronimo. Those brothers chose to die rather than live in squalor and deprivation. Their concern for their plight and the plight of their Black brothers and sisters all over the world led them to sacrifice the ultimate for a remedy to their situation. Those of us who are left can only be inspired by their revolutionary deaths.

AHMED

That's right, my brother. Even in death the brothers have provided impetus for the revolution.

(*During the last exchange the* SISTER *has moved to* GERON-
IMO's *side to inspect his bandages*)

SISTER

Mkuu Geronimo, you movin' so much you startin' to bleed
again.

GERONIMO

(*Looking at the wound*) Wow. Dig that.
   (HE *touches the wound then pulls his hand away, marveling
at the sight of the blood. Then,* HE *clenches his fist and
closes his eyes*)
Oh man, oh man! I can feel it, my brothers! The revolution,
Victor, Juney-bugs and Ramon. I can feel it all. Oh, my God!
   (*The* SISTER *tries to redress his wound, but* HE *pushes her
hand away*)
No, don't!! Not yet.
   (HE *places his hand over the wound once more*)
Yeah . . . yeah . . . Now, I know what Victor felt when he
touched Ramon's blood. My wrist! Alla y'all grab aholda my
wrist.
   (HE *clenches his fist.* ALL *grab his wrist*)
Can you feel it? You feel the spirits? You feel 'em? Oh God,
it's beautiful. Can you feel it, brothers? Can you feel it, sister?
It's the spirit of the revolution. Can't nothin' hurt me, now; I
know it!! Oh wow, man! The blood! The feeling! It's really
taking me out.

SISTER

Geronimo, you're trembling all over.

AHMED

He must be gettin' the fever.

GERONIMO

(*Angry*) It ain't no goddamn fever!! It's the revolution. It's
my only reason for being alive from this moment on! To fight
and die for the revolution. I won't live beyond it! I don't
want to. I don't care what goes down after we win. I only

want to live to destroy my enemy. Once that has been, my
usefulness to the revolution will be done. From now on, I'm
a revolutionary warrior. I live for the battle. Peace would kill
me. I only want to live to destroy my enemy. That's my goal.
Death and destruction will be my weapons of war.

(*Clenching his fist tighter*)

Oh God, can ya'll feel it? The blood is burning in my fist.

ANTAR

(*Looks warily at the* OTHERS) Geronimo, maybe you'd better
try and rest. You keep up like this and you'll lose a lot of blood
and that could lead to you dyin'.

GERONIMO

No, man, not! Not Geronimo! Geronimo ain't gonna die on
no hummer. I seen my death. I'm gonna die like a revolutionary with the blood of the enemy on my hands. To die for
the revolution is a glorious thing. It is, man, it is. Make no
mistake. I'll meet my moment in a true revolutionary manner.

My brothers, I ain't splittin' into no goddamn exile. I'm
stayin' here to fight and die in the revolution. Let me join you.
I need to hook up with some revolutionary freedom fighters.
Let me work with you. Please. Y'all are revolutionaries, an'
I'm one, too. Don't deny me the chance to get even for Victor,
Ramon and Juney-bugs.

ANTAR

(*Smiling*) Geronimo, you were always one of us, my
brother. We would be honored to have you serve with us.

(THEY *embrace*)

AHMED

Death to the oppressors!!

ANTAR

Long life to the revolution!!!

GERONIMO

Death and destruction! Pain and agony! Let the blood of the

enemy flow in the streets purifying the revolutionary cause. Let nothing remain standing before the power of the revolution!!!

ALL
AAAAAAIIIIIIIIEEEEEEEE!!!!!!!!!!!!!
(*Blackness*)

Scene IV

A few days later in the apartment occupied by KEUSI *and* M'BALIA. HE *and* M'BALIA *are eating. The radio blares in the background.*

RADIO NEWSMAN
. . . And now the top news story of the week: Some eighty-five policemen, members of the elite Night Rangers, earlier this week raided the headquarters of the American Liberation Front at 221 Chapel Street in the Penny Lane District. Twenty-two persons, including thirteen policemen, were killed in the blazing twenty-minute gun battle that ensued when police reported that they were met with gunfire when they sought entrance to the headquarters to ask the ownership of a Volkswagen double-parked illegally outside. Police eventually had to use a special cannon and dynamite to gain entrance to the building, which was destroyed by fire in a successful attempt to destroy certain records and files that the ALF members apparently did not want the police to obtain. The bodies of nine members of the ALF, seven males and two females, were found in the rubble. Police have also had to deal with increasing sniping incidents in the surrounding neighborhood, as well as with rampaging bands of Black youths who have been attacking foot patrolmen from rooftops.

Now, as we had promised earlier, here is a tape of the telephone call the WORL newsroom received from the ALF headquarters during the height of the gun battle that has been declared the bloodiest in the annals of modern American law enforcement:

(*We hear the sound of a* WOMAN'S VOICE *amid the reports of gunfire and explosions, shouts and screams*)

REVOLUTIONARY SISTER

. . . The revolutionary headquarters of the American Liberation Front are now under siege from the racist, fascist, reactionary army of the pig power structure. They are attacking us with everything but we are holding firm. Already, at least three pigs have been barbecued, with minimal losses to ourselves.

(*Explosion. Screams.* VOICE *more excited*)

Now the pigs look like they usin' cannon, but we still holdin' on. The revolution is moving to a higher level. Right on! Death to the fascist dogs and the imperialist criminals who control them! Death to the enemies of the lumpenproletariat! Long live the revolution!!

(*More shots, screams, more explosions*)

They throwin' everything at us, yet we will persevere because we must! . . .

(*Tape is abruptly cut. The* NEWSMAN *takes over*)

RADIO NEWSMAN

That was the voice of one of the members of the American Liberation Front speaking to this office in the midst of the shoot-out with the Night Rangers that took the lives . . .

(M'BALIA *rises from the table and cuts off the radio*)

M'BALIA

Yessir! The American Liberation Front stone took care of business.

KEUSI

(*Nonchalantly*) Yeah.

M'BALIA

They really did the job, man. I bet the oppressors never expected to be met with such revolutionary fervor. Thirteen oppressors revolutionized to death.

KEUSI

At the cost of the lives of nine ALF warriors. Alla that death and gun play was unnecessary, if you can dig it.

M'BALIA

Unnecessary? Their deaths had meaning. They died in order that the revolution might carry on. In that respect, their deaths were necessary.

KEUSI

You know you got too much idealism. That's your problem. You gotta recognize that at this stage, the death of *any* revolutionary is needless. We haven't the strength to face the honky on a large scale, yet. We can't even keep pushers outa our neighborhood with any real success, so how can we run down a program of armed struggle against the beast? Hit-and-run tactics, at best, are all we can do. The ALF had an out and didn't use it.

M'BALIA

They had no out. They had to fight. They had no choice other than to fight and die like men, or surrender and be herded to the electric chair in shackles. Those brothers and sisters chose to commit revolutionary suicide and in doing so advanced the revolution even farther. There is no tragedy in their deaths; only glory.

KEUSI

Hey, baby, how you gonna talk about glorious death, when to get killed now is really not necessary?

M'BALIA

In our daily struggles against the oppressor, the possibility of death is always present, no matter what level the revolution is being waged on. We acknowledge death and do not fear it.

KEUSI

But the revolution is about life—I thought. Our first duties as revolutionaries is to live.

M'BALIA

Is it? The first duty of the true revolutionary is to kill the oppressor and destroy his works.

KEUSI

But don't that come when the revolutionaries have got strength? Until that time he got to live, and he can't do that practicing revolutionary suicide.

M'BALIA

(*Angry*) And when the tables are turned against him, when every avenue is blocked, every alternative closed to him, what then must the revolutionary do?
(*Without waiting for answer*)
He must fight! He must fight or die. He has no choice. When his back is to the wall, he can't die like a lamb waiting the slaughter. No, let him have his gun and his manhood.

KEUSI

(*Silent a moment*) Yeah, okay, my sister. But I still think Geronimo was crazy to pursue a gun battle with the police. See, like, his back wasn't totally to the wall. What he did was cause his headquarters to get burned down, nine brothers and sisters to lose their lives, and for the revolution to suffer another bad day.

M'BALIA

How can you say that?

KEUSI

'Cause from listening to the reports and from having known some brothers who belonged to that chapter of the ALF, I know that the gunfight wasn't necessary.

M'BALIA

Are you accusing him of being a traitor?

KEUSI

No. I'm accusin' him of piss-poor leadership.

M'BALIA

What the hell do you know about it?! Who are you to say
something like that?

KEUSI

I can't say what I want?

M'BALIA

Not when you go around disparaging one of the baddest
brothers walkin'. I think you should watch your mouth. Ahmed
is right. One of these days you're gonna be stepped on.

KEUSI

I guess I'll have to worry about that when the time comes,
'cause when I see things I feel are goin' wrong I gotta speak
out. I've seen some things in the past week that have got me
wonderin' what's happenin'. Suddenly, you know, I'm like,
questioning which way the revolution is going.

M'BALIA

You're just afraid of revolution. That's what it is. You're afraid
of a real revolution.

KEUSI

Damn right, if people like Geronimo are gonna be leadin' it.
All the revolutionaries I've seen ever since I came outa
the indoctrination classes got a colossal death wish. We all
bein' oriented toward death. Once you get hooked goin' that
way, everything you do is geared toward destruction and
finally you can't think positively or constructively.

M'BALIA

Oh, I can think positive, alright. The most positive thing I
can think of is the death of the oppressor. Ahmed once said
that we shall bathe in the oppressor's blood on the day of
our victory.

KEUSI

Suppose I was to say that we could build the Black nation without even firing a shot, if we really wanted to do that?

M'BALIA

I'd call you an insufferable romantic fool and a threat to the revolutionary fervor we are trying to promote in the people.

KEUSI

Yeah, M'Balia, I can see why Antar has placed you with me. I'm sure gonna learn a lot from you.

M'BALIA

You need to. You lack all kinds of revolutionary zeal.

KEUSI

Baby, I'm a trained killer. I've seen shit that would have you vomitin' all over this place and I seen buddies of mine die right in my arms. So what the hell're you talkin' about? Zeal? What the hell is some goddamn zeal? Zeal don't mean shit when it comes down to it. What counts then is quick thinking, discipline, holdin' up under pressure and common sense. Zeal will get you killed if you don't watch out.

M'BALIA

Your incorrect mouth may get *you* killed.

(M'BALIA *rises without further comment and begins moving about the apartment straightening up. Her movements are graceful and very feminine. This is brought about by the lapa* SHE *wears.* KEUSI *lights a cigarette and watches her awhile, a wry and gentle smile coming over his face*)

KEUSI

Hey, baby, tell me somethin'. When's the last time you been treated like a woman.

M'BALIA

I don't know what you're talking about. I'm always treated like a woman.

KEUSI

Well, Antar said that you was to be my wife and do everything a man expects of a woman.

M'BALIA

Provided I'm in the mood. Now look, I told you about this once before. Don't be disrespectful.

KEUSI

I'm not being disrespectful. I'm being a man.

M'BALIA

Well, I don't think I want you to make love to me.

KEUSI

A fine-lookin' sister like you? I'm sure you must need *some* lovin' *some*time.

M'BALIA

I'm—a Black Terrorist. Sex isn't a thing with me any more.
  (KEUSI *bursts into a great laugh*)
Well, what's so funny?

KEUSI

(*Laughing*) Yeah, okay, baby, we all must make sacrifices for the revolution.
  (*Laughs harder*)

M'BALIA

You stop laughing at me! There's nothing funny. It's the truth. A true revolutionary has no time for such emotions. I'm a Black Terrorist . . .

KEUSI

(*Interrupting*) You're a woman . . .

M'BALIA

I'm an expert assassin . . .

KEUSI

You're supposed to get fucked and have babies. Let the men fight.

M'BALIA

That's not true. The Black Terrorist Women's Organization said that my main function was that of a revolutionary, not those mundane feminine things. I'm a free woman, not a whore.

KEUSI

Aw, woman, ain't nobody said you wasn't a revolutionary. Now, c'mere and shut up!!
  (*Moves toward her*)

M'BALIA

(*Backing away*) Keep away from me.
  (SHE *strikes a karate stance*)
You keep away from me, you hear!
  (KEUSI *moves on her whereupon* SHE *tosses his behind on the floor.* KEUSI *looks up at her in angered bewilderment.* HE *rises slowly and faces her. Gradually* HE *begins to relax, then smiles. Eventually,* M'BALIA, *feeling* SHE *has made her point, lets her guard down. At that instant* KEUSI *smacks the shit outa her.* SHE *hits the ground hard on her behind.* SHE *fights back a few tears.* KEUSI *kneels beside her*)

KEUSI

Awww, what's these? Revolutionary tears? I thought you was beyond such emotion.
  (*Laughs, reaches into pocket and wipes her tears away with a handkerchief*)
You're a woman before anything else. When I get through with you, you'll never want to forget that. Now, come here and don't hand me nunna that "I'm a revolutionary" bullshit.
  (*Pulls her close*)
Hey, baby, you lookin' g-o-o-o-o-d.
  (KEUSI *begins to undress her as the lights go down.*
  Lights up on KEUSI *and* M'BALIA *lying together*)
Hey, baby, I'm sorry I hit you.

M'BALIA

You could have broken my jaw.

KEUSI

Aw, the only thing hurt was your pride. I half pushed you, anyway. I'm sorry, though, honest.

(SHE *does not answer him*)

Hey, baby, I really mean it.

(*Leans over and kisses* M'BALIA *long and hard*)

See?

M'BALIA

Yes. I believe you, but . . . well, Keusi, you know this can't lead to anything. I can't get involved with you in any deep way because I'm an assassin and because of what I do, I won't always be able to see you. Let's end it, now. We had a good little time, but—

KEUSI

Uh-uh. We ain't endin' nothin'. I dug you the first time I laid eyes on you an' I ain't gonna lose you now.

M'BALIA

Keusi, my life belongs to the revolution. I live it and breathe it. Anything beyond that just isn't real for me. To become your woman, I'd have to leave the Female Assassins unit, and I could never do that. I've been with them for two and a half years; I've lived with them, and laughed and cried with them. They're my family, my sisters in the revolution. I just can't up and leave them.

KEUSI

Yes, you can.

M'BALIA

No. It's impossible.

(*Hoping to change the subject*)

Hey, you'd better get some sleep. Tomorrow's the day you eliminate the oppressor.

KEUSI

(*Smiling*) Sleep is somethin' I don't wanna do, right now.

(*Half whisper*)
Now, c'mere.
(HE *kisses* M'BALIA *as the lights go down*)

Scene V

Lights up. The next day—very late . . . evening. M'BALIA
worriedly paces the floor. KEUSI *appears in the doorway.* HE
carries a duffle bag with him, his appearance grim. M'BALIA
stands in frozen expectation, watching him. KEUSI *slowly nods
his head. Excitedly,* M'BALIA *approaches him.*

M'BALIA
There's no doubt? He's dead?

KEUSI
(*Quietly*) They should find his body in his driveway a coupla
hours from now. Maybe sooner.
(M'BALIA *embraces him.* KEUSI *gently pushes her away.
Reaches into his pocket and takes out a slip of paper and
pencil.* HE *writes a telephone number down*)
Here, call this number. Let the phone ring three times. Then
hang up. That'll signal success.
(M'BALIA *does as* SHE *is told.* KEUSI *moves into room and
sits wearily.* HE *removes his shoes and begins to unwind.*
M'BALIA *finishes the telephone call, then approaches* KEUSI)

M'BALIA
(*Looking at duffle bag with curiosity*) How . . . how did you
do it? I got worried when I looked into the room and saw you
didn't take any of your weapons.
(*As* SHE *rummages thru the bag* SHE *comes up with the crossbow and takes it out of the bag.* KEUSI *sits quietly, not really
paying any attention.* M'BALIA *eyes it, both repulsed and fascinated at the same time*)
Keusi, did you use this?

KEUSI

(*Remembering every detail of the assassination*) Yeah . . . it was simple.

(*Laughs sardonically, then becomes silent again.*

Noticing M'BALIA *with the crossbow,* KEUSI *takes it from her and puts it back in duffle bag. Tired and drawn*)
Yeah . . . so simple.

M'BALIA

Did anyone spot you?

KEUSI

No.

M'BALIA

But a crossbow? I don't understand.

KEUSI

Quick, silent and very accurate.

M'BALIA

That's all you got to say?

KEUSI

What else is there to say?

M'BALIA

I suppose you're right. Um . . . are you hungry?
    (KEUSI *looks at her, then looks away*)
Is there . . . is there anything I can do?
    (KEUSI *lies down.* M'BALIA *gets some oils, moves to him, and begins massaging* KEUSI's *back*)

KEUSI

Oh, baby . . . I'm tired. So goddamn tired.

M'BALIA

(*Massaging*) This will help you relax.

KEUSI

He looked right at me . . . right at me . . . I saw him get out of his car. I took aim an' I fired. The arrow hit him in the back of the neck. He turned around and he had this weird, twisted and frightened look on his face. He saw me . . . he reached out, and started staggering toward me, bleedin' and coughin' blood. . . . Then he fell dead. But his eyes was open, lookin' right at me. . . . Right at me.

(*With suddenness* KEUSI *takes* M'BALIA *in his arms*)
Baby . . . baby . . . baby. Lemme just hold you.

(*Holds her tight*)
God, it's so good to be alive. Living, breathing, loving. Never aware it can end on a hummer in a minute. Baby, lemme just hold you an' be glad I'm alive . . .

(THEY *embrace and kiss as lights go down*)

Scene VI

The headquarters of the Black Terrorists. ANTAR, AHMED *and* GERONIMO *are seated together. Laid out before them is what appears to be a large diagram. Also, an assortment of maps are strewn about.*

GERONIMO
There, that's it. Whatchall think? We can plant bombs under the sewers
(*Pointing to diagram*)
along here. And here. You see? When they blow, those streets will be rendered useless. Also, looka here.
(*Reaches for another diagram*)
This one's of the police station itself and shows that we can plant another bomb here and disrupt their whole communications thing. We can drop charges in other places. Look, me, Juney-bugs, Ramon and Victor went over these plans backwards and forwards, in and out, day and night.

ANTAR
I don't know, Geronimo. I'm hesitant to try something like that.

GERONIMO

Me and my three chiefs went over this thing for months, man.
It can work. Why you against it?

ANTAR

It's risky, man. It doesn't sound all that foolproof. I'm not all
that sure it can work.

GERONIMO

You tryin' to say somethin'?

ANTAR

No, Geronimo—

GERONIMO

Don't be disparaging the memory of those three young
brothers. They had good minds, man. They don't put together
no shoddy shit.

ANTAR

I'm well aware of that. But I still feel that it's too risky. How
do we know that the oppressors won't be guarding against
just such a maneuver?

GERONIMO

(*Annoyed*) The whole goddamn revolution is risky, Antar.
Any revolutionary move you make involves the element of
risk. What the hell you rappin' about?

AHMED

(*To* ANTAR) I think it's a good idea, Antar. Psychologically,
it'll blow the Man's mind.

ANTAR

I don't know. That kind of terrorism involves high risk. We've
usually operated against lesser targets and much closer to
home. I think more planning is needed. We have to look into
every angle.

GERONIMO

What's there to look at? We have a target, we destroy it. No bullshit, no questions; destroy the target. Hey, man, you brother terrorists or not?

ANTAR

(*Calmly*) We're terrorists.

GERONIMO

Then what the fuck's the problem?

ANTAR

That kind of guerrilla tactic is the problem. It may be beyond our particular training. I think we should be more cautious.

GERONIMO

Motherfuck, caution!!

(AHMED *looks angrily at* GERONIMO, *but* ANTAR *restrains him with a silent gesture*)

Hey, man, look! All you do is get in the goddamn sewers, crawl through 'em, plant the bombs and split. The men be underground. Who the fuck's gonna spot them?!

ANTAR

(*Calmly*) Listen. Your idea is a good one. But I'm only trying to say that the nature of the venture requires more careful planning. Yes, I could give you some of my men, but they will run the risk of being detected in an action against a target all the way across town from the nearest Black neighborhood. If they are discovered, they can be trapped in those sewers and slaughtered like animals. All you've done is show me some diagrams, blueprints. Juney-bugs was the only one of the three of you who had ever been in that jail before, and that was only for a brief stay. He couldn't have possibly gotten the most precise information needed for an operation of this sort. Add to that the possibility of those diagrams y'all stole being old as anything and we could really have problems. Suppose the oppressors have renovated those buildings? We wouldn't even know it. And tell me, have you been in those sewers out there? Have you studied the logistics of getting men— *Black* men and bombs undetected into a white neighborhood that is already cringing in fear because of our activities? You

know as well as I do that that area is heavily patrolled by the
police. Have you taken that into account. My brother—

GERONIMO

(*Hurt; interrupting*) Man, why you trying to stop this plan?

ANTAR

I'm not trying to stop the plan. I actually tend to agree with
Ahmed. It would be a major psychological blow to the oppressor. But I want a more carefully laid out plan. I'd like to
see all my people get back safely.

GERONIMO

Yeah well, okay, Mkuu Antar. But you should recognize the
inevitability of revolutionary death.

ANTAR

I do. But I don't want all my revolutionaries dying at once.

AHMED

I like the idea, Antar. If it's the implementation of it that wor-
ries you then I'd like to volunteer to work with Geronimo on
a new plan that will meet with your approval.
    (*To* GERONIMO)
Provided that's alright with you, brother.

GERONIMO

I'd be very proud, Ahmed. I've always had the highest respect
for you. So did Victor, Ramon and Juney-bugs.
    (*Just then, sounds of squeals of delight, shouts and pande-
monium are heard. A* BROTHER *enters with a wide smile on his
face.* HE *snaps smartly to attention, salutes*)

BROTHER

Antar! I am pleased to report to you that Ndugu Keusi Kifo
has eliminated Commissioner Savage. The brother has offed
the pig!! Keusi Kifo has offed the pig!!

AHMED

Wooooeeeeeee!!!
    (*Joyous laughing*)

GERONIMO

(*At first, unbelieving*) The motherfucker's dead?! He's dead?!
(*The* BROTHER *nods*)
AAAAIIIIEEEE!!!! He's dead! The beast is dead! His blood
shall feed the revolution!!! Victor, Ramon, Juney-bugs! The
motherfucker is dead! AAAIIIIEEEEE!!!!

ANTAR

(*As* OTHERS *enter; amid the shouts*) This is the greatest moment in our brief history. The most brutal of all oppressors
outside the federal government has been successfully eliminated. His death has opened the floodgates. The very founda-
tions on which the oppressive law and order machine of this
country is built is now quaking. But we can't stop here. The
revolution must continue. More oppressors must die! There
must be more victories! More life! More life for our parents,
our brothers and sisters. More life for generations of Black
people to come. Death to the oppressors! We shall be victorious.
(*Cheers*)

AHMED

We are the Black Terrorists, sworn to the liberation of our
people!

ALL

May we never lose sight of our duty!

AHMED

We seek the death of those who oppress us!

ALL

May our vengeance be as swift as lightning! AAAAIIIIEEEE!!!
(*More celebration. After a while,* KEUSI *and* M'BALIA *enter
amid cheers and congratulatory remarks.* HE *moves to* ANTAR,
salutes him, and is embraced by ANTAR, AHMED *and* GERONIMO.
M'BALIA *receives the same greeting, then is whisked off by the*
WOMEN. *Cheering continues as lights dim to denote passage
of time. Lights up on the aftermath of the celebration. Enter
a* SISTER *with refreshments and places them before* KEUSI, AH-

MED, M'BALIA, ANTAR *and* GERONIMO *who are seated in that order. The* SISTER *exits*)

ANTAR

A job well done, Ndugu Keusi. Zaidi ya asante.
   (KEUSI *smiles*)
But we gathered here not only to express our thanks. We have another assignment for you.

KEUSI

(*Surprised*) Wow, I just . . .

ANTAR

We know, but this man is even more dangerous than Savage.

GERONIMO

(*Excited; interrupting*) Whatchu use on the beast, man?

KEUSI

A crossbow.

GERONIMO

(*Laughing*) Oh, wow! A crossbow? Check the cat out for gettin' into some Robin Hood.
   (ALL *laugh except for* KEUSI)

KEUSI

(*As if trying to provoke something*) That's historically incorrect, Ndugu Geronimo.

GERONIMO

Huh?

KEUSI

I said you're wrong. Your reference is historically incorrect. The crossbow came after Robin Hood.

GERONIMO

Oh, I didn't know.

KEUSI

A lotta things you don't know, Geronimo.

(*The* TWO MEN *stare at each other.* M'BALIA *attempts to intercede*)

M'BALIA

Antar, any new information on Radcliffe?

KEUSI

That's my new target?

(M'BALIA *nods and* KEUSI'S *face grows solemn.* HE *appears worried*)

ANTAR

Nothing beyond the information you supplied us with some time ago, M'Balia.

AHMED

Keusi, when you gonna get started on Radcliffe? That nigger's gotta go.

KEUSI

(*Quietly*) I guess I'll start first thing tomorrow. Anything special about him I oughta know?

M'BALIA

Nothing really. His son is dead, and his wife died of a heart attack years ago.

KEUSI

What happen, his son get killed in the Nam, or something?

GERONIMO

Hell no, he died fighting the enemy right here in the mother country.

M'BALIA

He died in a raid on a Panther headquarters two years ago. He was the only Panther to die. To show you what a lackey Radcliffe is, he refused to let any Panthers attend the funeral and swore to destroy Black militants because he said they had destroyed his son.

KEUSI

He must have loved his son a lot to be feelin' like that.

M'BALIA

That's beside the point. Radcliffe is an oppressor. He must die.

KEUSI

No doubt. But actually, to tell you the truth, I hate to be the one to set the precedent for killing our own people. Fratricide oughta always be avoided 'cause it's the one kinda killin' that always gets outa hand. Look at Biafra and Nigeria. The death is appalling. Ain't there no other way to handle this misguided cat?

GERONIMO

No. He dies. Don't try to rationalize a way for this ass-licking scab to live. Off him!!

M'BALIA

He has sworn to destroy us, Keusi. It's almost an obsession with him. You heard him on that news broadcast when he turned three of our brothers in to the oppressors.

(*Lights go out. Stage black. Spot picks up on* CHAUNCEY RADCLIFFE *standing in a remote part of the stage*)

RADCLIFFE

It's time the decent, law-abiding Negro citizens of this country stood up and shouted "Enough!" It's time for us to bring to an end this lunacy, this—this madness being perpetrated on our society today. We are fed up with being identified with these young fools. They are trying to tear down the greatest country in the world. America may have her faults, but there is no place on earth where the Negro has it this good. We're better off today than at any time in our history. We go to better schools, we have better jobs—better housing. Our middle class is growing stronger every day. What right do these disgruntled young thugs—for that's just what they are—thugs—what right have they to trample upon the rights and land for which so many Americans, colored and white, have died. These young disgruntles—spoiled brats and hooligans—are the creation of the television age. The sensationalist news media ignore the legitimate Negro leaders who are making positive contributions to Negro progress. They ignore those of us in my generation who've toiled for years, battling against mindless white racists on the one hand and Black fanatics on the other. Quiet but steady progress can't fit into the late news, so the media cover the misinformed Black power boys. Why? Because they make sensational news copy.

Well, I tell you, such madness has to stop. The responsible Negro element, the only true voice of the Negro since he first set foot on these shores; the responsible Negro element, which has survived the likes of Paul Cuffe, David Walker, Martin Delaney, Garvey and the brilliant but misguided Malcolm X, now declares war on these young thugs. We will assist all local, state and federal authorities in whatever way we can, in bringing to justice these criminals. They terrorize Negro communities and drive away our white friends who have suffered many humiliations while still standing at our sides. The three boys I have turned in today were only the beginning. By working with my good friend, Commissioner Charles Savage, I solemnly swear to you that all of the revolutionaries, Black or white, Jew or Gentile, will be brought to justice.

(*Lights down. Lights up on the headquarters*)

KEUSI

Yeah, sister. I guess you're right.

GERONIMO

When the French people staged the French Revolution, a lotta French heads rolled. When the Anarchists tried to rip off Paris in the 1850s, more Frenchmen died. When the Bolsheviks changed the course of world history in Russia, they offed thousands of fellow Russians, and so on down the line, brother. When Mao took China, the blood of fellow Chinamen flowed like a mighty river. Before we can move on the enemy without, we gotta move on the enemy within. Killing the archtraitor Radcliffe is necessary.

KEUSI

With you killing is always necessary.

AHMED

Look, man, we don't like the idea any more than you do, but the nigger's crimes can't be ignored. He cursed the name of the Panthers and assisted in the destruction of their headquarters, he turned in three of our men, and he drove his only daughter from his household when she refused to support his schemes. This lap dog seeks our deaths, man. What else we supposed to do?

M'BALIA

The faggot lackey is a scar on the face of the Black community. He must die.

GERONIMO

A pig is a pig is a pig, be he Black or white. When he oinks, his breath still stinks.

ANTAR

Ndugu Keusi, you must recognize that we have no other choice. To allow him to live is to invite our own deaths. Sooner or later the police may succeed in making one of those three prisoners talk and give away the location of this headquarters. A lot of blood's gonna flow. We have sworn it. And all of that will come about because of this man's treachery. Radcliffe is an oppressor—with the oppressor's values, the oppressor's way of life—

GERONIMO

(*Interrupting*) And with the oppressor's dick up his ass.
  (ALL *laugh except* KEUSI)

M'BALIA

When you were in the army, Keusi, wasn't it true that a man who deserted in the face of the enemy was shot?
  (KEUSI *nods*)
Well, Radcliffe has not only deserted, he has *defected*. We

are at war with the beast. Don't the rules count the same here?

KEUSI

Okay, okay, okay. Radcliffe will be taken care of. But I'm doin' it with reservations. Radcliffe looks and sounds like the kind of dude who's very active in the community. Is that true?

AHMED

Ndio. More or less.

KEUSI

So that means that he's into things like sending little kids to camp in the summer and young people to college in the fall. I'll betcha he's a member of a fraternity and he's probably a deacon in his church.

M'BALIA

Yeah, the society page of *Jet* magazine. That's him.

KEUSI

That means he's probably a hero in some segments of the Black community. A lotta Black mothers are grateful to him for helping to get their sons straightened out. You got any ideas of what that means to a lotta mothers? Working in the church automatically puts him in good with the older folks.

GERONIMO

So what?

KEUSI

So, even though he acts like a Tom to us, he could be regarded as a kind of hero to many of our people.

GERONIMO

Aw, bullshit. Radcliffe's an oppressor. He's got to go. And maybe those people who believe in him will have to go, too.

AHMED

When the target is eliminated, the people will understand.

KEUSI

I'm not so sure. Once you get a rep for killing your own people, popular support starts to dwindle.

GERONIMO

It depends on what Black people you kill, an' if the nigger is an oppressor, that's his ass.

KEUSI

Who are we to decide what Black people will live and what Black people will die? We got no mandate from the people.

GERONIMO

Fuck a mandate. We the vanguard of the righteous revolution. We don't need a mandate.

KEUSI

Y'all still don't understand.

M'BALIA

Chauncey Radcliffe is an oppressor. He oppresses the Black community and he oppresses the revolution.

AHMED

Hey, man, don't worry. The people will understand.

GERONIMO

It's not the revolutionary's job to take prisoners and rehabilitate. It's the revolutionary's job to eliminate.

AHMED

The people will understand.

KEUSI

The people will only understand that we are now killin' Black people. 'Cause, see, if we kill Radcliffe then we gonna haveta eventually do away with preachers 'cause a lotta them shuckin' and jivin', too. But if we do 'way with preachers we gonna haveta off teachers 'cause they teachin' in the oppressor's schools, an' if we off teachers we gonna haveta start on Black government officials 'cause they work in the oppressor's government administration an' they ain't gonna go for teachers gettin' offed. We kill city and government officials, then we gonna haveta start on our families next 'cause we all got people who're teachers, preachers, civil servants an' alla that. See what I'm gettin' at? Chauncey Radcliffe is more than just one man. He's a whole heap of people. His death is gonna open up a whole floodgate of death and destruction for Black people at the hands of other Black people. Us.

M'BALIA

When we became revolutionaries we recognized the probabilities of having to kill our own people. Even members of our own families. That's why we accepted the credo of the revolutionary which states in part that the revolutionary can have no family outside his "family" of other revolutionaries.

AHMED

Don't forget, man. Seven Panthers are dead in this city, and three Black Terrorists are rotting in pig pens because of this one man.

GERONIMO

He's not a man. He's an oppressor. A beast. A no-thing, a non-man. His death will be of little consequence.

AHMED

His blood's gonna feed the revolution.

ANTAR

Ndugu Keusi, there is no way this man can be allowed to live. Your considerations are wise ones, but these are revolutionary times. We have to take into account the survival of the revolution. I hate to say it, but there are times when the survival of the revolution must come before the desires of the people.

GERONIMO

That's right, Keusi. The people don't always know what they want.

KEUSI

But the people *are* the revolution.

AHMED

Precisely, my brother. We articulate the desires of the people.

KEUSI

But how are we gonna do that if as revolutionaries we live only among ourselves. How we know what the people want if we don't deal with their wishes?

ANTAR

We always deal with the wishes of the people. The people wished the oppressor Savage dead and we fulfilled that wish. Deep down they want Radcliffe dead. We will fulfill that wish, too.

KEUSI

But suppose the people don't want a revolution? Suppose they ain't really ready?

AHMED

That's what we mean when we say that the people don't always know what's good for them.

KEUSI

But if we represent the people, we gotta always be responsible to them. Revolutionaries are responsible to the people. If they say stop, we have to stop. We should never try to operate independent from the people. I don't know, man, but somewhere along the line I think we got a fucked-up set of values.

ANTAR

We have a correct value system, Ndugu Keusi. You shouldn't get into disparaging the revolution. Such a habit is counter-revolutionary.

AHMED

It's the same thing I was tellin' you about before, Antar. His personality and his makeup, man. Hey, Keusi, man, you gotta overcome that. You a good killer an' you got the makin's of a good revolutionary. But watch it, man. Your shit's raggedy.

KEUSI

(*Piqued*) Yeah, yeah, yeah. Yeah, man, okay.

GERONIMO

You should recognize that the revolutionary is responsible to the people only as long as they move forward to a revolutionary position. When the people falter the revolutionary must move on ahead as a righteous vanguard, smoothing the path for the people, so that when they catch up to the revolutionary in consciousness they will see what a glorious thing it is for a revolution to put into high gear. You gotta recognize that, my brother.

KEUSI

Bullshit. A revolutionary vanguard is impossible in this country 'cause without the people the revolution is lost. Can't no revolution be successfully carried out without the support of the people. If the people don't want a revolution there ain't gonna be none. And when you get into offin' Black people as though you were some omnipotent agents from heaven or someplace then, hey, man, you sealin' your own doom. "The saviors of the people must not become their tormentors as well."

GERONIMO

(*Very angry*) We ain't no tormentors!! Goddamnit, we righteous revolutionaries!!! Just assassins!! Black Terrorists! We *are* the revolutionary vanguard. An' we gonna keep on vanguardin' 'cause too many brothers and sisters have died to get us to this point. We goin' forward all the time!! The oppressors will die! Alla them!! 'Cause it's only right and just that they do so!! And any deaf, dumb, blind, incorrect nigger that gets in our way, gets his ass *blown* away. You understand?! His blood flows! Motherfuck the nigger! He dies!!

KEUSI

Is that all you got to offer the people, man? Death? Black people been dyin' in the most vicious manners imaginable for the past four hundred years. Hey, man, all you got to offer

people who seen too much death is more death? Why we
gotta fight a revolution with a value system directed toward
death? Why not wage a revolution directed toward life? Huh?

AHMED

Oh, will you listen to this romantic, idealistic motherfucker?

KEUSI

I mean it. Why y'all playin' up to death alla time? Don't nunna
y'all wanna live?

GERONIMO

That ain't got nothin' to do with it! If we gotta live under the
yoke of oppression then we choose death. At least in death
we can have some measure of freedom!!

AHMED

If it's gonna take our deaths to secure life for Black people,
then we say to our oppressors, "Take our lives, if you can!"

ANTAR

We don't glorify death. We just acknowledge its inevitability. To die for the revolution is the greatest thing in life.

KEUSI

To live for the revolution is even greater. To be alive to fight
the next—

GERONIMO

Aw, nigger, you just scared of death!

ANTAR

(*Comfortingly*) To be afraid of death is nothing to be
ashamed of, Keusi. It's a fear we must all overcome.

KEUSI

I ain't afraid of death. I've risked my life countless times. It's
the glorifyin' of death I'm afraid of.

AHMED

To be unafraid of death is not to glorify it!

KEUSI

Aw, why the hell don't you niggers stop sloganeering an' come down to earth. Y'all runnin' around here talkin' about you ain't afraid to die, waitin' for a chance to die to show the world that you meant what you said. Hell, if I'm scared of death, then y'all just as scared of life.

GERONIMO

Life at the price of slavery is unacceptable! Like the mother-fucker said, "Give me liberty or give me death."

KEUSI

Fucked-up references and fucked-up values.

GERONIMO

Ramon, Victor and Juney-bugs was real revolutionaries. Brave cats who met their moment in true revolutionary fashion. They weren't cowards. Not like you. They died valiantly.

KEUSI

They died needlessly.
 (*Shocked gasps from* OTHERS. GERONIMO *starts for* KEUSI)

GERONIMO

(*Being restrained by* OTHERS) You spittin' on they name?! You punk!! You punk motherfucker!!

KEUSI

I don't care what you call me. The facts are there for you to deal with. They died from an overdose of revolutionary fervor.

ANTAR

Don't be impudent!!
 (M'BALIA *bows her head in silence from this point on.* SHE *seems hurt and dismayed. After a while* SHE *should move from the group to an area by herself near the door*)

KEUSI

I'm not. I'm tellin' the truth. Hey, man, I'm sayin' that if cool

heads had been in charge not a single member of the ALF
would have died.

GERONIMO

The enemy was tryin' to kill us. We wasn't gonna cringe in
front of them. Not in front of the beast!!! We wasn't about to
give them that satisfaction.

KEUSI

You had an out, man, an' either you couldn't or you wouldn't
use it. You let revolutionary zeal get in the way of effective,
clear thinking and blew, man.

GERONIMO

What the hell you tryin' to say? We was attacked by the pigs.
We had no choice *but* to fight.

KEUSI

You had a choice, man. You had the option to postpone that
battle an' you refused.

GERONIMO

You sayin' we shoulda surrendered?! Huh?! Is that what you
think we shoulda done?! Man, you must be crazy. We ain't
scared of no pigs! You must be outa your mind!

KEUSI

You had a situation in which 'cause of the hour of the raid
your station was undermanned. In fact, from everything I've
learned about it, man, there was more sisters than brothers in
the headquarters at the time. You were outarmed and outnumbered from jump street. You were in charge of the most
crucial chapter of the ALF in the country because of the
alliance you made with the Black Terrorists. Also, because you
had built your headquarters into a fort valuable records from
the chapters all over the country were stored there. Even
though you had this fort everybody knew that no matter how
strong the damn thing was history showed that when the Man
wants to take it, he can. You can hold him off maybe six minutes, maybe six hours, maybe even six days, but eventually

the Devil can mount a successful assault. Geronimo, you knew that, and that's why the out was built. An' you didn't use it, man.

GERONIMO

Man, I didn't have no out! We was attacked. We recognized that we had to deal with the Night Rangers on the spot. We knew we might die but we knew that even in death we would set a revolutionary example.

AHMED

They gave impetus to the revolution. Ndugu Keusi, you got no right to jump on Geronimo like this.

KEUSI

Aw man, will y'all listen to reason?! Man, everything, all the records, weapons and personnel were lost in that battle, when the truth of the matter is that it didn't even have to happen.

GERONIMO

It had to happen! The moment dictated it!

KEUSI

You had an out, man, and because you didn't use it, the whole movement has been set back.

GERONIMO

What "out?" Whatchu keep talkin' about? Our backs was to the wall.

KEUSI

Man, don't you see? I'm talkin' about the escape tunnel.

GERONIMO

We used it, dunce! How you think me and the survivors escaped?

KEUSI

Why didn't you use it from the git?

GERONIMO

Because we had to fight! We was under attack!

KEUSI

But you was outnumbered and outarmed. You had valuable records and documents. To engage in such a battle woulda been useless. You faced losing your men, your records and possibly capture. Hey, man, that escape tunnel was your out.

GERONIMO

We was supposed to run from some cowardly oppressors, is that it? You expect us to run like those five white boys did?

KEUSI

I expected you, as the leader, to have kept a cool head and to have looked past the emotionalism of the moment. You dig?

GERONIMO

I ain't a coward, man, an' neither was the brothers and sisters who was with me. We weren't gonna run like those white boys did.

KEUSI

In they fear, those crackers showed you just what you shoulda done.

AHMED

(*Angry*) You takin' the side of white boys against your brother?!

KEUSI

No, man. They were even more wrong. In fact, we all know they shouldn't even have been there, in the first place. They coulda created panic and confusion runnin' like they did. But they got away, man. They alive walkin' around, totally useless to the revolution, while real revolutionaries are dead because their leader wasn't able to see the need to order an orderly retreat in the face of superior fire power.

GERONIMO

Meaning what?

KEUSI

Meaning you a piss-poor leader. You was so eager to fight the Man that you ignored the safety of your warriors and over-looked the need to protect those files.

GERONIMO

Goddamnit, we was under attack by half an army. How you expect me to think of everything at once?

KEUSI

'Cause you was the leader. Your first duty was to the safety of your warriors and to keep those records and files from being lost. You gotta think of all the contingencies, man.

GERONIMO

Look, motherfucker, I AM a leader, and a damn good one.

KEUSI

You jeopardized a whole movement when you did what you did. Revolutionary zeal got its place, man, but it's outa place in a situation like the one you was in.

GERONIMO

I'm a revolutionary. My job is to kill the enemy, foment revo-lution among the people and lay my life on the line if nec-essary.

KEUSI

You not a revolutionary. You just an angry nigger with a gun. You filled your head fulla a whole lotta slogans and you fol-lowin' an ideal that somebody lifted from the fucked-up minds of some nihilistic white boys who lived a hundred years ago.

GERONIMO

Keep it up an' I'm gonna bust a cap in your ass.

KEUSI

You had ample warnin' when those white boys did their thing. All you had to do was put the sisters in motion, carryin' the files out through the tunnel while the brothers fired to keep the police at bay. Then when the cops made their big push, y'all coulda gone underground, anything you wanted. Alla y'all woulda been alive to be *living* revolutionary examples, continuing to fight, instead of martyrs inspiring young impressionable kids to copy your suicidal deeds.

GERONIMO

You sayin' we shoulda run?! You sayin' we shoulda imitated those cowardly white boys?!

KEUSI

Man, ain't you listened to nothin' I said? I'm only runnin' down to you what the V.C. did to us every day. This is how Frelimo is kickin' the Portuguese outa Africa. Hey, man, I ain't sayin' y'all gotta be cowards. I'm sayin' to calm down and use your heads.

GERONIMO

(*Still ignoring* KEUSI) I'll die before I run!!

ANTAR

Hindsight is always easy, Ndugu Keusi. The brother described the situation to us, himself. We too questioned his tactics, but he correctly, we felt, pointed out to us that there is little time to take all that you said into account.

KEUSI

It don't take no time to burn some files and split. Geronimo allowed all this revolutionary zeal to get him all jammed up. The nigger got the most colossal death wish I ever seen. So does the whole goddamn revolution. We walkin' around practically worshippin' death. We so eager to die that we forgot how to live. The revolution gonna fail if we keep this up.

GERONIMO

Bullshit!! The revolution can't fail. We've seized the moment. Time is on our side. We can't fail!!! The French Revolution, the Anarchists, the Bolsheviks—ain't nunna them gonna have nothin' on us!!

KEUSI

You should realize, Ndugu Geronimo, that ultimately the French Revolution has failed 'cause after all those people got their heads cut off, after the motherfuckin' Reign of Terror, after eight republics, France is still fucked up. If you gonna use the Anarchists as a reference, then study they *whole* history; didn't a single one of those cats survive the Battle of Paris in the 1850s. The French cops and the citizenry killed them by the hundreds down to the last man and stacked their bodies like logs in the streets, and the fuckin' Bolsheviks unleashed Stalin on the world. See what I mean about references! It don't seem right to me that the crazy ideology of some sick Europeans should be passed off as the revolutionary ideology of Black people. We got to offer our people life, y'all. Not more death.

AHMED

But we're talking about constructive death!!
(*Pause.* ALL *look at* AHMED)

KEUSI

We are preparing ourselves to fight on the basis of a foreign ideology, brothers. We usin' the politics of the pig. And if we fight on that level then that fight's gonna be a futile, royal ass-kickin' with millions of our people dead, locked away in prisons or run out the country. I mean, if we gonna achieve some kinda change in this motherfucker we gonna haveta to do it without usin' the politics of the pig. We got to use all the economic, political and military know-how we got, but we gotta learn to use it wisely and cunningly. We got to wage our fight on a new level of thought and action. You dig? We gonna haveta run a master game down on this beast. Otherwise, Black people are gonna keep on gettin' wasted on bullshit hummers. We stay on this path an' we gonna fail our people.

AHMED

He's lying!!

GERONIMO

(*Drawing a gun; angry as hell*) Motherfucker, you standin' in the way of the revolution!!

(*Just as* HE *is about to fire,* ANTAR *hits his arm and the gun misfires.* M'BALIA *screams.* ANTAR *and* AHMED *restrain* GERONIMO *who breaks down and cries*)

He's a traitor! Kill him! That nigger's blockin' the revolution! He's downin' everything we stand for. The motherfucker's destroyin' our beliefs!!

(*Two* TERRORISTS *rush in, guns drawn*)

ANTAR

(*To the two* TERRORISTS) Help this brother to his quarters.

(*The two* TERRORISTS *help* GERONIMO *out*)

Ndugu Keusi Kifo, I will admit that some of what you say may have a ring of truth, but I cannot and I will not condone your conduct. You have behaved in a manner that, at best, can only be described as counterrevolutionary. You are a totally undisciplined individual and I, for one, found your little act here disgraceful. For all of your supposed knowledge you still have yet to learn that it is far wiser to be constructive in your criticism rather than insulting, arrogant and vicious. Your powers of persuasion are virtually nil. I think you're one colossal ass. In view of your attitude, I cannot trust you to carry out your mission against your other target. I'm relieving you of your responsibility to that mission. I am also suspending you from all other revolutionary activities except attendance at our indoctrination classes. I should have listened to Ahmed when he first told me of your maladjustment. You *are* dangerous. Despite his eccentricities, Geronimo is a very capable revolutionary leader. Your attack on him was excessive, biased and unforgivable. I only hope those indoctrination classes will help you. If not, I will expel you from this revolutionary cadre. You're dismissed, Kifo.

(KEUSI *starts out.* HE *stops near* M'BALIA *who is by the door.* THEY *look at each other but say nothing.* SHE *turns from him and* HE *exits*)

AHMED

You should have let Geronimo kill him, Antar.
(M'BALIA *buries her face in her hands.*
Lights go down)

Scene VII

Back at the apartment. KEUSI *is seen packing a knapsack.*
After a while, M'BALIA *enters.* SHE *watches him a moment, then*
moves toward him.

KEUSI

(*Noticing her*) Hey, how ya doin'?

M'BALIA

Alright.

KEUSI

You come to jump in my ass, too?

M'BALIA

No.

KEUSI

Uh-huh. I'll tell you one thing. I was really surprised by them.
I didn't think they were so reactionary.

M'BALIA

I didn't think you were so negative.

KEUSI

But I wasn't negative.

M'BALIA

Yes you were, Keusi. You tried to destroy Geronimo in front
of the other men.

KEUSI

I tried to correct him.

M'BALIA

Insulting him and trying to undermine him is no way to get
him to see your point of view.

KEUSI

I'm sorry, baby, but I got no patience with overzealous motherfuckers. I seen too much of that in the army an' I seen it get
a lotta people wasted. Y'all act like the revolution is just one
great big romantic gang war. It's serious business—

M'BALIA

(*Interrupting*) Don't lecture me. I know what revolution is,
and I know what death is, too.

KEUSI

Well, if you know what it's all about, then why you puttin'
me down for comin' down on Geronimo?

M'BALIA

Oh, I don't know. I didn't feel you had to be as malicious as
you were, but, Keusi, Ahmed wants you dead. He said as much
to Antar after you left.

KEUSI

Fuck that nigger. Shit, it doesn't matter anyway. I'm gettin'
out. I've had it. I would have thought that at least Antar
would have seen where I was comin' from, but he's let the
revolution blind him, too.

M'BALIA

You're going to run?

KEUSI

I'm not running. I don't believe in the Black Terrorists any
more. So it's just better that I split. I'll never sit in any indoctrination and listen to revolutionary bullshit that came from
the minds of crazy-ass Europeans.

M'BALIA

What will you do?

KEUSI

Keep on fighting. I don't know. I heard about these brothers who are into some new concepts and ideas. Maybe I'll join them.

M'BALIA

Can we really be that wrong?

KEUSI

Baby, times change. The whole world is different. You got to be flexible. An' the Black Terrorists just ain't flexible. They so dogmatic an' shit.

M'BALIA

I don't understand you. If you feel this way, why did you join us in the first place?

KEUSI

I don't know. Maybe then I was only beginning to see things. After meeting Geronimo and after listening to Antar take my ass over the coals an' shit, I began to realize that it was time for me to split.

M'BALIA

What if those other brothers don't meet with your approval? Will you leave them, too?

KEUSI

If they bullshittin', yeah, I'll leave them.

M'BALIA

Then I guess you'll always be on the outside, Keusi. It just don't look like you can ever really find anything to believe in. As soon as something goes wrong for you, you leave. If what you say about us is true, don't you even think that maybe you should stay here and try to straighten things out?

KEUSI

With Ahmed and Geronimo both ready to kill me? You kiddin'? Naw, I'm splittin'. Maybe I'll just go into the Black community and educate the kids as to what I have learned in the world. Maybe that's the only thing I can do. But I can't stay here. Not another minute longer.

M'BALIA

Oh.
(Pause)
Well, good-by.

KEUSI

M'Balia, I want you to come with me.

M'BALIA

No. You're asking me to be a traitor.

KEUSI

Please?
(Moves to her)

M'BALIA

I can't. The revolution—

KEUSI

You can still fight the revolution, but as the mother of my children.

M'BALIA

(As KEUSI *takes her into his arms)* I can't. Keusi, please. I'm an assassin. I've dedicated my life to what I do. Keusi, please don't. Please.

KEUSI

M'Balia, baby, baby, baby . . . please.
*(*HE *kisses her.* M'BALIA *starts to melt, but gains control and pushes* KEUSI *away from her)*

M'BALIA

I can't go with you, Keusi. Not now, not ever. I swore my life to the organization. I won't leave them.

KEUSI

M'Balia, I love you. I want you with me.

M'BALIA

No. My life is with my brothers and sisters. Anything beyond that is not real for me.

KEUSI

Not even me.

M'BALIA

Not even you. You don't seem to understand, Keusi. I told you before that the best you could ever be was my lover. I meant that. I could never let you get into my heart. I never have.

KEUSI

I'm not leaving here without you.

M'BALIA

And I'm not going anywhere with you.

KEUSI

Then you don't know me very well.

M'BALIA

I know you well enough. If you're going to, run, but don't expect me to run with you. I'll never run from the revolution.

KEUSI

(*Exasperated*) Goddamn!! Will you listen. Look, I'm not runnin' from the revolution. I'm runnin' from suicidal niggers who ain't got no idea of what they sayin' and doin'. Not really.

M'BALIA

We know what we're doing.

KEUSI

Is that so? When the revolution really begins and homes and neighborhoods get burned down, and blood really flows in the streets, and we face the full-scale cracker retaliation, you'll see what I was talkin' about. You'll see how far blind revolutionary zeal will get Black people living in white America.

M'BALIA

You're a defeatist.

KEUSI

I'm just tryin' to get y'all to see some truths, that's all.

M'BALIA

The revolution will be victorious no matter what you say, Keusi.

KEUSI

All we got is some semi-automatics, some carbines, some pistols, assorted rifles, knives and a whole lotta revolutionary zeal. That little bit of near *nothing* against the baddest, most vicious war machine in the world. We have no means of stopping a police car, much less a tank. It took the local cops only twenty minutes to run Geronimo outa his headquarters. How long you think it's gonna take the U.S. government to TCB in a Black neighborhood. All the zeal in the world ain't gonna help us unless we learn to get our shit truly together.

M'BALIA

For every one of us who falls it will cost them ten oppressors.

KEUSI

So, it's gonna be that? With only forty million Black people in this country against at least one hundred million crackers we supposed to fight a fuckin' war of attrition. This ain't Asia, baby. We ain't got an endless supply of manpower.

M'BALIA

We can fight urban guerrilla warfare. *The Battle of Algiers* demonstrated how it could be done.

KEUSI

This is America, not Algiers. See what I mean about references? M'Balia, get it into your head that the revolution in America is gonna be the most unique in history. We can't imitate nobody. Not the Viet Cong, or Frelimo or even the Chinese Eighth Route Army. We got to make up a whole new revolution, 'cause unlike other revolutions we in a minority,

and a highly visible one at that. All the beast gotta do is cage
us in, surround us and exterminate us, or, if he chooses, acti-
vate the McCarran Act.

M'BALIA

But we know the ghettos. They don't. We can hit and run
through alleys an' all kinds of things. We could fight guerrilla
war in the streets for months before the oppressor could do
any real damage to us.

KEUSI

You ever walk into a police station and look on the walls in
some of those offices. All over the place—maps. Maps of the
city, maps of the neighborhoods and maps of maps. The Man
knows all there is to know about the Black communities of
America. Don't forget, he built them.

M'BALIA

They wouldn't destroy their own property. We could always
be able to fight and hold them off. Besides, if they did bomb
us or try to kill the people off, world opinion would be very
much against them, and they couldn't afford that.

KEUSI

World opinion didn't mean shit when America invaded the
Dominican Republic. But that's beside the point. Look, as
revolutionaries, we also the protectors of the people. So, how
we gonna feed our people when the cracker stops sending food
to the A&P? How we gonna get water to the people when the
cracker turns off the water supply? How we gonna clothe the
people when we take off John's Bargain Store? When we
gonna get into educating the people as to how to take care
of themselves in a revolutionary situation? We ain't been
doin' this. All we been doin' is killin' cops, gangsters and a
few bullshit politicians, an' all that is doing is getting the
cracker in the mood to make a big bust. That means our
people are the ones who gonna suffer the most. An' that's all
we can offer them, now, you know. Nothing but empty slogans, pyrrhic victories and more death. How we gonna sell

them that kind of life? The kind of life we got off some dead Europeans?

M'BALIA

But we have to do *something!!* We can't just sit idly by and allow this oppression to continue. I don't know, your arguments are persuasive. You have a clever way with words. You can always make yourself sound so right, and I can't deal with that. But I know that unless we Black people take a stand and try to end this oppression, we'll never be free. We have to fight. We have to make war so that we can end this oppression and live as free men and women. How much longer are we supposed to put up with the terrible way so many of our people are forced to live?! What, are we insane or something? Are niggers a race of morons?! The Indians, the Africans, the Asians, all chose to fight. No people will submit forever to oppression. So, what's wrong with Black people? No, Keusi, no more generations of Black children will be born into a country that kills and oppresses us in the manner that this does. We must have our manhood and womanhood and we must have it now, or America will simply have to die. We're going to change this world, Keusi. We're going to place human values above market values, we're going to build governments that save lives rather than destroy them, and after the destruction we bring to the evil and wickedness on this planet, after we've cleansed the world of the beast and all his lackeys and all other counterrevolutionary elements, no one will dare pick up a gun in anger again. And we'll do all this because we must, or else we'll die trying. So go on and leave. What does it matter? You were never any good to the revolution, anyway. Geronimo was right. You *are* standing in the way of the revolution.

KEUSI

Then why don't you kill me?

M'BALIA

Because those weren't my orders.

KEUSI
And that's the only reason?

M'BALIA
Yes.

KEUSI
You could kill the man who loves you that simply?

M'BALIA
Without hesitation.

KEUSI
Nothing that's happened changed a thing, huh?

M'BALIA
No. I told you in the beginning that I was a revolutionary. I've pledged my life to what I do.
(*Mood changes*)
Keusi, if you intend to leave, just leave. I really don't want to deal with you any more.

KEUSI
I want you to come with me. There are more ways to fight a revolution than with a gun.

M'BALIA
A gun is the only way. Keusi, tonight I'm going to have to prepare myself for a mission. I'd like to be alone. So . . .

KEUSI
What's the mission?

M'BALIA
Radcliffe. It'll be the ultimate test for me. If I succeed, it'll provide me with the ultimate freedom a true revolutionary can have. I'll be able to begin a whole new life after this mission. That is really something for me to think about. It'll even free me from doubts about being totally dedicated as a revolutionary.

KEUSI

I don't understand what you talking about.

M'BALIA

You don't need to.

KEUSI

Wow, killin' Radcliffe is really gonna put y'all out there. I guess I'll have to read about it in the papers.

M'BALIA

It'll be headline news.

KEUSI

(*Trying to joke*) Don't miss.

M'BALIA

Oh, don't worry, I won't miss. I'm a very good assassin. I only miss when I want to.

KEUSI

Well, good luck.
  (*Pause*)
So you won't change your mind, huh?

M'BALIA

No.

KEUSI

M'Balia, I know . . . I know you gotta feel somethin', baby. You gotta feel *somethin'*.
  (M'BALIA *says nothing*)
M'Balia?
  (SHE *moves far from* KEUSI)

M'BALIA

You meant nothing to me, Keusi. I needed a man. You were available.

KEUSI

You're lying.

M'BALIA

Why should I lie? I have no time to be lying.

KEUSI

Am I so wrong to ask you to be my wife? Is it a crime for me to want to love you?

M'BALIA

(*Trying to remain emotionless*) You want me to make a choice between you and the revolution, and you're conceited enough to think you should come out on top. If Antar had told me to I would have killed you the minute I walked through the door.
(*Voice starts to break*)
You mean nothing to me, Keusi. You have no right to do this to me. These are not the days for trying to win a woman's love. The revolution takes preference over everything.

KEUSI

I'm not asking you to give up the revolution. Fight it at my side. Come with me, M'Balia. Hey, baby, I love you.

M'BALIA

Keusi, you're a fool. Leave me alone. Please. For me, there's no such thing as love. I'm a revolutionary. There's no love, or no male, no female; there's only the revolution . . . and victory. Do you understand?

KEUSI

M'Balia—

M'BALIA

(*Stifles a tear*) Get out! I mean it! Just get out of here and leave me alone! You've hurt me enough already! Leave me alone!

    (KEUSI *picks up the duffle bag and starts for the door.* HE *looks at* M'BALIA *but* SHE *refuses to acknowledge him. As the door closes,* M'BALIA *turns toward the door, stands silently a moment, then buries face in hands*)

Scene VIII

A lonely room in RADCLIFFE'S *house. We see him seated behind a desk; desk lamp burning. Busy reading, seems tired.* M'BALIA *enters unseen . . . watches him awhile. Inadvertently makes a sound . . .* RADCLIFFE *spies her.*

RADCLIFFE

(*Surprised*) You!

M'BALIA

(*Speaks in subdued terms*) Hello, Daddy.

RADCLIFFE

So, you've finally come home. You've been gone for a long time. No contact at all. I wanted to reach you to tell you how sorry I was . . . about . . . well, about everything.

M'BALIA

(*Quietly*) Well, that's okay.

RADCLIFFE

Where have you been?

M'BALIA

In the city.

RADCLIFFE

All this time?

M'BALIA

Yes.

RADCLIFFE

Rhea—

M'BALIA

My name is M'Balia.

RADCLIFFE

What?

M'BALIA

My name isn't Rhea any more. It's M'Balia.

RADCLIFFE

I see. What does it mean?

M'BALIA

It's the name of a sister who became a martyr and served as an inspiration for the revolution in Guinea.

RADCLIFFE

When did you change your name?

M'BALIA

I didn't change it. It was changed for me.

RADCLIFFE

When?

M'BALIA

A few days after I left you.

RADCLIFFE

I suppose that now you're a revolutionary too. Like David.

M'BALIA

Yes.

RADCLIFFE

Rhea—I'm sorry, er—er—

M'BALIA

M'Balia.

RADCLIFFE

Yes. M'Balia. It sounds nice. Has a pleasant ring to it.
(*Grins*)
M'Balia . . . you know you're the only child I have left.
David's dead . . . and your mother, too. I . . . I don't want
to see you lying dead as well. If you die violently and senselessly, like David, then what'll be left for me? What'll be
left for your father?

M'BALIA

(*Unemotionally*) Death.

RADCLIFFE

I suppose that's right.
   (*Pause*)
I'm sorry . . . I'm sorry that our lives have become so dismal.

M'BALIA

Mine has been very fruitful, Daddy.

RADCLIFFE

It has?

M'BALIA

I've found peace, contentment, and at the same time, great challenges.

RADCLIFFE

But you're a revolutionary . . . or better, I should say, a misguided young woman.

M'BALIA

I'm not the one who is misguided, Daddy. It's you.

RADCLIFFE

You young people amaze me. You all think you know so much. You all assume your ideas and opinions are fresh and spanking new. Well, they're not, you know. They're old hat. They've been hashed about for years and nothing has ever come of them.

M'BALIA

That's because they've always been betrayed by Negroes like you.

RADCLIFFE

(*Angry*) I do what I must.

M'BALIA

And so do I.

RADCLIFFE

Why did you come back? We're enemies now. You know how I feel about your revolution.

M'BALIA

I came back to . . . to . . . to say, well, to say . . . hello.

RADCLIFFE

(*Nods*) Yes. Whatever else, you're still my daughter, aren't you? Strange, this revolution you young people are trying to foment. It's pitting blood against blood. Whatever else, whatever new name you acquire, I can only see you as my only daughter. Just as I saw David as my only son.

M'BALIA

Daddy, please . . . believe me. I'm only doing what I think is right. I don't hate you. But my life is dedicated to the revolution. I have to do what's necessary to continue the revolution.

RADCLIFFE

I don't understand what you are talking about, Rhea. What you are doing and what David was doing are the things your mother and I have tried to keep you from—all our lives. Believe me, I understand your frustrations—your bitterness. But to lash out at this white man is to invite your death. I grew up in the South. I know what he's like. I know what he can do. Your mother and I had to swallow pride and dignity many times just to be sure you and David had enough to eat. When I was David's age—when I was a young man, I often thought of fighting—lashing out, but integration just seemed a better way to go. If we tommed a little, it was to feed you—to give you a chance for the good life—a life your mother and I never had. I'm fighting against your revolution because I don't want to see any of you dying in the streets at the hands of trigger-happy white policemen. At least, those boys I turned in will only get a prison sentence. And that's better than getting your head blown off. I don't want to see any more Black women crying over the bodies of their men like I saw my mother crying over my father. I just don't want to see you kids dying needlessly and senselessly against such hopeless odds, and I'll fight anyone who tries to lead you down that path. I mean it. I'm not going to stand by and see an entire people exterminated, because of some disgruntled, misguided children who only half read their history books!

M'BALIA

Daddy, you're hopeless.

RADCLIFFE

I'm sorry you feel that way, Rhea, but I'm going to finish the job I started.

M'BALIA

Then I guess I'll never see you again.

RADCLIFFE

(*Sadly*) Perhaps not.

M'BALIA

(*Almost pleading*) Daddy . . .

RADCLIFFE

Yes?

M'BALIA

(*Thinks better of it*) Nothing. Forget it.

RADCLIFFE

Oh.
    (*Trying to make conversation*)
So, tell me, are you still keeping a diary?

M'BALIA

Oh, no. I cut that kind of thing out. It's very childish, you know.

RADCLIFFE

I thought all young women kept a diary.

M'BALIA

(*Trying to make a joke*) I wouldn't know. I'm not all young women.

(*Laughs uneasily*)

RADCLIFFE

(*Smiling*) It's good to see you laugh again. I haven't seen that smile in a long time. I'd forgotten how much like your mother you really are.

(M'BALIA *bows her head*)

M'BALIA

Mom was very . . . beautiful.

RADCLIFFE

She would have been proud to see you grow into such a fine-looking woman.

M'BALIA

Daddy, it's getting late. It's time . . .

RADCLIFFE

(*Interrupting*) When you walk out of that door, part of me will die because I'll never see you again, Rhea.

M'BALIA

Yes . . . I . . . I know.

RADCLIFFE

Rhea, give up this madness and come back home. There is no life for any of you in the revolution. Leave there before you're killed or imprisoned. You can't cut yourself off from reality of the situation in this country. A revolution is suicide. You're a free woman. Don't *be led* into madness.

M'BALIA

(*Almost pleading*) You refuse to understand. The revolution is already here. If it's madness we're into then it's a madness that will change the world! If we're so wrong to fight then you ought to recognize that we were driven to this point by your cowardice and the inhumanity of the enemy. Don't be so

eager to put us down, especially since we're only doing now
what Negroes of your generation have failed to do for years.
Not another generation of Black children will have such an
assortment of cowards and lackeys as . . .

(*Voice chokes*)

. . . as . . . you . . . my father, Chauncey Radcliffe. They'll
have brave men and women as their parents, who'll teach them
to be true men and women. Free? I'm not totally free yet.
I'll never be free until I free myself of this oppression that I
have had to deal with all of my life.

(*Now looks directly at her* FATHER. *Lips tighten with deter-
mination as* SHE *tries to muster up the words* SHE *must somehow bring herself to say*)

And most of all, as a revolutionary, I can never be free until
I'm free of you.

RADCLIFFE

What a well-rehearsed diatribe that was.

(*Angrily*)

Don't you young people understand?! You're standing on our
shoulders.

(M'BALIA *is unmoved and seeing this* RADCLIFFE *becomes
dejected*)

Well then, Rhea, what is it you want from your father? Money?
My hatred? What do you want from me?

M'BALIA

(*Hesitant. Deep inside her voice tells her not to go through
with her assignment.* SHE *forces this inner voice into silence,
summons up a great inner strength and, trembling, faces her*
FATHER) Your death! Traitor!!

(M'BALIA *pulls gun, fires.* RADCLIFFE *grabs head, blood oozes.*
HE *falls. Gradually the realization of what* SHE *has done strikes*
M'BALIA. *The stage turns red.* M'BALIA *screams. We hear the
voice of a* RADIO NEWSMAN *as* M'BALIA *kneels at body of* RAD-
CLIFFE)

RADIO NEWSMAN

Acting on information obtained from three prisoners, local police and state troopers today raided the headquarters of a supersecret Black militant organization, the Black Terrorists. Reports are sketchy, but news reporters on the scene have said the picture here is one of horror and chaos. Scores of policemen lie dead or injured in the streets and in other sectors of the neighborhood policemen are being pelted with rocks, bottles and other missiles thrown by roving bands of Negro youths. Reporters on the scene have said that some policemen have shot a number of these youths, otherwise killing or capturing them all, while the Night Rangers, anti-riot unit of the police department, is now involved in the process of occupying and clearing out a number of homes in the immediate vicinity. There are indications that the area may have to be cordoned off for the quote, "safety of innocent citizens," unquote. There are no indications as to whether or not this cordoning off will cease once the operation against the Black Terrorists is completed.

(*Sounds; the* REPORTER *being interrupted*)

Uh, ladies and gentlemen, we take you to the scene of the action, live, where our local correspondent Neil Reiner has managed to get past security guards and is inside the headquarters to give us this exclusive report on the attack and probable capture of the Black Terrorists. Neil?

(*Sounds; gunfire, shouts, screams*)

VOICE #2

Yeah?! Harry?

RADIO NEWSMAN

Yeah, Neil. You're coming through nicely. Can you tell us what's happening down there?

VOICE #2

(*Anguish*) My God, it's awful. They're killing them all. The police are killing them all. Men, women, children—all dead!! All *dead!!* The police rampaged through the halls like madmen. They're covered with blood. They're like, like *savages*. Death is all around me. So far, I have not seen one Black alive. The police are killing them all. They're just shooting . . . it's unbelievable! I keep saying to myself, "This is America. It can't be happening! Not in America!"

(*In background, shots continue. We hear sounds of screams, death throughout until blackout*)

The Blacks are fighting like crazed animals. They are shouting chants and somewhere someone is beating a drum. I don't understand all this. Why are they fighting so hard?! All of this death and destruction. It's all around me!!! I can hear gunshots coming from everywhere. Blacks are dying, police are dying! Harry, it's like the death knell of America! Believe me!! My God! My God! These militants are frighteningly unreal, Harry. They seem to laugh at death. Almost worship it!! Rather than surrender, they fight on until dead! There's an escape tunnel, yet no one seems to have used it. I don't understand these people! All of this death!! Why?! Why?! Harry, there's a group of revolutionaries at the top of a flight of stairs. They're identified as Antar, Ahmed and M'Balia. They may be the only Blacks left alive in this building. They've got to surrender! They must! They *must!*

(*Lights on* M'BALIA *dim*)

Only death can be the final victor in this battle. Harry, these Blacks are fools. Why do they fight so hard?! They can't win. We're white! This is America, the greatest country in the world. We've proved we can survive any inner turmoil. Why do these Blacks continue?! Why would they rather be dead than alive in America. I don't understand! This is America! They can't win! They're foolish to continue. All of this violence. Harry, I don't—

(*Gunshots, screams, shouts*)

Oh no!! Oh, my God!! They've got DYNAMITE!!!!!!!!!!!!!!!!!!!!

(*Sound of explosion. Blackout*)

(*BLACKNESS*)

Peace   Power   Unity